Denatured Visions
Landscape and Culture
in the Twentieth Century

Edited by Stuart Wrede and William Howard Adams

THE MUSEUM OF MODERN ART, NEW YORK

Distributed by Harry N. Abrams, Inc., New York

PHOTO CREDITS

THIS PUBLICATION, SUPPORTED BY THE J. M. KAPLAN FUND AND THE MYRIN INSTITUTE, DERIVES FROM "LANDSCAPE AND ARCHITECTURE IN THE TWENTIETH CENTURY," A SYMPOSIUM HELD AT THE MUSEUM OF MODERN ART, NEW YORK, ON OCTOBER 21 AND 22, 1988.

LIBRARY OF CONGRESS CATALOG CARD NUMBER: 91-61459
ISBN 0-87070-422-2 (THE MUSEUM OF MODERN ART)
ISBN 0-8109-6105-9 (HARRY N. ABRAMS, INC.)

PRINTED IN THE UNITED STATES OF AMERICA

PRODUCED BY THE DEPARTMENT OF PUBLICATIONS
THE MUSEUM OF MODERN ART, NEW YORK
OSA BROWN, DIRECTOR OF PUBLICATIONS

EDITED BY HARRIET S. BEE, ALEXANDRA BONFANTE-WARREN, C. ALLAN BROWN, JOANNA EKMAN
DESIGNED BY THOS. WHITRIDGE, INK, INC.
PRODUCTION BY MARC SAPIR
PRINTED BY SCIENCE PRESS, EPHRATA, PENNSYLVANIA
BOUND BY MUELLER TRADE BINDERY, MIDDLETOWN, CONNECTICUT

DISTRIBUTED IN THE UNITED STATES AND CANADA BY HARRY N. ABRAMS, INC., NEW YORK.
A TIMES MIRROR COMPANY
DISTRIBUTED OUTSIDE THE UNITED STATES AND CANADA BY THAMES AND HUDSON LTD., LONDON

COVER: ANDRÉ AND PAUL VÉRA. GARDEN DESIGNED FOR A HOUSE OF THE VICOMTE DE NOAILLES. 1926. SAINT-GERMAIN-EN-LAYE, YVELINES, FRANCE

THE MUSEUM OF MODERN ART
11 WEST 53 STREET
NEW YORK, N.Y., 10019

CONTENTS

INTRODUCTION

TECHNOLOGICAL AND ECONOMIC TRANSFORMATIONS in the nineteenth and twentieth centuries have had a profound impact on the landscape and on our attitudes toward nature. Recognizing that the issue of landscape in the twentieth century was a fundamental but long-ignored subject that needed to be assessed critically, we organized a symposium of historians, scholars, architects, landscape architects, and artists in October 1988. As we are approaching the end of the century, it seemed a propitious time to take stock of the subject. We wished to examine the achievements in landscape design and the influences that have formed our culture's attitudes to nature as they are manifested in the relationship of modern building to nature and in the parks and gardens of this century.

Justified or not, we, like many others, came to the enterprise with the strong feeling that the aesthetics of the twentieth century, particularly in the visual arts, were fundamentally hostile to nature; that the modern movement had, on the whole, led to a divorce between architecture and nature; that this century had witnessed the fundamental demise of the park and the garden; and, in fact, that, generally, a vital, modern landscape tradition never emerged.

We set an ambitious agenda. The papers by Vincent Scully and John Dixon Hunt put architecture's relationship to landscape, and the park's and garden's relationships to culture, into historic perspective.

The papers by Robert Rosenblum, Kenneth Frampton, and Leo Marx address the ideas in art, architecture, literature, and the culture at large that have shaped attitudes to landscape in this century. In addition, members of the three panels delivered shorter papers that focus in greater detail on modern architecture and landscape, the twentieth-century park, and the twentieth-century garden.

What emerged was a confirmation of our original sense of the crisis of the designed landscape. There also emerged a more nuanced picture that brought forward the very serious ideas on landscape of a small group of designers and thinkers, reflected in important projects, built and unbuilt. Those achievements suggest that there is a stronger foundation in place than many observers have been willing to admit.

There was not much disagreement about the forces and circumstances that have distinguished this century from all preceding ones, with inevitable consequences for the arts and for landscape. The sheer velocity of the transformations in science, technology, mass production, and mass communication completely rearranged the environment, of which, among other elements, architecture and landscape architecture are a part. The preoccupation with production, transportation, and economic progress has scattered man-made development across the world landscape.

As Leo Marx makes clear in his paper, the dominant drives in the United States are those of market economies. He surveys some of the historic reasons why land and nature are seen mainly in economic and productive terms, despite a simultaneous tradition of pastoral idealism, which continues as a dissenting voice amid the clamor of a free-for-all "progress."

The fault lies not only with the larger societal forces. Another premise that emerged from discussions at the original symposium is that the crisis in landscape design is also reflected in the lack of critical analysis in the field. Other contemporary artists have drawn on and responded to the vitality of modern culture and have benefited from well-developed criticism both inside and outside their professions. This criticism expresses, implicitly or explicitly, a strong grasp of the artists' modern roots as well as a larger historic perspective. Landscape designers, however, have suffered from an almost total lack of critical discourse on the part of the landscape and architecture professions and their design schools. Unfortunately, landscape design is equally poor in metaphysical speculation. It is a field that has until now inspired few, if any, modern myths or manifestoes.

The three panel discussions on architecture, the park, and the garden underlined the confused state of each.

The relation between modern architecture and landscape has been complex and often contradictory, like the varied and sometimes contradictory aspirations of modern architecture itself. While on the one hand, modern architectural theory put stress on internal functional requirements and structural logic and seemed to have little to say about the relationship of building to site (with the notable exception of Wright), yet modern architecture aspired to a new relationship between buildings, their inhabitants, and nature. The shift was presented in utilitarian, if not sanitary, terms of light, air, exercise, and rest. The implications were most radical in urban design: the traditional city, its cohesive urban fabric done away with, was to be replaced by towers and slabs set in nature to achieve an immediate relation between nature and the inhabitants. But the dematerialization of the wall into glass in the house provided a similarly radical restructuring of the relations between inside and outside. Curious then that architects—except in some of the exceptional cases that Kenneth Frampton discusses—devoted so little time to the natural world outside. They embraced it, but on the whole dealt with it in the most diagrammatic fashion.

Radical early modern art, as Robert Rosenblum makes clear, displayed a strong bias against nature, or ignored it, as evidenced in the anti-nature transcendentalism of De Stijl, or the Futurists' glorification of the machine. Among architects there was a bias against active landscape design (which was identified with "artificial" aristocratic and bourgeois traditions) in favor of nature as found; this changed somewhat in the 1930s. Nevertheless, most of the great modern architects displayed a real sensitivity to the siting of their buildings (though few theorized about it). The larger legacy remains one of neglect, however, with landscape relegated to a secondary and subordinate concern.

The modern park, as Galen Cranz documents, has also increasingly moved away from its landscape roots. With the mass movement to the suburbs, and free access to the countryside provided by the automobile, the landscaped urban park seems to have lost its constituency. Recreation and amusement become the defining force, to the point where people speak of the city itself as the park. Parks are now designed as microcosms of the city; a strange inversion wherein the original impetus for urban parks no longer obtains at all.

The private garden has been perhaps the most problematic landscape type of this century. At a time when the design professions were shifting their emphasis to meeting the requirements of a modern mass society, the garden—which had tended to be the preserve of aristocracy and wealth—seemed to have no future and a dwindling constituency in a more egalitarian world. Yet gardens have mediated the deeper symbolic meanings and myths that nature holds for us. The demise in this century of the garden's previous form and the absence to date of any vital new tradition are two of the more troubling aspects of contemporary culture.

Beginning in the mid-sixties, artists stepped in to fill the increasing vacuum left by the design professions. While the impetus for "earth art" varies widely, much of it embodies the common need to give symbolic and aesthetic expression to our relation with nature—both our rediscovered need to live harmoniously with the earth, and our present alienation from it. As is so often the case, one suspects, the artists are considerably ahead in manifesting the deep and archetypal bonds between human beings and nature.

This symposium set out to examine landscape in the twentieth century and the cultural attitudes that have given it shape, beginning with the premise that our physical environment is a fundamental reflection of our culture. Today's parks and gardens, or the lack thereof, and the prevailing relations between buildings and nature are perhaps the most visible reflection and symptoms of the profound ecological crisis on a global scale. Not only must we deal with the fundamental ecological issues, but we must find new aesthetic and symbolic forms for our new faith in nature and the earth.

Having been in charge of the agenda for the gathering, we wish to thank the many distinguished speakers and participants whose contributions made this book worth doing. We are most grateful to C. Allan Brown for initially editing and organizing the diverse material of the book after the symposium. Our thanks also to Harriet S. Bee, Managing Editor, and Alexandra Bonfante-Warren, Associate Editor, Department of Publications, The Museum of Modern Art, New York, and to Joanna Ekman for their skillful editing of the papers.

Generous grants from the National Endowment for the Arts and the Graham Foundation for Advanced Studies in the Fine Arts underwrote the occasion. The J. M. Kaplan Fund, and its President, Mrs. Joan K. Davidson, generously supported the editing and publication of the papers. Concurrently, The Myrin Institute addressed some of the issues in its journal, *Orion*. To each of these organizations we owe a significant debt of gratitude.

Stuart Wrede
Director, Department of
Architecture and Design,
The Museum of Modern Art,
New York

William Howard Adams
Fellow, The Myrin Institute

VINCENT SCULLY

Architecture:
The Natural and the Manmade

THE WAY HUMAN BEINGS see themselves in relation to nature is fundamental to all cultures; thus the first fact of architecture is the natural world, the second is the relationship of human structures to the topography of the world, and the third is the relationship of all these structures to each other, comprising the human community as a whole. The question of the relationship of the manmade to the natural world is especially germane today for many reasons. The most obvious and surely the most important one is the threat to the existence of the natural environment itself that many kinds of human structures now pose. The second, perhaps less cataclysmic but closely related, is the general failure of canonical "modern" architecture to work out any set of relationships to nature that are special to itself. Modernism cast aside the lessons of the French classical tradition of garden design and urbanism with which earlier twentieth-century masters, like Sir Edwin Lutyens, were able to do so much and settled, generally, for watered-down versions of other relationships, such as those worked out in the English Romantic garden or in the architecture of ancient religions: in the case of Frank Lloyd Wright's late work, for example, that of pre-Columbian America; in Le Corbusier's, that of Greece.

These two ways of relating to nature—the pre-Columbian and the Greek—are in fact primordial opposites. In the first, manmade monumental structures imitate the shapes of nature: in the second, they contrast with them. Yet it is more accurate historically to say that the first approach seems to have been worldwide and to have characterized the way most human beings originally thought of the earth-man relationship, while the second was almost literally invented by Greece and has dominated world architecture, especially that of Europe, almost ever since. It is at once the glory of the modern age and its problem.

We who inhabit the American continent are especially fortunate to have a living culture which espouses the old way still active among us. I refer of course to the Pueblo people of the Southwest, in whom the ancient, non-Greek rituals and way of relating to nature are still wholly in force and can be read in their architecture. We also possess the great monuments of Mesoamerican civilization, where the operation of basically the same principle can still be seen. That principle is mimetic; it

This article is a shorter version of the talk given at the symposium. It is a précis of a book of the same title to be published by Collins Harvill and St. Martin's Press in 1991.

1. Temple of the Moon. Before third
century A.D. Teotihuacán, Mexico.
View of axis down the Avenue of the
Dead

2. Water Goddess from Teotihuacán.
Before third century A.D.
Museo Nacional de Antropologia,
Mexico City

3. Taos pueblo with Taos Mountain.
New Mexico

begins with imitation. At Teotihuacán, surely the greatest religious center this continent has ever known, the so-called Temple of the Moon lies at the end of the main ceremonial axis of the site, the Avenue of the Dead, and echoes with its shape the pyramidal form of the mountain that rises behind it (Fig. 1). That mountain, called Tenan, "Our Lady of Stone," is running with springs; in order to help draw the water out of it, its pyramidal geometry is intensified in the temple into which strong horizontal lines of fracture, like the faults through which underground water seeps, are introduced. Human beings are part of nature, building nature's shapes, but they must assist the idle gods in their work: hence, human sacrifice, whereby men feed the natural machine with their blood. Exactly so is the mountain echoed and its hydraulic structure intensified.

The water goddess from Teotihuacán, now in Mexico City (Fig. 2), can also show us that precisely this was intended. A great mass weighs down upon her head. It is notched in the center, exactly like the mountain above the temple. Its weight compresses her body, which compacts itself into horizontal lines of fracture, while water is squeezed out of her hands. The more or less *tablero* construction of her skirt is like that of the Temple of Quetzalcoatl at Teotihuacán. There the water from the earth and the water from the sky are squeezed out of the mountain, gushing forth in feathered serpent heads like so many fountains. The god of agriculture, the plumed serpent, the great divinity of the Americas, is thus drawn by human art out of nature's forms.

The same is true in any modern pueblo, most spectacularly and traditionally at Taos (Fig. 3). Here the set-back

4. Corn Dance with the Sangre de Cristo range. Left: "Old Baldy"; right: Lake Peak. Tesuque, New Mexico

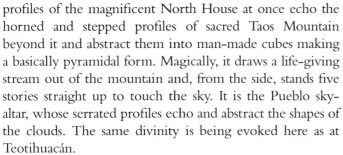

5. Temple I. Tomb of Ah Cacao. c. A.D. 600–900. Tikal, Mexico

profiles of the magnificent North House at once echo the horned and stepped profiles of sacred Taos Mountain beyond it and abstract them into man-made cubes making a basically pyramidal form. Magically, it draws a life-giving stream out of the mountain and, from the side, stands five stories straight up to touch the sky. It is the Pueblo sky-altar, whose serrated profiles echo and abstract the shapes of the clouds. The same divinity is being evoked here as at Teotihuacán.

The ritual dances of the Pueblos still complete those relationships today (Fig. 4). At Tesuque, a Tewa pueblo south of Taos, the profiles of the house of the governor pick up those of Lake Peak, the Sacred Mountain of the East, while the façade of the church, an intrusive European element, is shorn of its Hispanic towers so that it can repeat the conical profile of Old Baldy beyond it. In these ways the long horizontal profiles of the Sangre de Cristo range are reflected in the architectural forms and are further invoked by the long lines of dancers who pound the earth the whole day through, drawing the power of nature down into the pueblo, beating it into the plaza's dust.

From Teotihuacán to Taos and Tesuque—as from the Aztec's great Tenochtitlán to the Hopi towns—the major principle of imitation and intensification is everywhere the same. But at Tikal, in the Classic Maya area, it might at first appear that the principle does not apply (Fig. 5). No mountains are visible. The temple bases are springy and high. Is a more man-centered principle at work, such as historians have always wished to discern in Mayan art? Certainly the tall figure of Temple I suggests that of a standing, richly caparisoned priest-king, exactly like the king, Ah Cacao, buried within it. The shorter, squatter Temple II that faces it suggests the figure of Ah Cacao's queen, Lady Twelve Macaw, who is carved on its lintels and whose memorial it is. The royal couple is clearly there, king and queen facing each other. Yet the more general principle is at work as well, adjusted to the character of this site. The base of Temple I leaps high above the rain forest, as it once did above the houses of its town. The temple on the summit is built of concrete throughout, so that, unlike the temples of Mexico, it has survived the ages. Its interior is small and dank. When we climb up the steep stair to it in the heat we are greeted in the doorway by a wet rain breath, the very essence of its companion clouds, whose profiles its rich roof-comb amply enhances. It is one of the first skyscrapers of the Americas, literally scraping the clouds for rain.

Here the ziggurats of Mesopotamia come to mind. They, too, were manmade mountains, standing in the center of their cities, sacred mountains built down in the river basin where no mountains are. So they echo nothing. Hence their display is freer. They push out their masses, complicate the rhythmic variation of their set-backs, and in every way dramatize the heroic tread of the priest-king, like Gilgamesh, who mounted them as a conqueror and represented his people to the dangerous and capricious gods in the temple at the top. In the end, the only immortality Gilgamesh could count on was embodied in structures like these, and in the good, well-fired bricks out of which he built his city's walls.

At Sakkara in Egypt, at just about the same time, plenty of influence from Mesopotamia can be seen, including the manmade stepped mountain itself. There, however, the king did not climb the pyramid but was buried below it, and its massive presence was intended to ensure his immortality and to signal it from afar. Yet when the pyramid is viewed from within the temenos at Sakkara at the place where a wall of cobras, recalling the serpents of Quetzalcoatl, is obviously positioned to focus a straight axial view of it (Fig. 6), nothing whatever about it suggests three dimensions, as do the profiles of the pre-Columbian temples and those of Mesopotamia as well. Our minds supply no other sides to it beyond the one we see. It becomes a stairway climbing away into the sky. In this it already exhibits a special Egyptian character, wherein the pyramid, the sacred mountain, will be adjusted to evoke not primarily the power of the earth but that of the sky. That principle is completely exemplified at Gizeh (Fig. 7). There the true pyramids slant their faces away from the viewer and disappear at a point in the sky. Nor, seeing the corner of a pyramid, do we supply it mentally with its two other sides, but with one only: we reduce it to a tetrahedron. Moreover, the pyramids at Gizeh were all sheathed in blazing white limestone, shining dazzlingly in the sky, as they were seen from the river valley below them. For all their actual mass, they were visually pure light—the light of Re, the sun, into whose boat the pharaohs were thus magically introduced by them. They were a battery in echelon, deployed high on a shelf of desert above the west bank of the Nile, the side of sunset and death. They look east toward the morning sun; the Sphinx is the gunner. He wears his pharaoh's face. Multiple stone images of that pharaoh sat enthroned in the valley temple just below him. In them the king's head was held steady by the hawk, Horus, who alone could stare unwinking into the eye of the sun. So the Sphinx looks eastward unblinking, charging the whole great mechanism by focusing forever on the arising blinding brightness.

6. Pyramid complex of Zoser. South Tomb and Pyramid. c. 2600 B.C. Sakkara, Egypt

7. Pyramids looking east. c. 2530–2460 B.C. Gizeh, Egypt

In these ways, Egypt and Mesopotamia built their own sacred mountains but employed their energies in wholly different directions. In Crete, during the same period of the third and second millennia B.C., we find a situation more like that which prevailed in the Americas. Once again the sacred mountains are right there in nature, and human architecture found a way to adjust to them based on much the same mimetic principle. In Crete, it is true, there is much less direct imitation of the natural form: emphasis is placed instead on the central courtyard, placed so as to be axially directed toward the sacred mountain and to receive its force. At Knossos (Fig. 8), we are led to a stairway at the north end of the long court, beyond which rises Mount Jouctas, the home of the goddess of the earth, whose headdress is at once conical and horned, as is this mountain presence itself. It lies on the axis of the main south propylon of the palace, in the range of buildings behind which the throne room was placed. Here the king, perhaps bull-masked as Poseidon, received the earthquake tremors of the place seated on his quivering bucket-seated throne, draining the power of the goddess into the palace through his own body. At Phaistos (Fig. 9), where there was apparently no throne room, the axis of the court itself is directly on the mountain and is celebrated by the unique engaged columns that flank the doorway from the court on that side. Here the bull dance, like those of the American pueblos, took place under the mountain's own sanctifying horns, and both the natural form and the human ritual evoking it were visible to spectators who gathered on the flat roofs exactly as they do in the pueblos today. Indeed, the courtyards of Knossos and Puye above Santa Clara are almost exactly the same in conformation and mountain orientation, and the darkly looming buffalo dancers of the latter strongly recall the charging bull in relief above the northern entrance of the former.

In later Greek myth the conical shape of Mount Jouctas suggested the shape of the Mycenaean tholos tomb (and may indeed have inspired the building of that shape in the first place), so that Mount Jouctas came to be identified as the place where the Cretan Zeus was buried, while Mount Ida above Phaistos, opening as it does into a wide set of horns, became the mountain where Zeus was born.

Enter the Greeks, who took over Knossos and Phaistos by 1400 B.C. Although they clearly reverenced the goddess of the earth and wanted to live under her protection, they were driven by other passions and traditions as well. Their gods were to be wholly in the shape of mankind and would eventually embody all the characteristics of human thought and behavior that could be realistically imagined by human beings. Therefore the Greek temple, once fully developed, cast off the age-old imitation of natural forms in favor of the evocation of the human presence in landscape. The latter was still sacred, too, normally marked as such by the same horned and conical mountain forms. Thus the box of the cella of the temple was enclosed by a peripteral colonnade suggesting the vertically standing bodies of human beings. Each column is like a Greek hoplite, a self-contained, impenetrable geometric figure densely massed with other such figures in a human phalanx so that

8. View from north end of courtyard (c. 1600–1400 B.C.) to Mount Jouctas. Knossos, Greece

9. Courtyard (c. 1500 B.C.) and Mount Ida, Phaistos, Greece

10. Temple of Hera II (c. 450 B.C.) with conical hill. Paestum, Italy

11. Temple of Athena. c. 510 B.C. Paestum, Italy

12. Temple of Apollo. Sanctuary: sixth century B.C.; columns replaced in the fourth century B.C. Delphi, Greece

the power of all is made to act as one. The temple becomes one body. The Doric Temple of Hera at Paestum (Fig. 10), to take a well-preserved example, is built not only to bring the conical hill inland into the goddess's view from the cella across her altar, but also, as seen in the landscape, to contrast with the conical hill, so presenting the viewer with two images, the new, humanly conceived image of Hera and the traditional landscape form. This becomes the essential structure of classical Greek thought: fate and free will, nature and man, in tragic confrontation and ultimate harmony. Hence, each Greek temple is different from every other temple, since each embodies the special character of its particular divinity. Yet the temples had to be enough alike so that absolute differences of character could be perceived in their forms, as is possible only with creatures of the same species. So the Temple of Athena at Paestum is set on a slight rise and must be seen from below (Fig. 11). Its columns are more slender than those of Hera and their point of entasis is high rather than low; therefore they are read as lifting briskly rather than as weighing heavily on the ground, like those of Hera's temple. Moreover, and uniquely among Greek temples, the high pediment of Athena's temple never had a horizontal cornice, so that the whole body of the building lifts like Athena, the embodiment of the action of the *polis*, flourishing her aegis in defiance of the landscape forms. For the Greeks, from the very beginning, the hard edges of the city were a dangerous assault on nature, requiring the protection of the gods but certain to infuriate some among them.

At the same time, the columns of temples of Apollo of the same period have no entasis whatever. At Corinth they simply stand immovable, the phalanx of the Greek male god confronting nature's wildest natural forms. That defiance culminated at Delphi (Fig. 12), under the Horns of the Phaedriades, where the columns of Apollo's temple (the present ones are Hellenistic, but they, like those of the Archaic Period, are equally without entasis) stood out in triumph above the abyss of the Pleistos shining bright before the horns.

In the Classic Period of the mid-fifth century, the Greeks looked in two directions: back, at Olympia, to the time of kings and heroes, and forward, on the Acropolis at Athens, to democracy and empire. At Olympia the theme is law and limit, at Athens the breaking of limits and the victory of the human political system over everything—even, by implication, over nature itself. At Olympia, the site of the Sanctuary of Zeus is dominated, perhaps better to say protected, by a gentle conical hill that rises above the sacred grove and was the backdrop for all the activities, especially those of the Olympic Games, which took place below it (Fig. 13). Pindar tells us that Herakles named it the Hill of Kronos, where the dead god, the father of Zeus, was buried. Like Mount Jouctas, it was a tholos cone, and before it the man-made temple of the living god took its stand. The first Temple of Zeus, close under the flank of the hill, was renamed the Temple of Hera after the building of the second; and the Pelopion, the shrine of the human king of the Peloponnesos, lay between them, enclosed in a space formed by them and the hill. It is the place of the Olympic truce. The human crimes that threatened that truce are explored in the pediments of Zeus's temple, while Herakles goes about his labors in its metopes, humanizing the land, and the seated Zeus of Pheidias looms inside. Beyond that, everything about the site is calm, gentle, deeply quiet. To the deep roar of the crowd it must always have offered a commanding silence.

At Athens, everything is different. The Parthenon blazes on the top of a fortress hill (Fig. 14), a disquieting condensation of Doric and Ionic modes. Matchless, a wholly new unity, it rises in its sacred landscape but, like imperial Athens itself, it seems to lift free of earth and all the old ways. On the Acropolis one constantly hears people saying, "I can't take it in." The temple swells laterally like an Ionic temple but is still held to a Doric body. It looms, awesome, silently bursting to be free. Its sculptures bring the old antagonisms between men and nature into harmony. In the pediments nature consents to Athena's triumph; and the gods, in human form, become mountainous themselves. Political man is the measure of all. The Parthenon, still new, represents, literally, the victory of Western civilization over everything and was from the beginning the definitive embodiment of European hubris and pride. From this moment, one feels, the order of nature was everywhere endangered by the power of mankind.

Rome was different; she sought, primarily, not to win but to rule. The major topographical feature with which she first dealt was the chain of mountains that forms Italy's spine. Whereas Greece is shaped by bowls of small plains encircled by mountains, and its temples rise up in the center of the spaces so formed, Roman sacred sites are on mountain slopes, looking out toward the coastal plains. The Temple of Fortune at Praeneste is the archetypal sacred site, the most important in Italy. Fortuna Primigenia was at once the offspring and the nurse of Jupiter. Her waters nourished the land and were in fact led through the terraces of her temple down from the mountain to quicken the crops in the rich agricultural lands below. This recalls Teotihuacán; and at Praeneste profoundly pre-Greek forms do take shape once more, a suggestion of the ziggurat most of all. Yet Rome could hardly have identified those dreary piles of rubble far off in Mesopotamia for what they once had been. The form at Praeneste (Fig. 15) grows primarily out of the hill but was crowned with a sparkling Hellenistic colonnade, like that of the open altar of Zeus at Pergamon, but curved into a hemicycle, containing and shaping the space. We mount the ramps, turn up the central stair, climb to the hemicycle, and, turning within its embrace, look out over what seems to be the whole world of land and sea, of which we feel ourselves the commander. The columns spread out left and right from our body like the legion deploying. We recall that, unlike the Greek phalanx, which, like the Greek temple, formed a solid mass, the legion could fight in open order and often won its battles by enveloping the enemy in its wings. Moreover, the Latin *templum* means not a building but a

13. Sanctuary of Zeus. View from Temple of Zeus to Mount Kronos across Pelopion and Altar of Zeus. Temple of Hera left rear. Complex: c. 457 B.C. Olympia, Greece

14. Acropolis (fifth century B.C.) of Athens looking east

15. Temple of Fortuna Primigenia. c. 80 B.C. A Renaissance palace has replaced the original colonnade. Praeneste (Palestrina), Italy

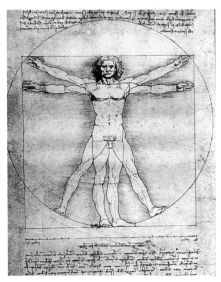

16. Hagia Sophia. A.D. 532–537. Nave looking toward apse. Constantinople

17. Leonardo da Vinci. Vitruvian man of perfect proportions. c. 1510

18. Water Organ fountain, Villa d'Este. Begun 1550. Tivoli, Italy

sacred space. Exactly so did Rome come to envelop the space of the Mediterranean world entire, and she built an exact image of that empire in the Pantheon. There the thick wall of Roman provinces surrounds "Our Sea," while the sun shines down from above and illuminates the planets standing in their niches around the walls. Why go outside? It is all here; the world enclosed, ordered, and made ideal by Rome. But it is the cosmos, too; stepping into the shaft of sun we are blinded by it and the walls around us disappear. We stand in the velvet blackness of interplanetary space. The Pantheon is, I suspect, the biggest space ever made by mankind, even bigger than those constructed later, as at San Vitale, when Christian Rome learned how to make the containing walls dissolve in a dazzle of light.

In this way, Rome set the major building program for the Middle Ages, whose concern was the creation of ideal interior spaces, not the experience of the natural world outside. Again, a late Roman monument shaped that internal world most fully: Hagia Sophia embodies the ideal order of the universe in the Pythagorean union of the circle and the square (Fig. 16). It reflects the famous passage in Vitruvius wherein he hails the fact that the human body seems to fit easily into these ideal shapes. Scores of medieval and Renaissance drawings illustrating that idea culminate in Leonardo's famous example (Fig. 17). The human image is sculptural and heroic, but the ideal shapes are drawn thin as wire, remaining pure Idea, untrammeled by matter. In this way the interior of Hagia Sophia avoids any indication of weight, and the circle of the dome, apparently unsupported, is made to float over the square as if "suspended on a golden chain." Where is nature now? The universe is perfected here. The great Gothic cathedrals of western Europe pursue similar aims, drawing the worshipper down the nave to the crossing, beyond which the gateway to heaven, the façade of the choir, rushes upward, and the circular rose windows of the transept arms spin up as well, transcending gravity at the very edges of our arc of vision and lifting us into the Pythagorean, finally Neoplatonic, harmony of the spheres.

When Western mankind finally goes outside again, so to speak, Praeneste becomes the model. Bramante introduced it into the Vatican gardens at the very moment he was rebuilding the ancient basilica. Its vast new dome, the ideal interior space, was balanced out in open nature by the ramps and hemicycle of the primary sacred site of pagan Rome: Fortuna's sacred mountain. Praeneste continued to be the fundamental model for most of the gardens of the sixteenth century: the Villa d'Este is the foremost example (Fig. 18). It, too, lies on a slope of the Apennines, opening out to the Latin plain. In antiquity it may well have had two shrines of Hercules, one above the other, at least nearby, and may itself have looked a good deal like

Praeneste at that time as well. Again, the point is water, Pindar's "best of all things," and the wonder of the Villa d'Este is how its waters, actually pumped from below, are made to seem as if bursting with a daemonic abundance out of the sacred slope itself, beyond which, in fact, the ancient pagan waters of Tivoli's grottoes still roar like Poseidon underground. In this way the Villa d'Este and the other important gardens of the sixteenth century, such as that of the Villa Lante at Bagnaia, all invoked the ancient sacred sites, embellished them, and keyed up their violence and awe in ways that are surely the very basis of modern Romanticism. The earth is seen as wild, dangerous, filled with at least the passions of the gods. The English Romantic garden of the eighteenth century was a gentled, softened, Anglicized product of similar intentions, and its roots lay in Italy.

The French Classic gardens of the seventeenth century are an entirely different matter. True enough, some of the earliest examples, like that at Saint-Germain-en-Laye, the ancient seat of the kings overlooking Paris, seem to derive directly from the Villa d'Este and are set on a slope. But when Nicolas Fouquet brought André LeNôtre, Louis Le Vau, and Charles Le Brun together at Vaux-le-Vicomte an entirely new type of garden emerged (Fig. 19). LeNôtre planted the site with trees—the forest that ennobled Fouquet—and then made the flat parterres appear to be pushing the trees back, exploding as they do out in space forward and aft of the château. Only the building itself has weight; therefore it is planted on an island within a moat, so that its weight will not seem to rest on the ground. That primary element, the flat surface of the earth, is kept paper-thin: the water of the *bassins* seems to slide through just below its taut surface. We are drawn into the château, only two rooms deep, and immediately propelled through the elliptical room behind the entrance out to the garden on the other side. There the view is all velocity: the evergreen hedges of the geometric parterres of Italy are cut down tight so as not to impede the rapid movement of the eye, and the *broderie* leaps out across the thin plane of the ground (Fig. 20). The effect is not of the imposition of an order upon the earth, as the English were to say it was, but of a vast release, not only of the

19. Vaux-le-Vicomte. 1656–61. Aerial view from the north

20a. and b. Vaux-le-Vicomte. 1656–61. The parterres from the château

21. Vaux-le-Vicomte. 1656–61. Aerial view from the the south

22. Robert Nanteuil. *Nicolas Fouquet. Superintendent of Finance.* 1661. Engraving

23. Versailles. Begun in 1662. View from the head of the stairs

24. Gian Lorenzo Bernini. Bust of Louis XIV. 1665. Versailles

human spirit, which is liberated into space, but also of some great order within the earth itself, now made visible, freed (Fig. 21).

The garden treatises written during the seventeenth century by Boyceau de la Barauderie, the Mollets, and others, are all very clear on the basic point of how and why this new topographical countenance was made. One starts with geometry, they say, but then the art of landscape architecture requires a knowledge of scale—*échelle*—in order to transfer the geometric figures to the surface of the earth at the proper size. That process, they say, is called *pourtraiture*: and it is indeed a portraying, on the one hand of the client himself, like Nanteuil's touching portrait of Fouquet of just these years (Fig. 22), and on the other, of the inner geometric framework of the earth itself, now brought forward in the only way such ideal order can be portrayed, as pure drawing upon its surface, free of all mass.

Louis XIV instantly saw all the possibilities inherent in this system. Imprisoning Fouquet, he brought the magic trio of collaborators to his father's hunting lodge at Versailles (Fig. 23) and built there a portrait of his new France: centralized, with straight new roads and long canals, and most of all at continental scale, extending, in Descartes's term, "indefinitely" beyond the horizon. The portrait is also of himself, as Vaux's was of Fouquet. Bernini alone of Louis's portraitists captures his aspiration in these years (Fig. 24). He is the Sun King, young, carried on a cloud, like those that float across the great open flat land of Versailles and the fields of France.

The sacred mountain is no more. The king is everywhere over France; his eyes are made to shine with light looking out to vast distances. His hair is water and fire, like the fountains that tell his story in transparent silver screens. Most of all, in the flat parterres (Fig. 25), drawn tight as wire and clothed in his livery, the king himself achieves the Neoplatonic dream: he is the individual at the center. The diagonals of his body's action project out across the circles and the squares and his will becomes more than regional, shaping the land of France in celestial *étoiles* and so, like the medieval kings before him, linking the kingdom to a cosmic order (Fig. 26).

Versailles was the first image of the modern nation-state at continental scale. Its plan thus became not only the model for the gardens, never very satisfactorily carried out, that were built by princelings of Europe, soon to pass away, but also for Washington, the ceremonial center of the first emergent republic of modern times, the very soul of American political aspiration, and the most wholly classical of modern capitals. The best of modern urbanism everywhere derives from Versailles:

modern Paris, the consummate work of art of modern times, most of all. There the fabric of the modern city is cut to the shapes of Versailles (Fig. 27). In the end, Paris is a garden, too. Its streets are *allées* defined by building masses like clumps of trees, with the mansards rounding them over at the top. It embodies a classicism blending north and south, and, like the Gothic cathedral, it is at last suggestive of the shapes of nature itself. No other urban scheme at great scale has improved upon its achievement or come near it. Peter Cook, the inventor of Archigram's science-fiction city, once said a true and touching thing: "Archigram is all right," he said, "so long as you still have Paris."

Inconceivable, therefore, the horror of the French New Towns where only the Catalan Ricardo Bofill seems to understand what Paris means. Nevertheless, Paris always carried the seeds of its own destruction, as all strong forms seem to do, since the plan of Versailles, perhaps as filtered through Washington, became Le Corbusier's model for his Ideal City of 1922 (Fig. 28). In it, however, the classical garden is destroyed. The boulevards are bereft of their trees and rush through an urban wasteland. The traditional street is progressively obliterated from the perimeter of the plan to the center, where only flat-topped skyscrapers stand in the superblocks as the automobiles speed by, like predators taking over the world. This vision became the model for the urbanism of the International Style, was there to complement the love of the automobile and the dislike of urban complexity that characterized American redevelopment in the 1960s, and is now the very image of all too large a part of our world. In recent years it has even begun to eat away at Paris itself.

In return, though, the classic garden, that of Versailles in particular, has helped shape the contemporary reaction to the cataclysmic planning of the International Style by healing the wounds it has inflicted on our cities and knitting up the urban fabric once again. Leon Krier's monumental drawing for La Villette, in Paris, is one of the first documents of that classical revival. It filled in the city blocks, disciplined the automobile, and seems in every way to have been based upon an aerial photograph of Versailles.

Classical France offers much more than this. Le Nôtre's *étoiles* at Versailles were matched by Vauban's *étoiles* along the Rhine. Louis XIV expanded the frontiers of Continental France exactly as he expanded the campaigns of building at Versailles.

25. Parterre du Sud and Pièce d'Eau des Suisses. Versailles

26. Versailles. Begun in 1662. Aerial view

27. Streets radiating out from the Arc de Triomphe de l'Étoile. Plan: mid-nineteenth-century. Aerial view. Paris

28. Le Corbusier. Ideal City. Presented at the 1922 Salon d'Automne, Paris

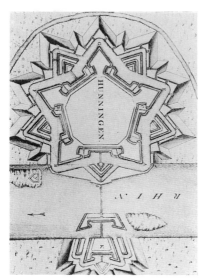

29. Sébastien Le Prestre de Vauban. Plan of his fortifications. Late seventeenth century. Huninque

He reached the Rhine, the Alps, and held the Pyrénées. And Vauban built his forts in echelon, in depth behind the frontiers everywhere; they were reflections of the same art that shaped the gardens, projecting as they did long lines of flat-trajectory cannon fire to the horizon (Fig. 29). As such, their outerworks, the *dehors*, kept expanding too. It always seemed advisable to have another *demi-lune, ravelin,* and *glacis* out there in space. Where can the Self stop in its defense against the Other?

Like the gardens, the fortifications became earth sculptures at ever-expanding scale. They held the frontiers from Flanders to Alsace and the borders of Andorra. When, therefore, the French built their railroads all at once in the 1840s, all of France became one great *étoile*, with long straight axes radiating from Paris to the frontiers, each railroad running to one of Vauban's citadels. Here is Ideal France, as every French schoolchild knows her, almost a pure geometric figure, but locked into the topography of Europe: centralized, organized, complete. Her shape belongs to Louis, made by his gardens and his forts. Colonial-minded historians of the nineteenth century criticized him for indulging these preoccupations while France's colonies fell. But was he wrong? All the colonies of Europe are gone, but France retains the viable Continental mass with which Louis endowed her. The threat to the frontiers, too, was not an illusory one. In the most recent invasion from the north, the traditional enemy from across the Rhine fell afoul of Vauban's flooded canals and *demi-lunes* at Gravelines and Bergues. Finally, French infantry, dug in at Bergues, kept them out of Dunkirk for a week, and the army got away. Right there, stumbling over Vauban's forts, Hitler lost his war.

Our reaction to that story reflects, I suppose, an identification with the nation-state and, especially, an aesthetic admiration for the first and most beautiful of them all—modern France—shaped as she is on the same principles from Versailles and Paris to the mountains and the sea. Clearly, such identification cannot be enough any longer, and it surely reflects one of the climactic victories of the human aggression against nature that is so splendidly embodied in the Parthenon.

We would seem to require broader and simpler modes of identification, based not upon political life, if that is possible for mankind, but upon the very fact of life itself. In a way, Taos is that, where all are one: man and mountain, snake, eagle, and cloud. Each is real, and worthy of respect as living: all are divine. Yet we cannot entirely cast aside that shining vision of the gods as human which was the Greeks' double-edged gift to mankind. We are torn two ways, but one thing is clear: in the modern age, and especially with that architecture we have most identified as "modern," we have on the whole shaped the earth badly. We need to revive our traditions and begin again.

JOHN DIXON HUNT

The Garden as Cultural Object

Let me begin by establishing four markers by which to orient the historical discussions that follow and to provide a context for consideration of the modern garden. They are, if you like, conclusions in advance of my concluding.

First, I would quote the first half of Wallace Stevens's "Anecdote of the Jar":

I placed a jar in Tennessee,
And round it was, upon a hill.
It made the slovenly wilderness
Surround that hill.

The Wilderness rose up to it,
And sprawled around, no longer wild.[1]

For our present purposes what interests me in this poem is its recognition that the introduction of a work of art into the unmediated wilderness of nature alters both, though it is wilderness that seems more changed. Gardens, too, are jars, set down in otherwise untouched landscape, and part of their function and interest is that they alter their surroundings by their presence.

Second, I would invoke two Renaissance writers, Jacopo Bonfadio and Bartolomeo Taegio, each of whom introduced a fundamental but unregarded concept into the study of gardens when he wrote of them as resolving the ancient antithesis of art and nature and, thereby, as creating or constituting a "third nature" (*terza natura*), whose name, one of them says, is unknown.[2] These first two propositions address the dialectic between culture and nature.

Third, gardens have often been, from the very earliest examples, an exercise in what modern historians have termed invented tradition.[3] Gardens are created, adapted, or used to provide spaces and forms of a ritual or symbolic nature that inculcate certain values and norms of behavior having an implied continuity with the past; indeed, they often seek to establish continuity with a suitable historic past that could be objective not idealized but is largely factitious. Some of the most conspicuous examples of invented garden traditions will occur (as the historians make clear about other forms) when society undergoes rapid transformations: in the Italian Renaissance new princes of church and state used gardens to signal their new place in the tradition of antique villa life; in the English nineteenth century, the remarkable, sometimes hilarious invocations of historical styles of gardening—Italianate or Dutch—suggest the instant formulation of "new" traditions to bolster the social aspirations of an emergent upper middle class. The cottage garden is another such invented tradition, but so was the medieval *jardin d'amour.*

Finally, gardens historically have been a representational art, until the late eighteenth century, although this perception of their function has been lost, or at least overlooked. With the same theoretical justifications as painting and literature, gardens have been said to represent the larger world outside them. Labyrinths represented the wilderness; mounts, mountains; pergola walks, paths through the forest; fountains, springs or waterfalls. When the idea of a garden as a representational work of art was abandoned at the end of the eighteenth century, a long-standing role of gardens was potentially lost, even though some late twentieth-century gardens seem to have recovered something of that function.

The Italian Renaissance saw the development of wholly new kinds of gardens, at least as far as western Europe was concerned. A more self-conscious, vital human control over space was evident in their axial organization, in the unity achieved between house and gardens, and in the elaborate disposition of space within the garden area. Though usually linked, especially in the Veneto or the Medici territories around Florence, to agricultural land, these villas also displayed the affluence of their owners by devoting space and expense to nonproductive ends, though that is not to say that plants in these villa gardens were not serviceable for the table or the pharmacy. But the age of the ornamental garden, dedicated to the delight in species for their own sakes, had to wait until the seventeenth century, in the Low Countries.

The contrivance of this third nature in Renaissance villas necessarily also changed the perception of the larger landscape in which these new gardens were established; one immediate effect of that change was that a villa complex, often including both regular, highly organized garden spaces and more "natural," less schematic groves, established a palpable gradation between culture and nature, a spectrum stretching from human control to unregenerate wildness. In their acknowledgment of classical precedents, these Renaissance gardens were also far more self-consciously dedicated to re-creating a tradition of garden and villa than even the monastic garden, with its allusions to the Garden of Eden and to the *hortus conclusus,* or enclosed garden, of the Canticles; for the new world of Renaissance humanism included an awareness of the modes and styles of country-house life in ancient Rome that merged with the Christian tradition to create a far more invigorating idea of a gardenist past.

Italian gardens of the sixteenth and seventeenth centuries were the source and inspiration for almost all the rest of northern European gardening. However different were social conditions, cultural objectives, or even climate, a country like England still found expression of its own concerns in the modish world of Italianate villas. Formal and aesthetic admiration of the new garden style was put at the service of political and social myths of an emergent nationhood. So it is no surprise that the

Italian garden appears prominently in Inigo Jones's masque designs for the lavish court entertainments enjoyed and promoted by James I and Charles I. Their appearances are explicit metaphors for the ideal world that the Stuart monarchy wished to create: out of rude and wild natural materials, out of chaos and disorder, are summoned forms of fine gardens that are enabled by the beneficent power of Stuart kingship, of which, in their turn, they are symbolic (Fig. 30). The stage directions in such instances are explicit: "The Britanides and their Prophetic Powers were to be re-established in this garden by the unanimous and magnificent virtues of the King and Queen Majesties' making this island a pattern to all nations as Greece was amongst the ancients." As yet another vista opens, soon afterwards in this masque of 1683—*Luminalia*, by William Davenant and Inigo Jones—Queen Henrietta Maria is herself discovered. The stage direction reads: "The scene was changed [sic] into a delicious prospect, wherein were rows of trees, fountains, statues, arbours, grottoes, walks, and all such things of delight as might express the beautiful garden of the Britanides."[4]

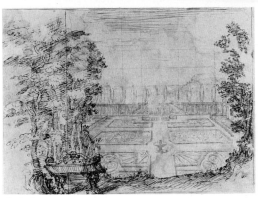

30. Inigo Jones. Design for the back shutter of *The Shepherd's Paradise*. 1631. Trustees of the Devonshire Collection, Chatsworth

A garden lent itself to this claim for the creation of order and power since it is a space, cleared, colonized, organized, and enabled by hard work and skill. And because the garden came (so to speak) ready-made with the implied imprimatur of Eden—for to establish a new garden is to re-create Paradise[5]—such claims for England's prestige and power were authorized by a potent myth for a century and country much preoccupied with millennial ambitions. The recovery of Eden is not the only myth at work here, however, for to establish England as the new Greece (a word frequently used to signal the classical world generally, Roman as well as Greek) invoked another contemporary obsession with the progress of the arts: namely, that what ancient Greece had authorized, classical Rome had inherited and augmented, and that these traditions were then reborn in Renaissance Italy after the interlude of the Dark Ages and thence were slowly but surely transmitted northward to their climax in England. Gardens that echoed Italian design motifs in northern countries could thus participate in the fiction that such and such a ruler had by his power and enterprise reestablished classical civilizations. The Dutch could claim for the United Provinces the same place at the apex of cultural progress as England, and virtually at the same historical moment.[6]

State entries frequently invoked garden imagery, for the entry of a new ruler into a city in his control gave his subjects the opportunity to admonish him as to his duties as well as to claim, via hyperbole, that he was capable of high achievement: thus Rubens utilized garden imagery on the structure designed to greet Archduke Ferdinand at Antwerp in 1635. When James I formally entered the City of London in 1604, the year after he succeeded to the English throne, he was greeted at one point in his progress with two triumphal arches where *tableaux vivants* (Fig. 31) enacted the visions that James should, could, and supposedly did nurture: one depicted the Fountain of Virtue, which flowed with real wine at His Majesty's approach.

It was the king's privilege, both at masques and on the road of entry into a sub-

31. From Stephen Harrison. *The Arches of Triumph* (London, 1604), plate 5. Folger Shakespeare Library, Washington, D.C. The figures in the alcoves above the arches are *tableaux vivants*

ject city, to be placed exactly on the central point of perspective: everything, especially on a stage with illusionist scenery, was designed to be seen from his position. (In contrast to the scheme of the Whitehall Banqueting Hall, the equality of the members of the Vicenza academy in the Teatro Olimpico was registered in Palladio's design through several street vistas on the perspectival stage from different points in the auditorium.)[7] The single-point perspective constituted, according to Alberti's treatise on painting, the sovereignty of vision,[8] with the king at the focal point enjoying "the prince of rays." Thus was the new architectural principle of house and garden, aligned on one axis, able to serve as well as be itself determined by political ends.

These ideal gardens in court masques and other political entertainments were, despite the vast sums spent on them, much more easily established than real ones. Doubtless it was this facility that fatally lured Charles I into mistaking the wish for the deed, the propaganda for the achievement. But actual gardens of the new model were also being created throughout England, and they served to maintain and extend the political imagery of the court. They were regional images of royal supremacy, all the more conspicuous when James I went on progress around the kingdom and visited his important subjects in their new houses and gardens. But they were also local instances of political and social power, for the landowners of these splendid creations acted in their local world precisely the same absolutist role that the king performed on the national stage. Hence the organization of gardens along perspectival lines privileged their owner at the center of the vista, while their imagery, too, announced his contribution to engineering the progress of art toward its English apotheosis.

At Wilton House, near Salisbury around 1640 the Earl of Pembroke may be understood to regard his fine garden from the lofty, central position that the engraver has by implication given him (see Fig. 32); the imagery of the garden and grottoes, which are housed in the far terrace, all declare the management by art, or *techne*, of the natural resources from which gardens, like estates and states, are made.[9] The power of lordship is made clear by the expense of technology that only the rich could afford ("The Grott & pipes did cost ten thousand pounds," relates John Aubrey); the entertainments that highlighted the manipulation of the elements of water and stone; and the representation by garden art of things outside its scope (His Lordship's gardener had custody of machinery that produced no fewer than three rainbows). Like the waterworks, a prime Italianate feature, the Wilton garden statuary declared Wilton's place in the declensions of classical culture. At the center of the final garden was a copy of the "Gladiator of brass the most famous statue of all that Antiquity hath left," and at the top of the hill was a copy of the famous equestrian statue of Marcus Aurelius that had been placed on the Capitol. Over the head of water that fed the grottoes presided a statue of Pegasus, the mythical beast whose hoof touched into being the springs of Helicon on Mount Olympus—an apt figure for an owner who wished to locate himself within literary traditions of the garden, for of course Pegasus had presided over other gardens of the

32. Isaac de Caus. *Wilton House Gardens*. 1645(?). Engraving. The British Library

Italian Renaissance, like that of the Villa Lante. Moreover, the amphitheater on the Wilton hillside claimed direct descent from the one Bramante had created in the Vatican Belvedere courtyard in the early sixteenth century (a design later codified in Serlio's treatise), a configuration of steps that in its turn had been borrowed from the remains of a classical temple at Palestrina. No wonder visitors such as William Stukeley applauded the success of "bringing as it were all Athens to Wilton" and took particular notice that the gardens instructed them in the "great illustrations of history": "The curious spectator may be reminded . . . of the character of so many illustrious personages famous in ancient times . . . a double pleasure in improving the mind and fixing in the memory a stronger impression of the qualitys & endowments, of the virtues and vices each was distinguished for; whilst the eye is surveying the living portraits." Clearly, whatever the beauty of the new garden style, the pleasure it gave was premised upon political and cultural motives that shaped its creation as surely as they did visitors' admiration.

Now we may ask what happened to these gardens when the informing ideas and forms no longer held sway, when the political climate changed, when the Stuart monarchy succumbed to republican ideologies after the Civil Wars. By the mid-eighteenth century Wilton House Garden had been completely altered, its Italianate structures largely wiped away and apparently a wholly new imagery substituted, as Richard Wilson's later painting suggests (Fig. 33). What we see is a fine example of the English landscape garden, which, we are accustomed to hear, is eloquent of a new love of nature that swept Europe in the second half of the eighteenth century. It is true that such an enthusiasm was widespread, just as it is true that some landscapes came into being as imitations of landscape paintings by Claude Lorrain or the Poussins, or were determined by the economic need for gardens that were easier to maintain. But all that is neither the whole story nor, I'd suggest, the accurate story. The new landscapes were, at least in their early stages, just as much the product of political and cultural ideas and ambitions as the earlier English gardens had been: this is signaled by the eighteenth-century Palladian Bridge, as indeed it alerts us to some continuities between garden styles otherwise wholly opposed to each other.

33. Richard Wilson. *Wilton House from the Southeast*. c. 1758–60. Oil on canvas (unfinished), 39 x 56¾". Yale Center for British Art, New Haven

On the map of political ideologies in seventeenth- and early eighteenth-century England, a conspicuous element was a form of civic humanism that ultimately drew its inspiration from classical, republican Rome, mediated along the way by Machiavelli in Renaissance Italy and by Sir John Harington and John Toland in England. This civic humanism has been studied by a cluster of modern historians, most notably John Pocock in his 1975 study, *The Machiavellian Moment*. They have demonstrated how powerful and vivifying was the classical model of a mixed government of consuls, patricians, and *comitiae*—or, in English terms, monarchy, a House of Lords, and a House of Commons. An additional attraction of this political model to the British was that it maintained the fiction of a tradition of constitutional progress from classical Rome to seventeenth- and even eighteenth-century

England, which paralleled the progress of the arts that we have already noted. It was by invoking this tradition of a political system that prospered by each of its three elements checking and restraining the other two that the Glorious Revolution of 1688 was engineered, bringing William III to the British throne at the expense of James II; thereafter, it kept alive a spirit of reasonable, balanced, and nonabsolutist government that featured prominently in the British mythology of civil liberties.

This brief sketch of a complex tradition in political thought is intended to convey how classical Rome continued to inspire English culture: one consequence was that Renaissance Italianate gardens, always considered as somehow revivals of antique gardening, continued to attract attention as a symbol of continuing English adherence to classical ideologies. Lords and other nonaristocratic landed gentry who subscribed to the politics of civic humanism (and who indeed provided two-thirds of its structure) could declare their loyalties by insisting, as Cobham did at Stowe, upon gardens in the Italian style rather than, for example, in the French, which smacked precisely of that absolutism that the 1688 revolution had fought peacefully against. Since both aristocracy (lords) and commons (the franchised gentry) were precisely those who sought to improve their estates while also serving the state, Italianate garden designs were a ready-at-hand imagery of political commitment.

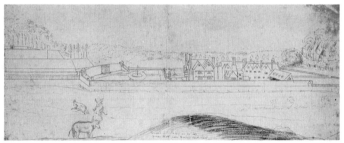

Here we may note two curious factors. What seems to modern eyes the same style of gardens was susceptible to more discriminations by contemporaries, who would distinguish, for example, between Dutch and Italian modes. Both could be opposed to the French, yet each could be seen to be very different from the other. Equally, different political ideologies might invoke the same garden style. Thus the Earl of Pembroke, owner of that single-vista, lordly garden at Wilton, fought on Parliament's side in the Civil War; while John Evelyn, a royalist who wisely absented himself in Italy during the conflicts, espoused the style of axial gardens and associated Italian imagery when he redesigned the family seat at Wotton in Surrey (Fig. 34). What Evelyn recreated here and at nearby Albury for the banished Earl of Arundel were gardens that breathed the spirit of old Rome; in practice this meant locating on British soil imagery that would recall villa life after the classical and modern Italian fashion. The garden and groves of Wotton were Evelyn's quite deliberate reinvention of classical traditions of husbandry: as he said of his neighbor, "Mithought I saw old Cato or Varro in Him."[10] The Earl of Arundel also deliberately used the term *villa*, a Latin and an Italian word, to describe Albury, and Evelyn's redesigning of this hillside specifically invoked classical Rome in its imagery of terraces, exedra, and tunnel through the Surrey hillside.[11] John Aubrey, who himself never went to Italy nor even built his ideal country house, nevertheless left us a manuscript in which the formal elements of Italian gardens—regular terraces, groves, fountains, grottoes, statuary— are introduced by a mock title page where a cartouche with the key term VILLA inscribed within it is buttressed by quotations from classical authors (Fig. 35).

Gardens, then, were utilized as a series or congeries of signs. As with all signs—

34. John Evelyn. Drawing of the gardens of his family home at Wotton, Surrey. 1650s (?). Christ Church College, Oxford: Trustees of the Will of the late J. H. C. Evelyn

35. John Aubrey. Cartouche for VILLA. 1669. The Bodleian Library, Oxford

all verbal or visual language used to communicate—one thing has to be transmitted via another. (This explains, for example, how Italian gardens could sustain both the world of Pembroke, Arundel, and Aubrey as well as the English Palladians in the eighteenth century.)   How, if you like, was John Aubrey to translate his classical authors and his sense of Italian design into the forms of an English country estate? It was a problem that faced (and always faces) good literary translators. Thus, John Oldham, a contemporary of Aubrey, said his job was to put Horace into "a more modern dress than hitherto he has appear'd in, that is, by making him speak, as if here living and writing." Early in the eighteenth century, a friend of Alexander Pope urged him to continue translating Homer so as to "make him speak good English."[12]

Contemporary architectural and gardening activities were also translations in this way: Lord Burlington and other lords of creation translated Palladianism from Italy to England, all along perfectly aware that Palladio himself had translated classical remains into modern Italian forms. Pope's gardening activities were also an effort of translating: making classical and modern Italian gardens into English ones, making Pliny or Horace as villa dwellers speak good English.[13] The crucial challenge of all such translation is to be modern, speaking the contemporary idiom of one's readers, while also giving them a clear impression of the original. What did this mean, then, in garden-design practice?

The example of Castle Howard, in Yorkshire, may serve to provide an answer as well as to inaugurate another aspect of this topic. John Vanbrugh and his adjutant, and later successor, Nicholas Hawksmoor, created one of the earliest examples of the so-called English landscape garden at Castle Howard from the 1710s. The ancient castle of Henderskelfe had burned down in 1693, but its associations were maintained in the title of Castle Howard (for the Howard family). This verbal emphasis was given visual focus in Vanbrugh's mock battlements and double "ring" of walls that confront the visitor, while the essential Palladian-villa ground plan of the house is given, at least from a distance, something other than Palladian classicism, if not a castle air. Similarly, the second gateway of the "castle" has the distinct character of a Roman triumphal arch rather than a medieval postern. Such mingled forms are signs of a larger enterprise. The old castle, like the woods and hills of the estate, was old English; it recalled ancient British liberties (the example of King Alfred was often invoked on other estates, like Bathurst's Cirencester) which were annexed to the classical traditions of civic republicanism. To highlight this endemic Englishness and at the same time to assert its classical origins, the Yorkshire landscape was completed with temples. Vanbrugh and Hawksmoor were adamant that this meant classical temples. The latter inscribed a design (Fig. 36) for one such temple, or belvedere, with the words *After the Antique, Vid[e] Herodotus, Pliny and M: Varo.* It looks very unlike any Italian building, ancient or modern, but the aspiration is there, and it is interesting how strongly the Italian influence was felt by Hawksmoor who, like Aubrey before him, never traveled. The temples that do survive are more Italian in form—Hawksmoor's

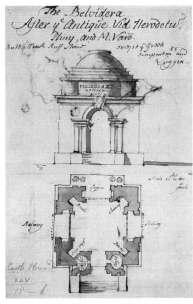

36. Nicholas Hawksmoor. Design for a temple or belvedere. 1720s. Castle Howard, Yorkshire. The British Library

37. View of Temple of the Four Winds on the "ramparts" beside Wray Wood, Castle Howard, Yorkshire

38. Castle Howard. Engraving from Colen Campbell. *Vitruvius Britannicus*. 1725. London. Collections of Dumbarton Oaks, Washington, D.C.

39. Pyramid in Pretty Wood, Castle Howard, Yorkshire. From Christopher Hussey. *English Gardens and Landscape 1700–1750*. (London, 1967)

Mausoleum out in the fields recalls round antique temples. Vanbrugh's Temple of the Four Winds, however, while it gestures to Palladian buildings, is sited on a bastion that echoes the "medieval" ramparts encountered earlier (Fig. 37). We know that Vanbrugh's patron, the third Earl of Carlisle, was "utterly against anything but an Italian building in that place" and that the wood on the edge of which the temple is set was called "Belvedere," which, a contemporary manuscript still surviving in the family insists, is "Italian for the Fine View." Yet, from these Italian-inspired vantage points, what is viewed is purely indigenous—the beauties of Yorkshire and, in particular, the Howardian Hills. The owner, Charles Howard, was a prominent Whig, a member of the Kit-Cat Club, which celebrated the fresh English continuations of civic republicanism. It was therefore apt that Castle Howard should be featured in the third installment of the significantly named *Vitruvius Britannicus* (Fig. 38): the engraving depicts the south bastion, with more views over the English countryside, laid out in groves decorated with classical statues and temples.[14]

Castle Howard shows how an English landed family chose to situate itself within an invented tradition of gardens and politics and how it could encode meanings within the materials available to its designers. But we must also understand how its creation of a third nature within the garden space had repercussions for the perception of a much larger landscape. Looking out, past a Palladian temple or past temples in groves, into an unmediated English landscape beyond the control of designers (because it is too large, above all), we do not see simply nature: the very context of our looking changes what we see, and what we are invited to see, I suggest, is a representation of Englishness. It is, in fact, a phenomenon encountered in many early gardens of the landscape movement—like Rousham, for example—and Jane Austen, as late as 1816, takes its point exactly when she has her heroine Emma see a "sweet view, sweet to the eye and the mind. English verdure, English culture, English comfort, seen under a bright sun, without being oppressive."[15]

Castle Howard and Rousham provide excellent examples of a garden experience we have totally lost. We no longer register a representation of English landscape; we just see it. As Wallace Stevens's jar upon the Tennessee hillside makes lucidly clear, however, a juxtaposition changes how we see things, and viewing the Yorkshire countryside from a garden so carefully encoded with meaning must change it. With an uncanny anticipation of the Stevens jar, Hawksmoor placed in the heart of the Yorkshire woodland on the Castle Howard estate a couple of monuments that a distinguished modern authority has termed "utterly pointless." In fact, the whole point of the pyramid (Fig. 39) or the Four Faces is that they recall one's attention to the way in which the landscape is made to represent itself.

It is doubtless a difficult notion to appreciate today, but in the eighteenth century all the fine arts were deemed to have representation at their center, and gardening aspired to *beaux-arts* status. It is also during the eighteenth century that this notion was lost. Jane Austen's Emma may be required by her creator to see a representation of Englishness, since it is part of her process of education; but for many visitors to country estates at the time, the prospects from the garden into the surrounding countryside were nothing but of nature itself. By using natural forms to represent English nature, the English landscape garden defeated its ambition to be a representative art. The medium was the message, and nobody could tell them apart.[16]

The designers responsible for this crucial *démarche* were William Kent and Lancelot Brown, known as "Capability." As I have argued elsewhere, the former's gradual suppression of busy Italian imagery in his designs follows his determination to let English nature speak on his patrons' country estates.[17] In the 1730s at Holkham, in Norfolk, he planned an elaborate context for a seat upon a mount: in fact, a viewing platform from which to watch the building of the Palladian mansion below (Fig. 40). Like the house itself the design is firmly Italianate, with its pergola tunnel; its classical seat at the center and its two classical entries to the tunnel; and even its exedral shape, contrived by the hemicycle of hedges, which in another drawing is given a much more explicitly theatrical dimension with ranged seats in tiers like an antique theater. That was what Kent proposed in about 1733, and the proposal was entirely consonant with his and his patron's determined love of Italy. Ten years later, however, the design was substantially altered (Fig. 41): the classical seat is there, but the tunnel and its architectural entrances, together with the exedral seats, have been eliminated. Why? A conventional answer is that Kent is becoming more natural, but that simply begs the question and, in fact, probably interprets Kent in the light of merely aesthetic criteria that were not his. I would suggest instead that Kent was learning how to make Palladio and Italian gardening speak good English, retaining the Italian accent, so to speak, in that classical seat flanked by herms and the suggestion, still, of a classical amphitheater but rendering the language and syntax in the English forms of Norfolk countryside. The seat is his jar that transforms how we see the surrounding hillside.

Kent's successor, Capability Brown, took this naturalization of the garden to its logical conclusion. He eliminated even more of the Italian accent—banishing terraces, statues, grottoes, temples, exedras—to give Englishness its fullest voice. One must insist that Brown was not simply letting country estates become natural, but was representing in its most perfect forms a nature that was British, and to do so he invoked the general, abstract forms of his materials—trees, woods, waters, hills. His was one of the last public, political statements of English gardening that was wholly in line with the demands of spokesmen like Sir Joshua Reynolds who urged the political obligations of the arts. After Brown, garden design succumbed, as John Barrell has recently argued in his *Political Theory of Painting*, to the pressures of privatization, and garden art, like its other more established sisters, became an expression of private ideas and sensibilities.[18]

It is unwise to describe gardens or to explain garden history simply in stylistic terms: that way lie the banal alternatives of "formal" or "informal," labels that continue to dog and clog garden analysis. No, we must ask far more searching questions, probe

40. William Kent. Proposal for the seat on the mount at Holkham Hall, Norfolk. Before 1733. The Earl of Leicester

41. William Kent, new proposal for the seat on the mount at Holkham Hall, Norfolk. Mid-1740s. The Earl of Leicester

more deeply into cultural assumptions, asking about the uses of gardens, uses both physical and metaphysical, visible and invisible. What Roland Barthes has written about photography is relevant to the study of historical gardens: "We saw that the code of connotation was in all likelihood neither 'natural' nor 'artificial' but historical, or, if it be preferred, 'cultural.' Its signs are gestures, attitudes, expressions, colors or effects, endowed with certain meanings by virtue of the practice of a certain society: the link between signifier and signified remains if not unmotivated, at least entirely historical."[19] Gardens, too, mean rather than are. Their various signs are constituted of all the elements that compose them—elements of technical human intervention like terraces or the shape of flowerbeds, elements of nature like water and trees—but they are nonetheless signs, to be read by outsiders in time and space for what they tell of a certain society. Everything in a garden is, then, what Roland Barthes calls signifiers in photographs, and I would argue that successful gardens always have been those where the ensemble of elements is not only just beautiful, but also answers to a particular society's deepest needs.

Thus, we may register in representations of late medieval gardens, for example, how precious and precarious they were. Vulnerable because they were often established outside the walls of fortifications—expendable spaces when under siege from either human enemies or beasts of the wilderness—they were status symbols, too, privileged in terms of class and gender. Other garden images recall not just their preciousness to a few socially superior folk (Fig. 42), but also their associations variously with the Virgin Mary or with the Garden of Love, associations that confirm them as principally female preserves.

If we go back even further to examine the garden world of ancient Pompeii, assessing from the ruined spaces and the miraculously discovered garden paintings what gardens meant to their creators and users, we are confronted with a strange sense of intimacy.[20] It is a social and familial intimacy, for the garden images are brought into the living areas of the houses, which themselves extend out into the garden areas. But it is also an even stranger intimacy of humans with the numinous world, the world of spirit and *genius loci*, for however "realistic" we may wish to judge the paintings and statues that survive, they also represent another world to which the religious Pompeian wanted constant and intimate access.

42. Woman listening to music in a garden. From Pietro de Crescenzi. *Il libro della agricultura.* (Venice, 1495). Collections of Dumbarton Oaks, Washington, D.C.

Does it not follow, then, that successful garden designers have succeeded precisely because they were able to give gardenist expression to their patron's or their patron's society's urgent and most desired—even if not always declared—ambitions and assumptions?   In the English garden of the nineteenth century, for instance, the political and cultural expression of civic humanism, which I have traced in various earlier forms, lost its point. As William Hazlitt, acknowledging the new status of art as a private transaction, put it, "Whatever is genuine in art must proceed from the impulse of nature and individual genius."[21] The republic of arts, including gardening, had become a private realm which was wholly separate from the political republic and which Hazlitt now projected in democratic forms. This change did not imply by any means that gardens were any less the expression of ideas and sensibilities, only that ceasing to serve an explicit polity, their meanings were, and still often are, obscure.

Public gardens, whether royal preserves opened to the public like some of London's parks or freehold land donated to the citizenry as in some northern English cities, gave the politically disfranchised and the newly franchised their own garden. While essentially offering a utility, an amenity, they also had clearly ideological intentions. It is not surprising that these large public gardens took as their models the forms of the final flowering of civic humanist gardens under Capability Brown, even if they gradually introduced new facilities into them; public gardens always aped the private gardens of the privileged, invoking ancient traditions for the citizenry's new purposes. The famous pleasure gardens of the eighteenth century like Vauxhall or Ranelagh invoked the imagery and layouts of the patrician gardens of Europe,[22] just as the much more extensive public emparking of the nineteenth century looked back to the landscape estates of the previous century.

43. Camille Pissarro. *Garden of Les Mathurins at Pontoise*. 1876. Oil on canvas, 44⅝ x 65⅛". Nelson-Atkins Museum of Art, Kansas City, Missouri

Private gardens, meanwhile, rapidly acquired a new imagery, which mirrored even as it also sanctioned new bourgeois values. The professionals identifying and creating them were, first, Humphry Repton, who typically provided clients with Red Books, which addressed local sites and local ideas, and his successor, J. C. Loudon, who virtually invented the suburban villa garden. The prime value expressed by these new private gardens was ownership, sought by increasing numbers of citizens, as well as a desire for privacy and security. These ambitions of the nineteenth-century private garden are perhaps given their most eloquent expression in Impressionist paintings (Fig. 43), which show gardens designed to allow all members of a family to congregate, but also with local spots where some solitariness was possible. These private gardens were spaces where, hidden from full public scrutiny, the newly privileged could indulge their wishes and fantasies. To fence off and set apart some space of land as a garden constitutes not only a third nature, but a world where the owner may see him/herself as partaking in tradition, now reinvented for consumption by either one single person or by a very small group.

The mass production of housing—whether in the form of row or town house, or of housing development or subdivision—means that gardens, too, are likely to be mass-produced, as expressed in a cartoon by Stefan Verwey (Fig. 44); while they still may answer dreams and desires, the individual's freedom of expression is at best curtailed because preempted. The subject of mass production raises the whole question of a new relationship, if any, between client and designer: these days, the Repton or Loudon is likely to be the anonymous designer who provides the garden center with its wholesale merchandise. Standardization of forms and taste through this commercialization of small-garden design does not lessen, strangely, the social rivalries that garden ads exploit. It tends to create a homogeneous imagery that its consumers can credit with being tasteful, in contrast to the creations of those who cannot afford to patronize the garden center. The poorish *quartiers* in the Parisian conurbation that Bernard Lassus explored in his 1977 study *Les Jardins imaginaires* have no inhibitions

44. Stefan Verwey. Cartoon. Originally published in *De Volkskrant*

45. Stefan Verwey. Cartoon. Originally published in *De Volkskrant*

46. Stephen Dowling. From R. J. Yeatman and W. C. Sellar. *Garden Rubbish*. (London, 1936)

about what imagery is apt or tasteful: the local gardenists (Lassus terms them "les habitants paysagistes") pillage Walt Disney, Batman, comic strips, and girlie magazines. The imagery is, interestingly, as public and available as the dreams and fantasies that the imagery expresses are hidden.

Another cartoon by Verwey (Fig. 45) suggests that besides confronting matters of acceptable imagery, the modern gardener is locked uncertainly into a historical conflict between nature and culture or artifice. What should be the extent of human intervention into the natural world within the modern garden? Should the modern gardener regulate his tulips, eliminating untidy growth, or, rather, give free expression to nature's sensual fecundity? And do these questions receive different answers today because the late twentieth-century garden inhabitant has more immediate and frequent access to large areas of wild landscape? Does the suburban garden not become a jar upon the hillside of the national park?

The guidelines or criteria by which such questions may be answered seem elusive, as another, older, set of cartoons implies. In 1936, together with W. C. Sellar as coauthor and Stephen Dowling as illustrator, R. J. Yeatman produced a volume called *Garden Rubbish*; among its themes is that of garden design for the English upwardly mobile, middle-class, suburban dweller. The garden lover (Fig. 46) with thatched cottage, winding and crazy-paving path, garden gnome, and rabbit and sundial, wants to locate herself in an invented tradition that ignores her urban location, striving for a natural garden, fecund with rabbits and even instinct with preternatural spirits (the gnome). But if the sundial suggests a wish to live a life closer to nature, however, the wristwatch amusingly declares that the advantages of technology have not been abandoned.

Such modern suburban gardens locate themselves in earlier and more spacious traditions of gardening, with an eclecticism that is familiar to us from postmodernist architecture. Pergolas, serpentine paths, pools, and terraces are invoked sparsely in one Dowling drawing; crammed and jammed in another (Fig. 47). What Yeatman and Dowling identify above all is a garden's hugely inclusive realm. In it are concentrated, as perhaps nowhere else in human technology or art, a whole cluster of ideas and aspirations, some conscious and declared, others no less apparent for being unconscious. They point to the appeal of mythology, particularly that originating myth of the Fall: hence the resonantly lone fruit tree in their garden with its shades of the Garden of Eden, as well as the attempt of a diminutive herbaceous border bursting at the seams to recover the fullness of Eden, which seventeenth-century botanical gardens sought briefly to recover, before the profusion of new plants overwhelmed the ambition. Also registered is a garden's traditional purveying of messages, for there, iconographically, is the winding primrose path (which leads suburbanly only to the garden sheds). The authors are alert to the garden as botanical treasure cabinet, parodying that lure of exotica with eucalyptus and monkey-puzzle tree; to the garden as laboratory, indicated by the sundial and rain gauge; to the garden's representation in miniature of a larger world, with the rockery eloquent of sublime alp and the pergola, of forest avenue. The garden is also shown as a crucial social space—a series of rooms that extend the opportunities of the house for social discourse and recreation (tennis and swimming). Clearly, garden owners and designers need to determine the relationship of the relatively small areas under their control to the larger landscape, to which television and the automobile have variously given us greater access. In turn, this evaluation will require assessments of what balance is appropriate between art and nature, of what is, or should be, the accessibility of garden imagery to individuals or groups, and what traditions of gardens are available to what sections of the public and what "new" ones we might usefully invent. The medieval peasant toiling to obtain a basic subsistence from a small vegetable garden has perspectives upon that plot that are wholly different from those of the modern, suburban man who reinvents contact with the soil or re-creates, if not Eden, an ecologically virtuous spot, a *cordon sanitaire* against biochemical pollution.

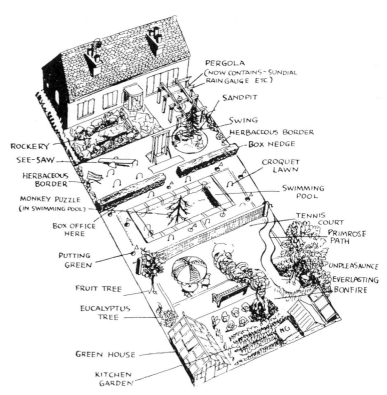

47. Stephen Dowling. From R. J. Yeatman and W. C. Sellar. *Garden Rubbish*. (London, 1936)

The Scots poet and designer Ian Hamilton Finlay, whatever the (mis)judgments of his ideology or his actual practice, seems to me exemplary in precisely the proportion that he addresses these questions. In particular, he confronts one dialectical tension between culture and nature, as in his tree sculptures at the Kröller-Müller Museum in the Netherlands, and another between history and the present, as in the garden he designed at Versailles to celebrate the French Revolution.[23] He is alert to the strange changes that have taken place in our perception of the world of the garden in relation to that of nature—hence, perhaps, the miniaturization of his own garden at Little Sparta or the Country Lane he designed for the 1988 Garden Festival in Glasgow, where it was uncertain whether the countryside was to be replicated in little inside a garden space, or some actual country land colonized as a garden. Above all he has committed himself, as we must, to the revival of the garden as a coherent and comprehensive art form.

1. In *The Palm at the End of the Mind*, ed. by Holly Stevens (New York, 1972) p. 46.

2. J. Bonfadio to R. Tomacelli, *Lettere del Cinquecento* (Turin, 1967), p. 501, and B. Taegio, *La Villa* (Milan, 1559), [p. 58].

3. See *The Invention of Tradition*, ed. Eric Hobsbawn and Terence Ranger (Cambridge, 1983), especially Hobsbawn's "Introduction: Inventing Traditions," pp. 1ff.

4. Stephen Orgel and Roy Strong, *Inigo Jones: The Theatre of the Stuart Court* (London, 1973), vol. 2, pp. 706, 708.

5. See John Prest, *The Garden of Eden: The Botanic Garden and the Recreation of Paradise* (New Haven, 1981).

6. See John Dixon Hunt, "But Who Does Not Know What a Dutch Garden Is? The Dutch Garden in the English Imagination," in *The Dutch Garden in the Seventeenth Century*, ed. J. D. Hunt (Washington, D.C., 1990).

7. Stephen Orgel, *The Illusion of Power: The Political Theater in the English Renaissance* (Berkeley, 1975), p. 11.

8. Leone Battista Alberti, *On Painting*, trans. and with introduction and notes by John R. Spencer (London, 1956), p. 48.

9. The gardens at Wilton are discussed, references to the remarks quoted here are given, and Serlio's exedra is illustrated in John Dixon Hunt, *Garden & Grove: The Italian Garden in the English Imagination* (London, 1986), pp. 139–42.

10. For Evelyn's work at Wotton see ibid., pp. 145–52.

11. See ibid., figs. 82, 83.

12. Ibid., p. 201.

13. I have taken this theme further in two separate but interlocking essays: "Pope's Twickenham Revisited," in *British and American Gardens in the Eighteenth Century*, ed. Robert P. Maccubbin and Peter Martin (Williamsburg, Va., 1984), and "Pope, Kent and 'Palladian' Gardening," in *Alexander Pope: The Enduring Legacy*, ed. Pat Rogers and George S. Rousseau (Cambridge, 1988), pp. 121–31.

14. A much expanded version of this section on Castle Howard will appear in my collection of essays, *Gardens and the Picturesque,* to be published by the M. I. T. Press in Spring 1992. For discussions of the estate and its principles see Wolfgang Kaiser, *Castle Howard: Ein englischer Landsitz des frühen 18. Jahrhunderts* (Freiburg im Breisgau, 1984).

15. Jane Austen, *Emma*, chap. 42.

16. We can see the extent to which an understanding of garden representation was eroding in the early nineteenth century by looking at J. C. Loudon, *Observations on the Formation and Management of Useful and Ornamental Plantations* (London, 1804).

17. John Dixon Hunt, *William Kent: Landscape Garden Designer* (London, 1987).

18. John Barrell, *Political Theory of Painting from Reynolds to Hazlitt: The Body of the Public* (New Haven, 1986).

19. Roland Barthes, *Image—Music—Text*, essays selected and trans. Stephen Heath (Glasgow, 1977), p. 27.

20. See Michael Conan, "Nature into Art: Garden and Landscapes in the Everyday Life of Ancient Rome," *Journal of Garden History* 6 (1986): 348–56.

21. Quoted in Barrell, *Political Theory of Painting from Reynolds to Hazlitt: The Body of the Public*, p. 322.

22. See John Dixon Hunt, *Vauxhall and London's Garden Theatres* (Cambridge, 1985).

23. See Yves Abrioux, *Ian Hamilton Finlay: A Visual Primer* (Edinburgh, 1985), and the pamphlet by Finlay and Alexandre Chemetoff, with Sue Finlay and Nicholas Sloan, *Proposition pour un Jardin Commémorant la Révolution Française et les Droits de l'Homme, 1789–1989: Hôtel des Menus Plaisirs, Versailles* (Little Sparta, Scotland, 1988).

ROBERT ROSENBLUM

The Withering Greenbelt: Aspects of Landscape in Twentieth-Century Painting

RECENTLY WE RECEIVED AT HOME what was meant to be a sort of botanical decoration. It was a very chic little black box, containing not a potted plant, but just a clipped row of beautiful green grass that looked like a time capsule from a Steven Spielberg movie. This was a very peculiar bit of science-fiction landscape in a New York apartment. On a similar note, our children are always coming back after what they call a nature walk in Washington Square, and they say, producing something like one pitiful autumn leaf, "We brought back some nature," as if they were coming from another planet. These free associations will give some idea of how remote the topic of landscape in modern art seemed to me on first consideration.

The color green is, of course, associated with landscape, and it also occurred to me that this color is relatively rare in twentieth-century art, especially in more recent art. The artist who immediately comes to mind for a subliminal, or perhaps even willful, exclusion of the color green—green equaling nature—is Jasper Johns, as represented, for example, in two works of 1955 in The Museum of Modern Art's collection, each a *Target*: one red, yellow, and blue; the other, all green. One of the things that is so arresting about the green *Target* is, in fact, its color, which somehow translates green into a total abstraction. Nothing could have fewer associations with nature. It is as if green had suddenly been lifted from the spectrum of colors and singled out as isolated and unreal, something totally inorganic. Nevertheless, the strong effect of green in that work is made all the more potent because green is so frequently absent from Johns's palette. In a famous work from 1959, *False Start* (Mr. and Mrs. S. I. Newhouse Collection), the names of all the basic colors are stenciled; the word "green" does occur, but there is no green in the picture.

Generally, Johns's palette sticks to red, yellow, orange, blue, and sometimes purple, but green is rare or peripheral, occurring as a cerebral fact, as in the case of variations of the primary flag images of the 1950s. In a 1967–68 lithograph about memory, we are supposed to stare at the red, white, and blue flag above and see an afterimage in the space provided below. When green appears, it is as the complement of red, as a completely abstract concept that has nothing to do with the experience of landscape.

48. Rudolf von Alt. *Makart's Studio.*
1885. Watercolor, 27⅜ x 39½".
Kunsthistorisches Museum, Vienna

49. Narcisse-Virgile Diaz de La Peña.
Sous-bois. 1855. Oil on canvas,
19⅝ x 23⅛". Musée du Louvre, Paris

50. Claude Monet. *The Train in the
Countryside.* 1870–71. Oil on canvas,
50 x 65". Musée du Louvre, Paris

All of these thoughts are an introduction to an extremely complicated story that I hope to tell not consecutively and probably not very coherently, but in a buckshot variety of associations concerning what I will call the withering greenbelt around us.

As one way of presenting the change we've experienced in our century, we can compare two famous artists' studios: one of Hans Makart, in Vienna, in 1885 (Fig. 48); the other of Piet Mondrian, in Paris, in 1926. Essential to Makart's artistic environment, in the most florid nineteenth-century tradition, was lots of greenery, and one can imagine all the potted palms that were part of this *Wintergarten* milieu that seemed to fertilize his mind and art. The 1920s approach to an artist's studio, as seen in the famous André Kertész photograph of Mondrian's studio in 1926 (The Museum of Modern Art, New York), shows that all nature, with the exception of the perfect flower, has been banished from this austere sanctuary of purity. Here, nature would be a strange intruder, most unwelcome, especially in the Machine Age decades.

This separation from nature had not always been the case. As anyone who flips through the history of nineteenth-century art knows, the last century produced, in both public and private arenas, acres of paintings that had to do with the veneration of unspoiled nature. Nature was all over the place, at least in terms of the Salon walls at mid-century. For example, a Barbizon painting of 1855 by Narcisse-Virgile Diaz de La Peña (Fig. 49) offers a full-scale embrace of the peace, comfort, and serenity that can be found in the woods. The painting, which has the generic title *Sous-bois*, is a kind of underbrush scene in which the participants, a young boy and his dogs, have gone into the woods to seek refuge from some nearby community; but more to the point, for the spectator weary of the restraints of life in nineteenth-century Paris, pictures like this one seemed to provide an antidote—a mythic, pastoral alternative that could totally engulf one in a fantasy about the woods, about a natural, escapist environment that offered relief from the realities of the city.

The history of Impressionism, as it has been written and rewritten in recent decades, is full of accounts of the way in which the distinction between city and country began to be blurred in the 1860s and 1870s; the suburban site of Argenteuil on the Seine, just a short trip from Paris, has usually been the locus for this kind of study.

In views of Argenteuil from the early 1870s, an industrial scruffiness is beginning to emerge on the horizon, contaminating this once-innocent stretch of woods by the Seine, invaded more and more by citified ideas. This theme is pinpointed in a most unforgettable way in a painting by Claude Monet of 1870–71 (Fig. 50), showing a railroad train running along the horizon, belching forth smoke, and polluting the air around the people who are enjoying the green. This is a picture, incidentally, that was used as the cover of the catalogue of the 1984 Impressionist exhibition in Los Angeles and Chicago called *A Day in the Country*, and that title suggests the way that people would move rapidly to and from these suburban land-scapes, thereby blurring more and more the distinction between city and country.

It is fascinating to see how at the same time, Monet could be interested in the most counterrural experiences, pausing to document, among other things, the unloading of coal on the banks of the Seine near Argenteuil in 1872. Back in Paris, he recorded the interior of the Gare Saint-Lazare at approximately the same time (1876–77) that he was exploring the luxurious and private gardens of the château belonging to his friends the Hoschedés at Montgeron. That Monet was capable of painting pictures like these during the same period may be an indication of the growing rupture, or the growing distinction, between nature and man-made that seemed to loom larger by the late 1870s. The pictures, which at first seem to be schematic black-and-white opposites, also can offer a curious point of convergence, so that the interpretation, for example, of the Gare Saint-Lazare almost resembles a day in the country, with the natural clouds of Monet's earlier paintings now trans-lated into the clouds of steam condensing within the glass-and-metal shed of the railway station.

Artists in Monet's wake could sometimes manage to synthesize what seemed to be the rhythms and images of a new industrial world with visions of a public land-scape. Of course the most famous example of this is Georges Seurat's *Sunday at the "Grande Jatte"* (1884–86, Art Institute of Chicago), which includes the first grass in the history of art that might be mistaken for Astroturf. The landscape appears totally synthetic in a manner prophetic of that little rectangle of perfect green grass we had in our home last year. More fascinating than such odd congruences between the natural and the man-made, however, is the sharper distinction that Monet and oth-ers began to draw at this time between city and country. The fact of the matter is that Monet and many artists and others in the late nineteenth and early twentieth century experienced such a complete about-face from city to country that, in the words of Voltaire, they cultivated their own gardens, to the point of creating her-metic worlds of nature, of individualized dreams, in which they could live and med-itate—rather like such musical fantasies of the turn of the century as Frederick Delius's *Walk to Paradise Garden*. The extreme statement of this is embodied in the now ultra-famous water gardens that Monet created at Giverny beginning in the 1890s. One of Steven Shore's beautiful photographs of the Japanese bridge, as well as Monet's painting of the same subject, *The Japanese Footbridge at Giverny* (1923, Musée Marmottan, Paris), wallow so deeply in this fictional nature that we feel the outside world has completely vanished. This kind of aestheticism, whereby a fantasy land-scape is constructed by an artist for the most refined delectation, is common to the experience of the turn of the century; one can find many international examples of paintings that take a rectangle of landscape, make it seem like the total cosmos, and emphasize the luxuriance of nature and its hedonistic character.

Such is the case in *Italian Countryside* (1917, Private collection), by Gustav Klimt. The picture gives a glimpse of the burgeoning Italian countryside, but it doesn't matter where the scene is, since the image is a displaced Persian carpet of gorgeous flowers, the equivalent of precious jewels rather than a commonplace

51. Augusto Giacometti. *An Ascent of the Piz Duan*. 1913. Oil on canvas, 33¼ x 33". Kunsthaus, Zürich

52. Frederick Carl Frieseke. *Lady in a Garden*. c. 1912. Oil on canvas, 31 x 26½". Terra Museum of American Art, Chicago

53. Ferdinand Hodler. *Autumn Evening*. 1892–93. Oil on canvas, 39⅜ x 51⅛". Musée d'Art et d'Histoire, Neuchâtel

landscape. That same aesthetic of nature as an exquisite tapestry can be seen in another painting (Fig. 51) by the insufficiently known Swiss painter Augusto Giacometti (a relative of the much more famous Alberto), which fits into the luxuriant-garden motif flourishing at the time. Other flower gardens on both sides of the Atlantic may be considered: some of those by the German Expressionist Emil Nolde are insular and hermetic, with more Nordic, mysterious overtones than the examples considered previously; from this side of the Atlantic, a painting of c. 1912 by Frederick Frieseke (Fig. 52) of a lady in a garden suggests a world of aesthetic choice and harmony. We can be sure that the lady depicted by Frieseke was a subscriber to a magazine like *House Beautiful* or *Better Homes and Gardens*. In this milieu of private elegance and sensibility, one takes from nature only a rarified selection, which belongs exclusively to the aristocratic owner's world. This work, it seems to me, represents another fascinating category of the artistic response to nature at the turn of the century. Another approach to the removal of landscape from ordinary experience was the almost spooky sanctification of nature, which could become so magically pure as to lead to divinity itself. This point can be demonstrated in the work of any number of artists from the turn of the century, but I choose here the work of the Swiss master Ferdinand Hodler. In a painting from 1885, *Beech Forest* (Kunstmuseum, Solothurn), we find ourselves in a beautiful but quite familiar kind of landscape, but in an autumn scene of 1892–93 (Fig. 53) we suddenly have the feeling of something more dramatic, sharply focused into one-point perspective. It is a picture that makes us feel we are lonely wanderers in a landscape whose significance can even be made religious in character—a point that is emphatically clear in *The Path of the Chosen Souls* (Private collection), a painting of 1893–94, in which we see looming high on the horizon the Cross, the salvation for those who follow on this straight, and narrow, and flowered path. This kind of sanctification of nature became a commonplace at the turn of the century.

Consider one more example from Hodler's work (Fig. 54), a painting from 1893–94 that is a hymn about six angels who are protecting Hodler's young son on a mountaintop. Here is an equivalent of that little rectangular grass plot I received—a perfect, newly planted tree. Its hermetic purity is echoed by the symbol of the naked child, so that the domain of man-made landscape blurs into that of a kind of Christian ritual. The site also seems to be a very sacred spot, as sacred as a shrine in prehistory; it might be Stonehenge, though in this case it is inspired by some height in the Swiss Alps. A kind of universal view is also represented, with the earth rounded below. In the spring meadow, angels hover above a sacred mound, in which the natural and the spiritual have finally become one. This feeling of a regression in nature to something that is spiritually elemental, for those of a religious persuasion, or organically elemental, for those a little more empirical in orientation, is found constantly in the art of the turn of the century, exemplified most breathtakingly in a pair of great paintings by Henri Matisse, *Music* and *Dance* (1910, Hermitage, Leningrad).

Like the picture by Hodler—which Matisse may well have seen and thought about in creating his own images—these landscapes take us to what seem to be prehistoric sacred sites, a very generalized nature consisting of nothing but the green of the fertile earth (so unlike the abstract green of Johns) and the blue of the sky (or is it the blue of the water?). These elemental colors of landscape—blue and green—are as distilled as the red-ocher of the figures' flesh. The two paintings seem to announce Igor Stravinsky's *Rite of Spring* of 1913, taking us to a landscape of primordial character. The roots of music, the roots of dance, and the roots of landscape experience have now become so mythical that we cannot associate them with any place or time.

54. Ferdinand Hodler. *The Consecrated One.* 1893–94. Tempera and oil on canvas, 8⅝ x 11⅝". Kunstmuseum, Bern

This archaic landscape of the imagination was plumbed by any number of major artists at the turn of the century, and of course Pablo Picasso was among them. In 1908, for example, he began to explore what seems to be a kind of primeval nature, often inspired by a little village north of Paris, La Rue des Bois (*Landscape*, Collection Hermann Ruff, Bern). If one had to imagine the kind of humanoid creature who lived in such a landscape, it probably would be someone like the prehistoric, Druidic woman in another painting by Picasso of the same year (*The Dryad*, Hermitage, Leningrad). No contemporary city dweller could survive in these landscapes by Picasso or Matisse; the scenes have become mythical, primeval, taking us back to the origins of things, as is the case in a much more innocent, wide-eyed way in *Eve*, a painting by Henri Rousseau of 1906–07 (Fig. 55). Here, Rousseau represents the mother of us all, placing her within a landscape that is rare for its verdancy. The image manifests almost a childlike belief in the greenness of nature—something of an anachronism by the early twentieth century, especially for urbanites like Picasso.

Such regression to the deepest recesses of nature can be paralleled in much architecture of the period, but the most famous example may be on the outskirts of Barcelona, in Antoni Gaudí's Park Güell of 1900–1914. There, the entrance leads to a Doric hypostyle temple, but as one moves to the outer reaches of the park, one enters, shall we say, Picasso and Matisse territory; suddenly these columns have become prehistoric, the sort of thing troglodytes might have lived in. Moving further into the recesses of these galleries, one can hardly decipher whether they are man-made or natural. This kind of conceit of regression is familiar in images of landscape from the years before 1914.

55. Henri Rousseau. *Eve.* 1906–8. Oil on canvas, 24 x 18⅛". Kunsthalle, Hamburg

Other fantasy trips, especially east of the Rhine, involved Oz-like landscapes, completely unreal, with their rainbow colors and utterly molten quality. Such is the case in a pair of landscapes of 1910: one by Franz Marc (Fig. 56) and the other by Vasily Kandinsky (Fig. 57). Although both landscapes were inspired by the Bavarian Alps outside Munich, they give the effect of an extraterrestrial, fairy-tale world where nature, animals, and rustic buildings become one, fused in a melting spectrum of prismatic intensity. Such images of a lost Eden must have provided balm for the wounds of many Europeans just before 1914.

Characteristically, both of these artists and many of their contemporaries, especially in Germany, also turned to the converse view of this pastoral dream—an apocalyptic vision of landscape—in exactly the same years preceding the outbreak of

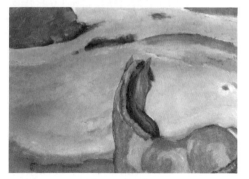  

56. Franz Marc. *Horse in Landscape.*
1910. Oil on canvas, 33½ x 44".
Museum Folkwang, Essen

57. Vasily Kandinsky. *Mountain Landscape with Church.* 1910. Oil on cardboard, 12⅞ x 17⅝". Stadtische Galeries im Lenbachhaus, Munich

58. Franz Marc. *Tirol.* 1914. Oil on canvas, 53½ x 56⅞". Staatsgalerie moderner Kunst, Munich

the war. Another painting by Franz Marc (Fig. 58) is, again, inspired by the Tyrolean mountains, but here one senses a version of *Götterdämmerung*, very prophetic, too, of Anselm Kiefer. Marc depicts a huge explosion of a symbolic tree and an eclipse of sun and moon over a vision of the Virgin and Child, offering us a private myth of a cosmic earthquake in which the whole earth is being destroyed before our eyes. Nature itself is at the core of this destruction. That feeling of violent, apocalyptic tragedy is also evoked in many prewar works of Kandinsky, of which *Improvisation No. 30* (1913, Art Institute of Chicago) is probably the best-known example, especially because of the spectral presence of a cannon in the lower right-hand corner, a reference, as Kandinsky himself avowed, of the talk about the war that was coming.

In Germany, this sense of explosiveness on the eve of the war can be felt in the art of lesser masters as well, as in a painting (Fig. 59) by the strange artist Ludwig Meidner of an apocalyptic landscape that for us, living after 1945, has a shattering quality of prophecy. In Meidner's vision, all the world, both nature and city, seems blighted at this ultimate moment. It is interesting to see that from the ashes of this "explosion" all kinds of irrational new shapes, some of them even architectural in character, began to reemerge in Germany. Those interested in the history of Expressionism certainly know the curious studies by Hermann Finsterlin, most executed during the First World War, including one of a little dwelling that looks as though it might be the first shelter built by the only survivor in a rubbled landscape (*Architectural Fantasy*, 1917, SMPK Kunstbibliothek, Berlin). That sense of cosmic desolation and despair joined with some kind of new hope, is echoed in many of the images of the period.

59. Ludwig Meidner. *Apocalyptic Landscape.* 1913. Oil on canvas, 26 x 31½". Collection Mr. and Mrs. Marvin Fishman

Yet another approach to the resurrection of landscape, or what was left of it after the First World War, can be seen in the activities of artists and architects west of the Rhine, especially in Paris, from 1918 on. One might look at a typical 1921 landscape by Fernand Léger—although nominally a rural scene, it has fragments of industrial imagery in the background, but most strikingly, there is a blasted, leafless tree on the left that evokes a bit of potential green, a survivor, even a memory of the French classical landscape tradition.

Images like Léger's clarify the growing fusion of city and country, of nature and industry, that had existed in the grand constructive tradition of French painting stretching back from Cubism to Paul Cézanne and Seurat. For instance, in the foreground of a famous painting by Cézanne, *The Bay from L'Estaque* (c. 1886, Art Institute of Chicago), there is an almost camouflaging mix of domestic homes (in the foreground) and industrial plants, with factory smoke beginning to pollute the deep blue of Mediterranean sky and water in this site at L'Estaque, outside Marseilles. Artists like Picasso and Georges Braque would also include such unexpected things as industrial buildings and factories in what might otherwise be an unpolluted tourist landscape. In a 1910 painting (Fig. 60) by Braque of the same place, L'Estaque, the artist clearly is nodding in Cézanne's direction, also representing (though it may not be immediately legible) the new factory buildings, which have a powerful, young industrial life of their own. Braque thoroughly suppresses the sense of nature, of greenery, of sky, that still clings to Cézanne's imagery of related Mediterranean sites.

60. Georges Braque. *Rio Tinto Factories at l'Estaque*. 1910. Oil on canvas, 28⅜ x 23⅝". Musée National d'Art Moderne, Paris

Traditional aspects of landscape have also been annihilated in comparable paintings by Picasso, such as one of 1909 of a Pyrenean hill town (*Factory at Horta de Ebro*, Hermitage, Leningrad), in which the verdant palm trees of the nineteenth century have turned into abstract chimneys that rhyme with the actual factory buildings in the foreground. Such works belong to a tradition that goes back to the artist of the 1880s who had most firmly synthesized the facts of nature with the facts of the industrial world—Seurat. *The Bridge at Courbevoie* (c. 1886–87, Courtauld Institute, London), showing an industrial suburb of Paris, not only has the usual factory blight on the Seine, but also offers us what becomes almost a lone, symbolic tree, a sturdy but irregular silhouette of a leafless form. The perfect architectural expression of this imagery and the almost paradoxical conceit of nature within a newly constructed world are found in the famous Pavillon de l'Esprit Nouveau (Fig. 61) by Le Corbusier at the Paris Exposition des Arts Décoratifs of 1925: a single tree rises through the circle of a hole in the roof. This design provides a three-dimensional counterpart to the prop-like trees that Léger—and before him, Seurat—so often included in their machine-age landscapes.

That sense of everything as totally synthetic, of nature as turned out on an assembly line, was also emphasized by Picasso, with his usual wit, in a little postwar landscape of 1919 (Fig. 62), in which the verdure of the landscape is painted with an extraordinarily unreal, synthetic green. Picasso has transformed the French tradition of Poussinesque, classical landscape into something that looks like a totally flat and artificial stage set.

The artist of the twentieth century who most schematically represents the collision between nature and the modern world is Mondrian, whose career offers an almost complete turnabout, from an espousal of nature and its mysteries, to a rejection of it in favor of an imagery rooted in the utopian city conceived during and just after the First World War. The latter part of that career can be best seen in The Museum of Modern Art's painting *Broadway Boogie Woogie* (Fig. 63), executed during the Second World War, in 1942–43. A contemporary photograph of Manhattan shows Central Park as a perfect rectangle, an

61. Le Corbusier. Pavillon de l'Esprit Nouveau. 1925. Presented at the Paris Exposition des Arts Décoratifs

62. Pablo Picasso. *Landscape with Dead and Live Trees*. 1919. Oil on canvas, 19⅜ x 25¾". Bridgestone Museum of Art, Tokyo

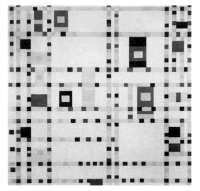

63. Piet Mondrian. *Broadway Boogie Woogie.* 1942–43. Oil on canvas, 50 x 50". The Museum of Modern Art, New York

isolation chamber for nature, as well as the skyscrapers from Central Park southward, an image that Mondrian transformed. This later work is particularly dramatic in view of his early work as a landscape painter: for instance, an almost van Gogh–like flat landscape near Amsterdam (*Landscape Near Amsterdam*, c. 1902, M. Seuphor Collection). At the beginning of this century, he seemed both literally and figuratively to move farther and farther away from the city, and even from the countryside, ending up about 1909–11 at the very brink of land, the dunes on the cold northern shores where he felt he could immerse himself in the void. All of this is a far cry from the embrace of industry and urban imagery that characterizes his later work.

The sharp distinction between the modern city and the most remote, primordial landscape was hardly unique to Mondrian; there is almost a perfect parallel on this side of the Atlantic in the works of Georgia O'Keeffe. She, too, very often split her work into city versus country. Her 1927 view of the then brand-new American Radiator Building by Raymond Hood, *Radiator Building—Night* (Fisk University, Nashville), may even be among the pictures that inspired the skyscraper-fenestration look later abstracted by Mondrian. At the same time, however, O'Keeffe escaped the city in her life and art, traveling as she did to the remote areas of North America to experience a timeless nature that could not be clocked by the years of the nineteenth and twentieth centuries.

After the Second World War, the schism between the organic and the inorganic, the natural and the man-made, reached a point of both maximum divergence and collision. Two pop artists of the 1960s give us some idea of how remote nature had become in this country by that decade. In Andy Warhol's *Do It Yourself (Landscape)* of 1962 (Museum Ludwig, Cologne), an American landscape icon has turned into a commercial diagram. If you want, Warhol's title is saying, you can mentally fill in the green parts, but you can make that choice for yourself. Roy Lichtenstein in 1964 offered an equally synthetic, urban product—*Sinking Sun* (Private collection), a corny sunset, which also mocks any old-fashioned ideas of nature. Nevertheless, nature persisted in various covert and overt ways: covert, in the very organic imagery of a master like Mark Rothko, whose sunsetlike vision could not be more different from that of Lichtenstein; or more overt, in the tradition of earthworks that began to be explored in the late 1960s and 1970s by the likes of Robert Smithson, as in the famous *Spiral Jetty* of 1970, in the Great Salt Lake, Utah. On the other side of the Atlantic, Richard Long, a British nature lover, wandered about the globe like a visitor from another planet, carefully treasuring such finds as wood from California, which he preserved and put in a magical circle in a SoHo gallery; or documenting his own snakelike trail on the Isle of Skye, the modern version of a walk through the woods by, say, Dorothy and William Wordsworth. Even more like a time capsule from which future civilizations could learn what we thought about landscape is Long's written account of a walk straight northward across Dartmoor.

The feeling of growing remoteness, as if nature were not only an endangered species but practically extinct, emerges constantly in the sixties and seventies. I vividly remember seeing in 1969 an installation at The Museum of Modern Art by

Robert Morris, who had magically preserved Japanese bonsai trees—strange mutants, it seemed, from another planet—in rectangular tanks, rather like that little box of grass I received. Related to this concept is *Varese Window Room* (1973, Collection Panza), Robert Irwin's installation in Count Panza di Biumo's residence in Varese—a glimpse of greenery, equally remote and magical, as seen through the precision of a geometric cube.

The landscape of the present can also conjure up memories of our experience of the landscapes of the past. There are, to be sure, any number of artists who try just to paint in a would-be matter-of-fact way the facts of a pleasant American landscape. That is certainly the case with Jane Freilicher in *View Over Mecox Bay* (Collection of Mr. Edward E. Robbins), which shows a bay in the Hamptons with a big house—a canvas that, in today's world, has a willfully innocent or anachronistic look. More to the point might be a picture by Alfred Leslie of a breathtaking view of the Connecticut River from Mount Holyoke (Fig. 64). The landscape in this painting is really a landscape in quotation marks because it alludes quite clearly to one of the most famous of American landscape paintings, Thomas Cole's *The Ox Bow* of 1836 (The Metropolitan Museum of Art, New York). Leslie's picture offers an art-historical, or synthetic, revision of the nineteenth-century image of nature, recalling, from the other side of an unbridgeable historical gulf, the American landscape past.

64. Alfred Leslie. *View of the Connecticut River, as Seen from Mount Holyoke.* 1971–72. Oil on canvas, 71⅝ x 106¼". Neue Galerie, Aachen

One of the most telling landscapes of that retrospective category is an Anselm Kiefer of 1974 (Fig. 65) that represents the Märkische Heide, near East Berlin, a site fraught with German cultural memories, not only of the early nineteenth-century Romantic pastorals as told by Theodor Fontane, but also of momentous and horrific military conflicts. It is a vision of scorched earth, an earth that may never be regenerated, and it is a picture that, like Alfred Leslie's, tells a great deal about the way that landscape seems to have been relegated in the 1970s and 1980s to the domain of myth, history, and memory.

65. Anselm Kiefer. *March Heath.* 1974. Oil, acrylic, and shellac on burlap, 46½ x 100". Courtesy of the artist

KENNETH FRAMPTON

In Search of the Modern Landscape

The Baroque system had operated as a kind of double intersection. It had often contrasted with rationalized gardens, building façades decorated with plant motifs. The reign of man and the reign of nature had certainly remained distinct, but they had exchanged their characteristics, merging into each other for the sake of ornamentation and prestige. On the other hand, the "English style" park, in which man's intervention was supposed to remain invisible, was intended to offer the purposefulness of nature; while within, but separate from the actual park, the houses constructed by Morris or Adam manifested the will of man isolating clearly the presence of human reason in the midst of the irrational domains of freely growing vegetation. The Baroque interpenetration of man and nature was now replaced by a separation, thus establishing the distance between man and nature which was a prerequisite for nostalgic contemplation. Now . . . this contemplative separation arose as a compensatory or expiatory reaction against the growing attitude of practical men toward nature. While technical exploitation tended to wage war on nature, houses and parks attempted a reconciliation, a local armistice, introducing the dream of an impossible peace; and to this end man has continued to retain the image of untouched natural surroundings.

—Jean Starobinski
The Invention of Liberty, 1964[1]

Surprising as it may seem, there is to date no decent account of the history of twentieth-century landscape design. Thus, as the above title suggests, this essay is little more than an attempt to redress a certain imbalance, by providing a map of a relatively uncharted field, a foray, so to speak, into an unknown domain, emphasizing certain salient features and, of necessity, ignoring others. It is an unavoidably provisional undertaking, standing in lieu of a much more comprehensive historical work.

The material selected here has been organized according to the following schema. The first section, under the heading "Beginning with the Pioneers," addresses the role that landscape has assumed in the hands of professional architects, as an integral part of the development of "progressive" architectural form. The second section, doubling back chronologically, deals, albeit briefly, with the emergence of a modern sensibility in twentieth-century landscape practice, with a particular stress on three distinctly different cultural experiences. The first is the Anglo-

American modernist school of garden design, directly or indirectly initiated by Christopher Tunnard in the late thirties and pursued through the
forties, first at Harvard and then at Yale. The second, equally seminal,
experience is the Brazilian tropical garden movement that was jointly
founded in São Paolo by Victor Brecheret and Mina Klabin, both of
whom created their first abstract cactus garden in 1927. The third experience brings us closer to our point of departure, to the somewhat tran-
scendental midwestern American landscape tradition, initiated in Chicago
in part by the Danish emigrant Jens Jensen, and in part by the Prairie
School. A unique synthesis of these two quite different approaches will
emerge in the mid-century work of Alfred Caldwell and in that of his collaborator,
the emigré, ex-Bauhaus architect-planner Ludwig Hilbersheimer. This critical
model, proclaimed by Hilbersheimer as the New Regional Pattern, will be extended
as a general policy in the low-rise, high-density, land-settlement theses independent-
ly advanced by Christopher Alexander and the Austrian architect Roland Rainer.
This reformist, but nonetheless radical critique from an ecological standpoint, has its
roots in the anarcho-Socialist horticultural settlement model first advocated by Peter
Kropotkin in his 1896 book *Factories, Fields, and Workshops*.

66. From Claude Nicolas Ledoux.
*L'Architecture considérée sous le rapport de
l'art des moeurs et de la législation.*
Frontispiece

The essay ends with a brief look at a series of relatively recent topographical
transformations, grouped together under the heading "Shifting Sites," after the title
of Georges Descombes's book, in which he documents a critical, haptic approach to
the design of landscape as a kind of reparatory itinerant perception, wherein, despite
distinct topographic features, relationships cannot be precisely defined, since everything is in a perpetual state of partial recovery and ruination.

BEGINNING WITH THE PIONEERS[2]

The frontispiece depicting the poor man's abode in Claude Nicolas Ledoux's *L'architecture considérée sous le rapport de l'art des moeurs et de la législation* (1804) conveys, as no
other image, the vision of an essentially benevolent nature, even if the ultimate fate
of the naked primordial man beneath his sheltering trees, rests in the hands of the
gods (Fig. 66). This vision of an unspoilt Edenic landscape, ostensibly accessible to
all, will be embraced as a compensatory assumption through the development of
twentieth-century architecture. Thus the avant-garde architects of the early modern
movement would not so much cultivate nature as they would cradle their buildings
within it. This is surely the context for Le Corbusier's idealistic setting of the Ville
Contemporaine (1922), and a similar assumption would obtain a few years later in
the first row-house settlements of the Weimar Republic. In the later twenties, however, this naïve assumption undergoes a change and we begin to encounter works
that are specifically modulated in respect of their sites. One of the most dramatic
shifts in this regard occurs in the work of Hannes Meyer, wherein he passes from
the *tabula rasa* site of his entry for the Société des Nations competition (1927) to the
subtly contoured organic landscape that surrounds his Trade Union School (1930) in
Bernau (Fig. 67).

I use the term *organic* here to indicate a sensitively inflected approach toward the

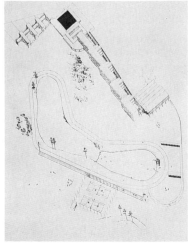

67. Hannes Meyer. Trade Union
School. 1928. Bernau. Site plan

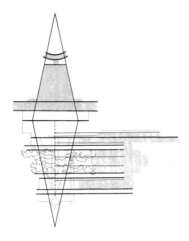

68. Le Corbusier. Palace of the League of Nations. Competition entry. 1927. Layered plan

placement of the building in its site: one that synthesizes the sometimes conflicting demands of access, orientation, landfall, water table, prevailing wind, ecological imperatives, and so on, without having immediate recourse to picturesque aesthetic effects. The more sophisticated members of the Soviet avant-garde in the late twenties were to assume a similar attitude, as were the later European functionalists of the Weimar Republic and the Swedish welfare state. Such an attitude is evident, for example, in Moisei Ginzburg and Mikhail Barshch's linear-city proposal known as the Green City (1930) and in Ivan Leonidov's dematerialized urban project of virtually the same date, his Culture Park for Moscow and his linear city for Magnitogorsk.

Three fundamentally different concepts seem to run through the evolution of the modern landscape, as far as the "progressive" architects of the twentieth century are concerned. The first of these is Greek in origin and conceives of built form in the likeness of a *temenos* set against the vastness of space and time; the second is Japanese in inspiration and presupposes an introspective garden shielded from the turbulence of everyday life. The Greek line is evident to different degrees in the work of Le Corbusier and Ludwig Mies van der Rohe, whereas the Japanese line, initiated by Frank Lloyd Wright, is fully articulated by the pioneer architects of the southern Californian school, by Wright's pupils, Rudolf Schindler and Richard Neutra. Finally, some notice has to be taken of the third concept, the Islamic "Paradise garden" tradition, as it also appears in the work of such diverse architects as Wright and Hans Poelzig. This tradition resurfaces as an abstracted modern form in the work of the Mexican architect Luis Barragán and in that of the school that has since borne his name.

While Le Corbusier displayed little interest in the niceties of garden design, he was nonetheless deeply susceptible to the evocative power of landscape. He was possessed by a panoramic vision that seemed to incorporate in its trajectory the literal sweep of history. His early vision of the Acropolis as set forth in *Towards a New Architecture*[3] anticipates his later concept of an acoustical centripetal space in which the temple form draws the landscape into its gravitational field.

This feeling for the Greco-picturesque reappears throughout Le Corbusier's career and alternates in his Purist period with the intimacy of the *promenade architecturale*. This last is a complex painterly vision that, conceived as a kinetic experience, passes from a middle-ground perception of the surrounding landscape as a framed, flat, figure-ground field to a close-up identification with the real possibility of penetrating the same layered vegetation in depth—a shallow-to-deep spatial oscillation comparable to that which exists within the interior of the house. This neo-Cubist sense of space is first combined with the Greco-picturesque in Le Corbusier's project for the Société des Nations, where alternating bands of artificial and natural forms are arrayed against the horizontal datum of Lake Leman and the Alps (Fig. 68). That Le Corbusier possessed a unique capacity for combining the monumental and the intimate is evident from his own characterization of his 1925 Plan Voisin:

69. Le Corbusier. Penthouse for Charles de Beistegui. 1930–31. Paris

On one side the floors of the luxury houses—the new rue de la Paix—on the other side, green spaces extending far from the city. This is a sea of trees, and here and there are the pure prismatic forms of majestic crystals, gigantic and limpid. Majesty, serenity, joy, sprightliness.... Night has fallen. Like a crowd of meteors on a summer equinox, the cars trace trails of fire along the autoroute. Two hundred meters above on the roof gardens of the skyscrapers, are large paved terraces planted with spindle trees, bay trees, ivy and embellished with tulips or geraniums set in parterres or crossed by paths lined with a mixture of vivacious colors...electric light bestows a quiet joy, night makes the calm grow deeper, here and there are armchairs, talkers, orchestras and dancers and other gardens far away on every side, at the same level seem like flat platforms of suspended gold. The offices are dark, the façades are extinguished, the city sleeps.[4]

Against this romantic vision we may set the normative space of the Purist picture plane as it seems to appear in Le Corbusier's Pessac housing (1926):

The site at Pessac is very dry. The gray concrete houses produce an insupportable compressed mass, lacking in air. Colour is able to bring us space. Here is how we have established certain invisible points. Some façades are painted in burnt sienna. We have made the lines of others recede, through clear ultramarine blue. Again we have confused certain sections with the foliage of gardens and trees, through the use of pale green façades.[5]

This seems to be a variation on the camouflage "dazzle" techniques employed during the First World War, wherein random advancing and receding colored planes were able to confuse the distant perception of a particular form.

Le Corbusier's Beistegui roof terrace (1931) is treated as an alchemical-cosmological space in which the ceiling is the sky and the roof deck is the earth, appropriately covered with turf. This substitution of the natural for the artificial, that is to say, grass standing in place of a fitted carpet, together with the chimneyless Rococo fireplace, evokes the Surreal antithesis of Purism: the dark side, so to speak, of Le Corbusier's imagination. Even here, the panoramic plays a role in the formal associations that serve to connect the Arc de Triomphe to the decorative chimney breast over the false fireplace (Fig. 69). This dramatic shift in scale and content is reinforced by the concealed presence of a voyeuristic periscope. Similar, if less contrived, scalar displacements may be found throughout Le Corbusier's more modest houses of the twenties and thirties, where the aim, in part, was to bestow an illusion of greater size.

The origin of Mies van der Rohe's architecture in the Prussian culture of romantic classicism largely accounts for the Italianate disposition of his classic houses of the thirties, in which he invariably combined an asymmetrical Schinkelesque format with a dematerialized aesthetic in which the artificial and the natural are fused together. Mies's unbuilt Gericke House (1930) is typical of this dialectical fusion,

70. Ludwig Mies van der Rohe. Tugendhat House. 1930. Brno, Czechoslovakia

71. Ludwig Mies van der Rohe. Farnsworth House. 1950. Plano, Illinois

combining panoramic views over the Wannsee with the tranquility of a dematerialized atrium. In one house after another, Mies's living volumes flow uninterruptedly into their attendant atria and vice versa, the overall volume being articulated in terms of plate-glass walls and freestanding screens. To this pristine vision is added a romantic sense of pleasing decay, a feature that is largely absent from Le Corbusier's work. Here and there, brick walls are covered with ivy, as a counterpoint, so to speak, to the fossilized vegetation that appears as real or virtual images in the marble and plate-glass walls. This play between fossilization, reflection, and transparency is a key to the aesthetic of Mies's Tugendhat House (1930) in Brno, where the winter garden seems to serve as a third term, mediating between the fossilized form of the onyx plane in the center of the living room and the natural verdure lying beyond (Fig. 70).

In Mies's Resor House (1938), projected for Jackson Hole, Wyoming, the surrounding landscape is framed and held at a distance by the glass, and from now on nature will lie beyond Mies's buildings rather than within them. Thus, his Farnsworth House (1950) in Plano, Illinois, frames the vegetation in which it is situated, the foliage being either obliquely reflected in the glass or, alternatively, framed by the fenestration as a kind of illusory "wallpaper" (Fig. 71). The house serves as a belvedere that bestows a perceptual intensity on its surroundings. Mies acknowledged this intention in an interview with Christian Norberg Schulz: "Nature should also live its own life, we should not destroy it with the colors of our houses and interiors. But we should try to bring nature, houses and human beings together in a higher unity. When you see nature through the glass walls of the Farnsworth House, it gets a deeper meaning than outside. More is asked for from nature, because it becomes part of a larger whole."[6]

While Le Corbusier and Mies were both influenced by the Greco-picturesque, Frank Lloyd Wright's feeling for landscape was much more naturalistic, as we may judge from his account of his rural origins:

On either side of the ridge lay fertile valleys luminously bathed and gentled by the moon. The different trees all made their special kinds of pattern when the moon shone on them and their favorite deep-dark silhouettes when it shone against them. The flowers had no color, but their cups and corollas glistening with dew were like pallid gems.... Broad, shallow mists, distilled from the heavy dews, floating in cool, broad sheets below were lying free over the treetops in long, thin, flat ribands. All would be quiet except for the drowsy singing undertone of summer insects. The ancient element of moisture seemed to prevail there as a kind of light flooding all. The deep shadows held mysteries alluring and friendly.[7]

Aside from the overt Beaux-Arts sense of order that tempers the naturalistic gardens of his early houses, there seem to have been three decisive phases in the evolution of Wright's landscapes. The first of these, dating from 1906, came with his initial visit to Japan. The second was his own direct experience of the landscape of southern California, while working with Aline Barnsdall on her famous Hollyhock House (1920) in Los Angeles. The third was his initial encounter with the southwestern desert of the United States, which he first experienced while building his Ocatilla Camp in Chandler, Arizona, in 1929.

While Wright had been influenced by Japanese culture ever since he saw the Ho-o-den temple and garden in the World's Columbian Exposition of 1893, his early gardens acquired their asymmetrical order through a series of countervailing Beaux-Arts axes rather than from the meandering promenade of a typical Kyōto stroll garden. This is evident in the layout of the Darwin D. Martin House (1904), Buffalo, and the Avery Coonley House (1908), Riverside, Illinois. In both instances, the formal axes of the houses contrast strongly with their informal surroundings. At the same time, the ordering principles of the house and the garden are often displaced by each other. Thus, while the living room at the front of the Martin House is axially bracketed by a semicircle of shrubbery, the formal gardens to the rear of the house are loosely organized around about a series of countervailing axes. A parallel arrangement obtains in the Avery Coonley House, where the main axial alignment between the living room and the ornamental pool stands in strong contrast to the irregular planting that occupies the remainder of the site. Here as elsewhere, low stone-capped brick walls, paralleled by planters and accented with basins, serve as the unifying element between the house and the garden. These low walls not only anchor the house into its site but they also contain areas within which herbaceous plants may be freely arranged without disturbing the overall composition.

A more plastic approach appears in the layout of the Barnsdall Hollyhock House, completed twelve years later, for here we seem to encounter for the first time a garden composed of freestanding sculptural plant forms, which assert themselves as contrasting figures to the almost windowless mass of the house. This part Islamic, part Japanese approach to the selection and positioning of plant material will later become an identifying motif in the architecture and garden design of southern California.

The southwestern desert of the United States stimulated Wright to rethink his attitude to both garden form and territorial context. This is already evident in the Ocatilla Camp, where plan and section are determined largely by the contours and by the positioning of giant saguaro cacti, dotted about the site. Pursuing his quasi-Japanese principles, Wright abandoned all symmetry in Arizona, predicating his sense of unity on the natural pattern of freestanding plants and rocks. Moreover, Wright saw the intrinsic structure of the local flora as an analogue for a new kind of organic architecture:

> The great nature-masonry we see rising from the great mesa floors is all the noble architecture Arizona has to show at present and that is not architecture at all. But it is inspiration. A pattern of what appropriate Arizona architecture might well be lies there hidden in the Sahuaro. The Sahuaro, perfect example of

reinforced building construction. Its interior vertical rods hold it rigidly upright maintaining its great fluted columnar mass for six centuries or more.

And all these desert remarkable growths show scientific building economy in the pattern of their construction. The stalks especially teach any architect or engineer who is modest and intelligent enough to apply for lessons. In these desert constructions he may not only see the reinforcing-rod scientifically employed as in the flesh of the Sahuaro but he may see the perfect lattice of the reed and welded tubular construction in the stalk of the cholla, or staghorn, and see it too in the cellular build-up of the water-barrel, Bignana. Even the flesh of the prickly pear is worth studying for scientific structure. In most cacti Nature employs cell to cell or continuous tubular or often plastic construction. By means of plasticity Nature makes continuity everywhere strongly effective without having to reduce the scheme to post and girder construction....

For our purpose we need fifteen cabins in all. Since all will be temporary we will call them ephemera. And you will soon see them like a group of gigantic butterflies with scarlet wing spots, conforming gracefully to the crown of the outcropping of black splintered rock gently uprising from the desert floor.[8]

Wright's desert experience caused him to reduce the syntax of his domestic manner to basic essentials. At the same time he consciously sought to bring out the natural characteristics of the site as much as possible. The so-called *genius loci* was of the utmost importance to Wright. Thus, when he built Taliesin West in Arizona in the early thirties, he chose a particular prominence and layered his built masses into the site in such a way as to suggest a long-standing settlement. This sense of historical, almost mystical continuity was reinforced by Wright's inclusion of petroglyphs found on or close to the site.

SURVIVAL THROUGH DESIGN

This Wrightian technique of literally inlaying the building into the site was taken over directly by Wright's California assistants in the twenties, that is to say, by Rudolf Schindler and Richard Neutra, both of whom were extremely responsive to landscape design throughout their joint and separate careers.

It is surprising that Neutra, who in his landscapes, was one of the most sensitive architects of the thirties and forties, should have written so little on garden design, particularly since he had been apprenticed for a brief period in 1919 to the Swiss gardener Gustav Ammann. The horticultural and site-planning skills that he acquired from Ammann were to stand him in good stead for the rest of his career, not least during his early years in Berlin, when he designed gardens for architects Erich Mendelsohn, Ernst Freud, and Arthur Korn. Moreover, after his emigration to Los Angeles in 1926, when he began to collaborate with his compatriot Schindler, Neutra's contribution seems to have been restricted to the field of garden design. Thus, Schindler's Howe House (1925) in Los Angeles and the Lovell House (1926) in Newport Beach had gardens from the hand of Neutra. Neutra's own first integrated work came with his famous Lovell Health House (1929) in Los Angeles,

72. Richard Neutra. Von Sternberg House. 1935. San Fernando Valley, California

where dark shrubbery and wisteria complement the white, gray, and blue-black color scheme of the house itself.

Between 1935 and 1947, Neutra realized five canonical houses: the von Sternberg House (1935) in the San Fernando Valley, California (Fig. 72), the McIntosh House (1937) and the Nesbitt House (1942) (Fig. 73), both built in Los Angeles, the Kaufmann House (1946) in Palm Springs (Fig. 74), and finally the Tremaine House (1947) in Santa Barbara (Fig. 75). In each instance, the landscaped extensions of the house played a dominant role in the composition, with the overall poetic quality deriving in large measure from the articulation of the garden. In all of this work, belated credit must be given to the little-known landscape gardener Gertrude Aronstein, who apparently collaborated with Neutra on many occasions and who obviously helped him specify and orchestrate plant material.

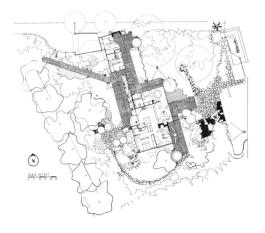

An idea of Neutra's landscaping approach can be found in his book *Mystery and Realities of the Site* (1951), where he wrote of the von Sternberg House: "The architect who is sensitive to his site is not content with merely digging a foundation.... As a further means of site-anchorage he may send out tentacles of structure to catch or hook some surrounding feature of the land.... This may be an elegantly curved metal wall, surrounded by a cooling moat, and containing a terrazzo-paved patio...."[9]

In the modest (Usonian) McIntosh House, the landscape elements are more understated, while the overall integration derives from the felicitous organization of a few decisive elements on a narrow site. The unifying thrust of the composition is initiated by a brick walkway that extends from the entrance into the house, while the opposing living-room terrace is inflected toward the prevailing breeze and southwesterly sun. Five years later Neutra completed his Nesbitt House, whose tactile presence largely depended on the contrast between vertically battered timber eaves and thick-jointed brickwork. These crude elements served to offset the delicacy of the Japanese garden within the back court. This whole sequence is concluded by a masterwork, the Kaufmann House in the desert, where the essential poetic stems from two complementary factors, from the hedonistic continuity of the horizontal living space and pool running out into the sparsely layered rock-strewn vegetation of the desert and the striking contrast between the vast rock outcrops of the site and the delicate light-weight aluminum framing of the house. The Tremaine House is in many respects the absolute reciprocal of the Kaufmann House for where the latter articulates, as it were, the uninterrupted flatness of the desert, the roof of the former posits itself as an artificial horizontal overhang under which the rough, rock-strewn, verdant house and garden descend in a series of controlled steps. In the Tremaine House Neutra combined a sense of hedonistic intimacy with a mountain backdrop of infinite extent:

73. Richard Neutra. Nesbitt House. 1942. Los Angeles. Site plan

74. Richard Neutra. Kaufmann House. 1946. Palm Springs

75. Richard Neutra. Tremaine House. 1948. Santa Barbara, California

A smooth terrace, really the sheltering roof of the play space beneath, pulls the domain of the habitation boldly out into the landscape.... At the head of the steps (leading up from the lower garden) is the dining terrace. It is radiantly heated so that, on still evenings, it can serve as an extension of the house floor. The glass panel doors of the living quarters can be thrown wide to the terrace and the soft, diffused light of the house can spill over it.... Because the living room is separated from Nature only by the full height, thin framed, sliding doors of glass, the living space sweeps on through and reaches out for miles until it is closed off by the mountain. The mountain is, indeed, the "back wall" of this stupendous living room.[10]

If the Neutra/Aronstein approach may be said to represent a subtle fusion of the typical tropical cactus garden of the Americas with the Japanese diminutive landscape tradition, then the gardens of the Mexican architect Luis Barragán may be said to derive from two equally antithetical sources: on the one hand, abstract Color Field painting (Barnett Newman, Josef Albers, and others), on the other, the Hispano-Islamic garden tradition, as this was embodied in Spanish colonial form.

76. Luis Barragán. Fuente del Bebedero. 1958–61. Las Arboledas, Mexico

Between 1927 and 1945, Barragán built some twenty buildings before turning his hand, at the age of forty-three, to garden design and to the creations of compositions in which the house is inseparable from the garden. This shift in focus led Barragán to the creation of ranchlike courtyard houses where the most important volumes were external, bounded by large blank walls and abstract surfaces, and often painted in pale pastels or sharply vibrant colors. This lyrical, minimalist expression reached its apotheosis in Barragán's El Pedregal development in the outer suburbs of Mexico City, where between 1945 and 1950 he transformed some seven hundred and fifty acres of barren lava outcrop into a series of forecourts, fountain pools, and courtyard houses (Fig. 76). Among the indigenous inspirations behind this evocative irrigation of a volcanic landscape was Barragán's childhood memory of the village of Mazamitla: "In this village, the water distribution system consisted of great gutted logs, in the form of troughs, which ran on a structure of tree forks 5 meters high, above the roofs. This aqueduct crossed over the town, reaching the patios, where there were great stone fountains to receive the water.... The channeled logs, covered with moss, dripped water all over the town, of course. It gave this village the ambience of a fairy tale."[11]

Through such a combination of monumental surfaces with minimal fenestration, relieved by aqueducts, pools, drinking troughs, and intermittent planting, Barragán and an entire generation of Mexican architects have brought into being a new regional landscape that is intrinsically critical of the placelessness of the megalopolis, by virtue of its emphasis on the place-defining boundary wall. As Barragán has put it, with regard to his general feeling for privacy: "Any work of architecture that does not express serenity is a mistake. That is why it has been an error to replace the protection of walls with today's intemperate use of enormous glass windows."[12]

From a stylistic point of view, Barragán, Neutra, and the Brazilian landscape architect Roberto Burle Marx could hardly have been more opposed to each other, yet each was to achieve a domestic garden culture oriented toward tranquility and the cultivation of the spirit which Neutra characterized as survival through design. Indeed, one may claim that the works of Neutra and Barragán jointly stand on that delicate frontier where architecture as such begins to dissolve into landscape design.

GARDENS IN THE MODERN LANDSCAPE

By the time Christopher Tunnard published *Gardens in the Modern Landscape* in 1938, landscape architects had already acquired the habit of integrating the abstractions of modern art with concepts drawn from the formal and picturesque traditions of the seventeenth and eighteenth centuries. Tunnard, for his part, was only too aware of the way in which the eighteenth-century park was in the process of being destroyed by suburbanization. Thus, he posited a villa and a garden, at Saint Anne's Hill, Chertsey (1936), designed with Raymond McGrath as a counterthesis, not only to the outworn paradigm of the picturesque but also to the invading sea of suburban semidetached houses surrounding it on every side. At Saint Anne's Hill, Tunnard attempted to reconcile three successive stages of historical transformations: first, the establishment of Saint Anne's Hill as an eighteenth-century park; second, its ornamentation by nineteenth-century horticultural exotica, extraneous monkey puzzles, rhododendrons, and so on; and last, his own rearrangement of the garden space as an abstract spatial domain. Two years later, Tunnard advocated a radical reconsideration of landscape, based on more complex notions of nature, art, and society than those of the eighteenth century, and this particular syndrome informed the remainder of his career. It was this that eventually led him to move away from landscape design toward the wider issue of environmental management.

As a designer, Tunnard thought that the seventeenth-century parterre was just as viable a legacy as the eighteenth-century park and that, in effect, one should strive to integrate both traditions within the modern garden form. To this end *Gardens in the Modern Landscape* advocates a number of formal arrangements ranging from Gabriel Guévrékian's ornamental terrace designed for the large terrace that Robert Mallet-Stevens built for the Vicomte de Noailles at Hyères (Fig. 77) to Jean Canneel-Claes's own house and garden built in Brussels in the late thirties (Fig. 78). Eschewing the petit bourgeois horticultural practice of English municipal gardens, Tunnard was attracted by the more organic naturalistic layouts favored by the architects of the European welfare state as it was then emerging in Holland, Switzerland, and Sweden. Tunnard cites with approval the address given by the president of the Swedish Garden Architects Association, on the occasion of the first International Congress of Garden Architects held at the Paris World Exhibition of 1937. Tunnard's own designs, however, were more astringent than the organic naturalism practiced by the Swedish *funkis* (functionalist) architects of the thirties, as is evident from the formal garden that he designed for Serge Chermayeff's timber-framed Halland House, Sussex (1938). Here the space of the house is extended into the

77. Gabriel Guévrékian. Garden terrace for the Vicomte de Noailles's villa. 1925. Hyères, France. The sculpture is by Jacques Lipchitz

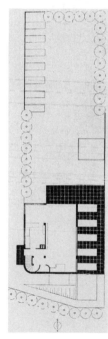

78. Jean Canneel-Claes. His own house and garden. Late 1930s. Brussels. Site plan

79. Serge Chermayeff. Chermayeff
House, 1938. Halland, Sussex. The
drawing is by Christopher Tunnard

landscape by a formal walkway and by an orthogonal screen that, aside from framing the vista, sets off a judiciously placed reclining figure by Henry Moore (Fig. 79).

Tunnard thought that there were three approaches by which an appropriate modern landscape tradition might be evolved: first, through a sociofunctional programming of open space; second, through a rhythmic use of plant material; and third, through the overall integration of the given plastic elements into the surrounding topography. The essentially sculptural nature of this last made him uneasy about adopting an unduly painterly approach to garden design, and in so doing he always tempered his own "palette" in such a way as to suit the site and the local ambient light. Thus, while influenced by contemporary painting, above all by Ben Nicholson's abstractions and by Paul Nash's *objets trouvés*, Tunnard was always conscious of the limitations of English light, its tendency toward glare or, alternatively, shadowless illumination where color tends to be absorbed. His sensitivity in this regard was close to that of the critic Adrian Stokes. Tunnard wrote in 1938:

In England, the light presses from above. It is not the clear white light of warmer countries, but it is dominant; there is a glitter at midday on glabrous leaves and lustrous glimmering flowers which drain the life from the colour so that only under a leaden sky or at twilight can a planned effect achieve its fullest value.... This is an argument for the use of mass plantings of one tone or of such combinations as will be effective in brilliant as well as subdued illumination. Elimination of light overplus is impossible; therefore, it is a fact that should be acknowledged. Elimination of incompatible greens is possible in some degree, so that colour can be liberated to perform its work.... Take, for example, the nebulous shape of a yew tree on the chalk downs, where it appears sporadically and grows to greater perfection than many other evergreens. Against rolling light green grassland it has no connection, no vital link of similarity or even of contrast to weld it to the surrounds. The grass lifts up, the yew tree weighs it down; there is a lack of balance in colours and in forms. See the same tree against the jagged whiteness of a chalk-pit, and the aesthetic effect is at once satisfactory. The dark shape looms strongly against a contrasting background, which welcomes it because the contrast is in kind. The intensity of tone in tree and soil is similar and therefore mutually enhancing; they draw together, yet individually gain a larger character. Similarly, a yew tree on a lawn is less powerful emotionally than one placed in relationship to buildings; from the grey stones of a churchyard it draws the necessary illumination to enhance its form.[13]

Modern landscape design came into its own in 1938, when Tunnard emigrated to the United States to teach at Harvard University, there to encounter not only the entrenched values of the Harvard Olmsted School, founded in 1900 by Frederick Law Olmsted, Jr., but also a number of young American students who would later contribute to a transcontinental movement in landscape design. Garrett Eckbo's revealing account of this moment warrants citing in full:

When I arrived at Harvard in 1936 as a green Californian from the frontier, I encountered a school in which the landscape faculty felt that since trees were not made in factories, it was not necessary for the profession to concern itself with new ideas in architecture or the arts. The old tried-and-true formal/informal system had worked since the 18th century and would continue to be comfortable and reliable.

Inasmuch as we were downstairs in Robinson Hall and architecture was upstairs, it was difficult for us to avoid what was going on up there. Dean Joseph Hudnut had arrived a few years before, determined to modernize architecture. In 1937, he brought Walter Gropius from England. The atmosphere of the Graduate School of Design was charged, controversial and exciting. Of the twenty students in landscape architecture, three—Dan Kiley, Jim Rose and I—were so turned on by the new ideas upstairs that on our own we began to explore new forms and arrangements which might reflect the new design ideas. In our experience at Harvard, we did learn about earlier efforts in Europe, particularly Christopher Tunnard in England and Pierre le Grand in France.

At the same time, in San Francisco, unbeknownst to us, Thomas Church, influenced by William Wurster and other modernising architects, began a similar exploration in his garden practice.

The results of these two parallel efforts are well known, and I need not belabor them. They became the modern design approach that has dominated American landscape architecture through the middle third of the century. Basically it made it possible to eliminate preconceived design vocabularies, and to develop forms and arrangements which spoke to specific sites, clients, users, local contexts and regional cultures.[14]

Eckbo's view of the role to be played by the landscape designer in modern society was to be altogether more ecological than the rather privatized northern Californian tradition of Church and his pupils, and in that sense his position lay closer to that of Tunnard. He saw landscape design as a necessary part of a wider environmental practice and thereby recognized that neither the planner nor the developer could perform this task alone. In his book *Landscape for Living* (1949) he wrote:

The contradiction between social relations and individual land use, which exists in all our communities, is not between subdivision itself and the community pattern, but rather between subdivision for unreasonable profit and land-use needs. The admission by all parties concerned, including most members of the banker-builder-realtor trinity, that earlier subdivision and practices have been unfunctional, unrealistic and irresponsible, is in itself an admission of this contradiction. The question now has become how much better are we to make those practices. The "community planning" of the operative (speculative) builders and the FHA is supposed to represent the sudden bursting of the promised land upon our dazzled eyes. But any objective examination of the

80. Garrett Eckbo. Private garden with glass-bottle wall. Late 1940s

81. Dan Kiley and Harry Wolf. North Carolina National Bank Headquarters Building, riverside park. 1988. Tampa, Florida

plans produced by these operations will indicate what a truly minute step forward they have taken.[15]

It is discouraging to recognize that nothing has changed at the level of public policy in the forty years that have elapsed since Eckbo wrote those words, despite his own specific suggestions for more responsible forms of future land settlement. Aside from his lifelong struggle for saner forms of environmental development, however, Eckbo has enjoyed an extensive career as a landscape architect. His practice has been characterized by a highly abstract, sculptural approach to garden design, as is evident in his private gardens of the late forties. Abstract art was once again the inspiration, but the attitude was glyptic rather than painterly, with the greatest emphasis falling on the tactile qualities of bounding walls, invariably made out of natural brick, paling, basketwork, and so on (Fig. 80). Eckbo's most important civic contribution of the forties lay in the pocket parks that he proposed for the United States Housing Authority and for the Farm Security Administration during the late New Deal. His public work during this period ranged from the layout and landscaping of migrant workers' camps in Texas to the design of the first postwar subdivisions as in his Mar Vista Homes project for West Los Angeles in 1948. In all these instances a similar syntax was employed, comprising shrub blocks, walkways, terraces, and certain tree forms that vaguely resembled the formal motifs of abstract art, although what Eckbo had in mind was a total cultural program rather than a one-shot aesthetic exercise.

One cannot conclude this very brief account of the Harvard landscaping tradition without mentioning the classic contribution of Dan Kiley and the landscape of Kiley's former apprentice Cornelia Oberlander. Despite a love for open landscape, Kiley has been at his best in urban situations. This inclination seems to be evident from the high points of Kiley's career, from the gardens that he laid out on the terraces of the Oakland Museum, Oakland, California (1962), to his garden court for the interior of the Ford Foundation Building, New York (1967), designed by Kevin Roche and John Dinkeloo. Kiley was to play an equally seminal role in the urban park that he recently completed in association with Harry Wolf, for the North Carolina National Bank Headquarters Building in Tampa, Florida (Fig. 81). It is significant that both Kiley's riverside park in Tampa and Oberlander's planting for Arthur Erickson's Robson Square complex, Vancouver (1979), are gardens established on (and indeed against) artificial sites, compounded out of a matrix of elevated concrete superstructures, the plant material being organized in such a way as to bring the matrix to life. Thus, Wolf's tartan infrastructure for the NCNB park and Erickson's tiered lawcourts at Robson Square, with their terraced extensions, are both matrices within which Kiley and Oberlander have laid out their respective planting. And while the architecture serves in each instance as an important catalyst, it would be nothing without the embellishment of botanical form.

Roberto Burle Marx was already heir to a local modern gardening tradition by the time he designed his first garden, for the Alfredo Schwartz House, in Rio de Janeiro (1933), the house itself having been designed by Gregori Warchavchik and Lucio Costa. Burle Marx based this garden on the pioneering work of Brecheret and Mina Warchavchik, née Klabin, who had been responsible for the gardens of Warchavchik's early houses.

Besides these self-taught designers, the botanist Henrique de Lahmeyer Mello Barreto was to exercise a lifelong influence on Burle Marx's work. Indeed, much of the landscapist's knowledge of plant material came from Barreto and from their joint botanical expeditions in the rain forests of Brazil. Burle Marx's familiarity with the subject was sufficient for him to be appointed director of the municipal parks in Recife in 1935.

Three years later, when he was twenty-nine years old, Burle Marx came into his own as an independent landscape designer with the remarkable garden that he designed for the Ministry of Education in Rio de Janeiro, where the Cubist principle of *mariage de contour* was given a three-dimensional rendering in terms of tropical planting and sinuous form (Fig. 82). This neo-Cubist landscape palette was first articulated at a topographic scale in Odette Monteiro's garden built at Correas, above Petrópolis, in 1947 (Fig. 83). Henrique Mindlin's description of this remarkable parkscape encapsulates the essential principles pursued by Burle Marx:

82. Roberto Burle Marx and Oscar Niemeyer. Ministry of Education. 1938. Rio de Janeiro

83. Roberto Burle Marx. Garden of the Monteiro House. 1947. Correias, Rio de Janeiro

> Boulders and sculptural plants echo the shapes of the mountains and plant fingers of red-hot poker . . . point strategically towards a "picturesque" tree which leads the eye towards forests on the lower slopes. An artificial amoeba-shaped lake reflects sky and mountains while providing a home for water plants. Stepping stones cross it and are spaced out into the grass beyond, rising towards a foliage bed restating the shape of the lake. From a distance, the reds, greens and grays are an abstract plant painting, but become an interplay of volume on close approach. Located in a gneiss-and-granite region, the garden makes ecological use of rock and quarry plants indigenous to this soil, and rarely used, before Burle Marx, in Brazilian gardens. A flowing garden path skirts the garden almost as in 18th century English style.[16]

The syntax just described would be reiterated in different permutations as Burle Marx passed from one scale to another—from, say, Affonso Reidy's Pedregulho housing development, to the Santos Dumont airport, or from his intimate Carlos Somlo garden, Rio de Janeiro (1948), to the Parque de Este, Caracas (1962).

Burle Marx's exceptional familiarity with many of the 50,000 different species of plants that enrich the tropical landscape of Brazil (as opposed to the 11,500 species of the European world) has made him a militant ecologist. As he put it in a recent

84. Alfred Caldwell. Caldwell Farm.
1948–73. Bristol, Wisconsin.
Perspective

interview: "People are so uneducated. Nature is always destroyed in the name of progress. Nature is a cycle of life that you must understand in order to take liberties with it in good conscience. The means at our disposal, like the great bulldozers, fire, defoliants, can be just as well used for good as for evil but in Brazil they are used to create misery."[17] Elsewhere in the same interview he remarked on the self-conscious ecological regionalism of his vision: "I don't say that in my gardens I don't plant foreign plants; I do. But they must fit to our landscape. It is important that a garden is a result of our existing landscape and our flora."[18]

Such postindustrial ecosystems and plant forms assume a particularly tragic cast as the rain forests of Brazil continue to be decimated. It is not only the laying waste of a particular ecology: it is also the destruction of an irreplaceable biochemical synthesis, not to mention the elimination of innumerable species of plants and animals, and the now-proven warming of the earth.

THE NEW REGIONAL PATTERN

Between the decline of the Olmsted school and the rise of Anglo-American modernism came the work of the Danish emigré Jens Jensen. Arriving in Chicago in 1884, Jensen served as park superintendent in the heyday of the Chicago parks system (1893–1920) and went on to a prosperous private practice, beginning around 1908 with his design for the irregular landscape attached to Wright's Avery Coonley House. Although Wright and Jensen collaborated very rarely, they were equally involved with the restoration of an aboriginal, almost mythic prairie landscape. In 1906 Jensen redesigned the West Park System of Chicago, which entailed an upgrading of Garfield, Douglas, and Humboldt parks, respectively, providing, among other features, a prairie-meadow for the first, a shallow lake for the second, and a reconstructed river channel for the third. In each instance Jensen tried to restore the Illinois landscape to what he thought it had been prior to the opening of the West. Soon after he founded the Chicago forest-reserve, Jensen created the public masterworks of his career: Chicago's Columbus Park and Knickerbocker Boulevard in Hammond, Indiana. This last amounted to an altogether more majestic suburban layout than anything Olmsted had achieved. Thus, as the Chicago architect Alfred Caldwell has written:

> The parks of Jensen are diametrically opposed to the Baroque; nature determines and not style—nature is style. The plant and the landscape have their own expressions. The expressions are not foisted on—they are out of it. The power of Jensen's park is the power of nature—not man's despotic power. In principle Jensen's parks are also opposed to the Romantic park of the 18th and 19th centuries. The Romantic park, like the Baroque, was a style too. It was concerned with the simulation of nature, and the provoking of mood melancholy or ideal. The raptures of Prince Puckler on seeing the ruins of Tintern Abbey—Wordsworth's Tintern Abbey—would scarcely be felt by Jensen who, in another age, was concerned with living nature, not with the patine of the dead past.[19]

Having served his apprenticeship with Jensen, Caldwell was himself to become something of a bridging figure, spanning from his neo-Wrightian landscapes of 1936, in Eagle Point Park in Dubuque, Iowa, and in Lincoln Park, Chicago, to his later collaboration with Mies van der Rohe on the design of Lafayette Park in Detroit. The trajectory of Caldwell's career does not end here, however, for he is as much an architect as a designer of landscapes, as we may judge from his own house and studio in Bristol, Wisconsin, under continual construction since 1948 (Fig. 84).

Caldwell's expression as an architect has covered a wide range, from an almost Zen-like attitude toward the intangible interplay of tectonic and natural elements to his later reinterpretation of Jensen's "prairie" culture. His mature sensibility, however, is virtually inseparable from Ludwig Hilberseimer's postwar vision, formulated in *The New Regional Pattern,* Hilberseimer's first book in English, published in 1949. It is clear that Caldwell's brilliance as a draftsman and an artist was essential to the representation of Hilberseimer's sublime de-urbanizing vision. At the same time, Caldwell's particular sensibility, more Chinese perhaps than Japanese, is most evident in the demolished garden court of his Eagle Point Park, now in the process of being restored. Of this stratified Jensen-like masonry, he has written:

> This small court shows the merging of Nature and Architecture, resulting in a kind of mysterious continuum of light and shadow, a wavering reality of a world glimpsed and undefinable, uncertain and mesmerizing. That, in brief, is its art and its defense. This visual quality as an idea—taking this detail as a symbol—presumes that actuality is not clear. Actuality has no hard edge of certainty. It is, like the meaning of life itself, illusive to the last. It can be analyzed, but it cannot be formulated. Such is the meaning of Nature in Architecture.[20]

Caldwell's regional-planning studies and his one-man demonstration project in regional planning practice, the farmhouse that he has been building in rural Wisconsin, may be compared to the critical environmental policies variously advocated by Wright, Tunnard, Eckbo, and Hilberseimer. Close to the spirit of Wright's Broadacre City but in some ways calling for a more symbiotic relationship between man and nature, Caldwell's regionalism has a marked political character. His deeply felt concern for a conscious return to a more fundamentally symbiotic way of life comes close to the latter-day "back to the land" strategies advocated by Helen and Scott Nearing.[21] Of his own regional land settlement model Caldwell has written:

> So these studies of small farms and gardens are in reality nothing but a few tentative notes on an ample page—a premonition, a hint—and nothing very much more. Just about everything remains to be solved. It is enough to see that, as the world is now going, the crisis of technology, by eliminating jobs by the tens of millions, will lead to mass unemployment, to economic impoverishment, and consequently to political dictatorship in the now democratic nations of the world. It is easy to see that such a situation will finally lead to nuclear war and a world-wide Armageddon.... However, I believe that unemployment and

poverty—which create modern wars—can be eliminated by part-time small farms and gardens for industrial and clerical workers. I believe that poverty can be transformed into what used to be called the good life. I believe that unemployment can be replaced by self-reliance. I haven't any proof. I have only an idea I have been working on for sixty years.[22]

Caldwell's delicate, oriental rendering of Hilberseimer's "new regional patterns" from the air—that is to say, this Kropotkinian vision of "almost-nothing," of low-rise, high-density, single-story dwellings shrouded in a sea of trees—is equally close to the spirit of both Jensen and Mies. It is predicated on a form of spiritual renewal and political praxis that is totally removed from our technologically distorted notions of nature, art, and society.

Hilberseimer's first low-rise, high-density settlement proposals date from the late twenties. Looked at retrospectively, after sixty years of megalopolitan development, they may be seen as the first indication of a critique wherein the single-story court-yard house pattern, the so-called *Teppischehauser*, is posited as a strategy with which to mediate the urban dispersal brought into being by the automobile. We may look back today over a half-century of critical environmental thought in which low-rise, high-density courtyard housing is projected at different times and even occasionally realized but rarely, if ever, adopted as a matter of public policy by any civic administration or large-scale developer. Thus, a similar critical impulse may be traced as it passes, say, from Rudolf Schindler's pioneering Pueblo Ribera Court (1923) in La Jolla, through Wright's Usonian houses, to Neutra's Strathmore Apartments (1937) in Los Angeles; or, alternatively, through Le Corbusier's Roq and Rob stepped-terrace patterns (1946) to a modified version of a similar barrel-vaulted typology realized outside Bern (1960) to the designs of Atelier 5.

A reworking of this low-rise, high-density residential line runs through the land-settlement patterns advanced by Serge Chermayeff and Christopher Alexander in their book *Community and Privacy* (1963), and much the same theme is picked up by Roland Rainer's *Livable Environments*, which was published three years later. That Rainer was to recapitulate the urban ecological arguments of his predecessors is borne out by the last paragraph of his book:

The basic social concept: to attain economic goals with technical means, is now, in view of the destruction of the environment, the unlivability of cities and the flight of their inhabitants, experiencing a crisis that is threatening society with total doom. Will society learn from the crisis, will it be able to learn that in the future there can no longer be any question of attaining economic ends with technical means, but society will have to become aware of the opposite approach: the subordination of all economic standpoints to the goal of human welfare, which at the same time means the careful preservation, tending and cultivating of its natural basis, i.e., the unconditional priority of psychological and biological standpoints and methods of working.[23]

Today, surely, one may trace a certain convergence between the early "biorealist" micro-environments of Neutra and Schindler, their luscious southern Californian gardens of the twenties, and these latter-day advocates of dense, low-rise, megalopolitan development. In all these instances, the burden of proof shifts away, so to speak, from the house to the garden and from the one-off aesthetic work to the landscape as a whole.

SHIFTING SITES

In his address to the Architectural League of New York in 1982, Vittorio Gregotti argued that the origin of architecture was not the primitive hut, but rather the primordial act of marking the ground. As he put it: "Before transforming a support into a column, a roof into a tympanum, before placing stone on stone, man placed the stone on the ground to recognize a site in the midst of a universe: in order to take account of it and modify it." This cosmological procedure is of particular import today, when there is a continuing proliferation of objects throughout the landscape. The dispersal of built "detritus" throughout the environment bestows a new importance on the creation of bounded domains and on subtle forms of modifying the landfall. In no single career has this new sensibility been more evident than in the work of the Greek architect Dimitrios Pikionis. The peculiarly Mediterranean quality of this innocent yet critical experience is evidenced in an essay that Pikionis published over half a century ago: "We rejoice in the progress of our body across the uneven surface of the earth and our spirit is gladdened by the endless interplay of the three dimensions that we encounter with every step,... Here the ground is hard, stony, precipitous, and the soil is brittle and dry. There the ground is level; water surges out of mossy patches. Further on, the breeze, the altitude and the configuration of the ground announce the vicinity of the sea."[24]

This recognition of a topographic narrative, experienced in terms of the body, informs the major work of Pikionis's career: his park and promenade running between the Philopapou Hill and the Acropolis in Athens. The single work was painstakingly achieved by the architect between 1955 and 1962. It may be seen, in retrospect, as a topographical mosaic, as a glyptic narrative, the stonebed of which varies according to the respective needs of pedestrian and vehicular movement. Where the incline steepens, Pikionis introduces rest spaces with stone benches, while throughout, intricate paving patterns allude to cosmic and mythical entities, to the ruins of past civilizations, and to the prophetic letters **A** and Ω, alpha and omega, embedded at random in the site.

A similar notion of a timeless topography was evoked in the Plaza del Tenis seafront, realized in San Sebastián in 1986 to the designs of Luis Peña Ganchegui and the sculptor Eduardo Chillida (Fig 85). That this place existed in the experiential memory of the sculptor prior to its realization was confirmed in an interview with Chillida: "That place captured my imagination before I knew I was going to do something in it . . . much before I became a sculptor . . . much before I finished my high school.... I could be fourteen then wondering where the waves would come

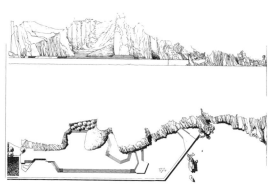

85. Luis Peña Ganchegui and Eduardo Chillida. *The Comb of the Wind.* 1976–86. San Sebastián, Spain. Plan of plaza and sculpture

from . . . I understood I had to make a preamble to the sculptures in a place that is the beginning and the end of the city . . . as a symbol of the meeting of the city with nature. Of a city that ends in an absolute which is the ocean."[25]

Peña Ganchegui's terraced *temenos* in pink Porrino granite is, in fact, bounded by two absolutes: the eroded volcanic rockface of the cliff and the restless turmoil of the sea. This last makes its presence felt not only through ceaseless pounding against the breakwater, but also by entering a disused sewer pipe under the plaza and bursting up as spray through small apertures let into the granite pavement. This connection with the sea produces miniature rainbow effects under the impact of light.

A topos of a more critical and compensatory nature is the "labyrinth" realized between 1980 and 1986 by Georges Descombes and Alain Leveille of the so-called CREX group in Geneva. Here, in the exurban municipality of Lancy, nothing now remains of an original rural landscape save the remnants of an interstitial space. Thus, unlike at the Philopapou Hill or at the Concha Beach in San Sebastián, here one is confronted with the ruination of modern development, with leftover space between characterless housing blocks and ubiquitous autoroutes. The CREX group had little option but to link up the fragmentary remains into an interstitial labyrinth. As Descombes has put it:

> The object was to attempt to "overturn" what hitherto had been a negation: negation of the place, of its history, of the sedimentary accumulations of the traces left by its processes of formation and transformation through pressures of economic expansion which negated . . . all relationships between the architectural objects and the overall morphology of their context.
>
> Thus the project amounts to a re-structuring, a restoration and a re-orientation of a "lost park." The straightness of the walls, their staggered dips distort the land and reveal its energies, the forces which shape it: folds, slope, streams. Upon this wounded, haggard territory forms are born again, rising up and resisting all levelling down.
>
> The fountain retains and then lets the water fall: in this "deconstruction" of the flow, the movement of water . . . here expresses its intrinsic forces, weight, gravity, and fluidity, making them more perceptible as renewed "presences."[26]

That the above all-too-adumbrated history is largely the account of a lost cause is surely still insufficiently appreciated, above all because the sociopolitical failure of the Enlightenment manifests itself today in a total disregard for all natural form. The imperatives of economic development and instrumental reason have effectively laid the world to waste. It is now generally accepted that if the production of fluorocarbons would cease tomorrow, the earth would not regain any kind of ecological stability for another two decades, and we need hardly dwell here on the global buildup of carbon dioxide that no amount of catalyzers will ever begin to address. In the long run, the cult of consumerism and infinite development will have to be brought to an end, or the species will not survive. We now see that the late Enlightenment ideal of infinite abundance, to be made available to all, was and is an illusion. To write of the modern landscape as though it were nothing more than a cultural discourse would be to trivialize values that are essential to our survival. To write of the modern is to entertain the hope of the postmodern; to evoke that which is not yet built, transformed, laid waste, or irrevocably ruined; and to conjure up that ineffable "other" world that lies beyond our present proliferation of useless objects.

1. Jean Starobinski, *The Invention of Liberty: 1700–1789*, trans. from the French by Bernard C. Swift (Geneva, 1964), p. 205.

2. A translation of the title *Begenung mit Pionieren*, by Alfred Roth (Basel and Stuttgart, 1973). In this partly autobiographical history, Roth traces the careers and the influence of the early modernists, including Le Corbusier, Piet Mondrian, Adolf Loos, Josef Hoffmann, Auguste Perret, and others. I have, of course, appropriated this title as a conceit.

3. Le Corbusier, *Towards a New Architecture*, trans. F. Etchells (London, 1927), pp. 189–90. Republished, 1981.

4. Le Corbusier, *L'Oeuvre complète* (Zurich, 1910–29), p. 114–15.

5. Ibid., p. 86.

6. Interview with Christian Norberg Schulz, in *L'Architecture d'Aujourd'hui* (Boulogne, 1954).

7. Frank Lloyd Wright, *An Autobiography* (New York, 1943), p. 47.

8. Frank Lloyd Wright, *An American Architecture*, ed. E. Kaufmann (New York, 1955), p. 196.

9. Richard Neutra, *Mystery and Realities of the Site* (Scarsdale, 1951), p. 41.

10. Ibid., pp. 21–24.

11. Emilio Ambasz, *The Architecture of Luis Barragán* (New York, 1976), p. 9.

12. Ibid., p. 8.

13. Christopher Tunnard, *Gardens in the Modern Landscape* (London, 1938), pp. 112–16.

14. Cited in Elizabeth K. Meyer, "The Modern Framework," in *Landscape Architecture* (March/April 1983): 50–53.

15. Garrett Eckbo, *Landscape for Living* (New York, 1950), p. 245.

16. Interview with Roberto Burle Marx in Denise Otis, "Artist of the Garden." *House and Garden*, vol. 158, no. 9 (Sept. 1986): 7.

17. Ibid., p. 220.

18. Ibid., p. 220.

19. Leonard K. Eaton, *Landscape Artists in America: The Life and Work of Jens Jensen* (Chicago and London, 1964), p. 61.

20. *Architecture and Nature: The Work of Alfred Caldwell* (Boston, 1984), p. 30.

21. Helen and Scott Nearing, *Living the Good Life (How to Live Sanely and Simply in a Troubled World)* (New York, 1970).

22. *Architecture and Nature*, p 30.

23. Roland Rainer, *Livable Environments* (Zurich, 1972).

24. Dimitrios Pikionis, "What the Limestone Said," *Keemena*, ed. Agnis Pikionis (Athens, 1988).

25. Fragments of a conversation with Eduardo Chillida (March 1985) in Jesus Bazel, *El Peine del Viento* (Pamplona, 1986), p. 27.

26. Georges Descombes, "Redefinition of a Site." *Georges Descombes: Shifting Sites*, ed. G. Tironi (Roma, 1988), pp. 57–58.

LEO MARX

The American Ideology of Space

LIKE ALL OTHER ASPECTS OF HUMAN EXPERIENCE, our distinctively American ideology of space has a history, and I propose to sketch something of its origin, its later development, and its presently visible consequences. I call my subject the ideology of "space" rather than "landscape" because space is an essential component of both architecture and landscape. Architecture and landscape architecture are two of the chief forms in which we shape and experience the spaces we inhabit. The term *space* also may remind us initially that a landscape is a physical entity whose meaning and value we construct and for which we have a variety of other names: land, topography, terrain, territory, environment, cityscape, country-side, scenery, place. One could go on, but all of these may be thought of as forms of space—geographical space. Indeed, the initial European conceptions of North America—the blank white areas often labeled *terra incognita* on early maps—had more in common with our shared idea of space (an empty three-dimensional field) than with the received idea of landscape (a pretty stretch of natural scenery).

The distinction points to another attraction of the word *space*: its relative neutrality. It does not carry the inescapably pictorial sense of place that the word *landscape* has carried since it first came into the English language in the early seventeenth century. (The word evidently was borrowed from the Dutch *landskip*, which closely associated it with the emergence of landscape painting as an independent genre.)[1] This pictorial idea of space was reinforced by eighteenth-century devotees of natural scenery, who developed elaborate theoretical distinctions among beautiful, sublime, and picturesque landscapes and representations thereof. By that time, *landscape* had become the essentially aesthetic concept it still is. *Space*, on the other hand, invites consideration of the actual state of the nation's terrain. The term may help to remind us of the differences among (1) ideas and images of topography, or its subjective existence; (2) the relatively small sector of the national terrain that might be called the designed landscape, consisting of deliberately planned gardens, parks, nature reserves, housing developments, and suburbs; and (3) the rest of the national terrain, most of which consists of a "built environment" shaped by the countless uncoordinated decisions of governmental bodies, firms, and individuals, and by the operation of various markets, especially that of real estate. I particularly want to emphasize the contrast between the small sector of the terrain shaped by the design professions—architecture, urban planning, and landscape architecture—and the rest of the national terrain, an immense unplanned area where the consequences of the prevailing American ideology of space are massively exhibited. This area is shaped by the decisions—in large measure market-driven—of countless real-estate investors, speculators, and developers.

My purpose, then, is first to consider the genesis of the ideology in the era of exploration and colonization, when Europeans began moving into the vast "deserts" of North America; second, to sketch the emergence, and relative importance, of three variants of that ideology—three more or less distinct ways of locating meaning, value, and social purpose in American space; and finally, to suggest where we are in America today, and where we seem to be heading, in our treatment of space.

THE MYTH OF AMERICAN ORIGINS

Anthropologists tell us that most self-conscious peoples possess a myth of national origins with a narrative core, and according to the American myth, our nation owes its being to the journey of Europeans from the Old to the New World. Among the features of our collective self-conception derived from that transatlantic migration is what the image geographers call a shared mental map. A nation's mental map, like the famous Bostonian's map of the United States (where that city fills a third of the national terrain and its western suburbs border on Chicago), is a shared, expressive, highly distorted representation of a people's actual geographic situation. It is a mental map, in other words, because the literal, objective geographic image has been reshaped by shared assumptions, beliefs, or ideology.[2]

The first principle of the American ideology of space derives from the initial European impression of the boundless immensity and seeming emptiness, or ahistorical character, of the New World. During the era of discovery, exploration, and settlement, the actual maps, with their conspicuous blank sectors and missing boundaries, comported with the European conception of North America as a vast, unbounded expanse of largely uninhabited, unclaimed, but potentially valuable space. The actual boundaries of the continent were, of course, unknown, and except for the land nearest the coast, so were the topographical details. The white interior space on the map reinforced the impression that this newly discovered place was nothing but raw nature, a cultural vacancy untouched by history and waiting to be filled by migrating Europeans. Of course, this view of the New World took little or no account of the Native Americans, but awareness of their presence did not conflict with the idea that North America consisted of little more than empty space: to most Europeans the "Indians," like other nonwhite peoples encountered by Europeans on other continents, were "savages" and hence not human, which is to say that they were a part of nature, not of civilization.

Another source of the emergent ideology of space, in addition to the perception of North America's immensity and cultural vacancy, was the sharp contrast between the built environment of the Old World and the unbuilt, or "natural," environment of the New World. For centuries most of Europe's habitable land had been preempted—owned or controlled—by privileged minorities. Thus the typical map of Europe revealed as much, perhaps more, about the alignment of human (political) power as it did about topography. It depicted a continent that had long since been dominated by the process of reproducing social institutions, or "civilization," whereas the unlined, unbounded map of North America figured forth a world still under the control of nature.

This early version of the American mental map, with its graphic opposition between an old, established civilization to the east and raw, unimproved nature to the west, provided the symbolic setting for the myth of national origins whose narrative core was a journey from east to west. That we are dealing with a "myth," in Roland Barthes's semiotic sense of the word—as a second-order discourse, which distorts or deforms the significance that signs possess in the ordinarily first-order semiological system—becomes evident if, for instance, we consider the density of meaning compressed into the three-word account of our national beginnings that young Americans learn in school: "Columbus discovered America."[3] The myth imparts immense creative power to the westward movement of Europeans: indeed, other places and peoples acquire a meaningful existence only if and when they have been incorporated into the consciousness of Western civilization. It is striking, once we recognize the weight of implication borne by the seemingly innocent verb *discovered*, drenched as it is in the Eurocentric presumptions of white racial superiority and domination, to recall that this implication was seldom noticed, much less challenged, before the heightened awareness of racial bias that accompanied the civil-rights movement of the 1960s.[4]

The transatlantic voyage was an indispensable feature of the myth, but the voyage was susceptible to divergent interpretations. Its significance varied according to the sector of the mental map identified with the highest values and meanings. The dominant version of the myth, exemplified by the mini–history lesson "Columbus discovered America," depicts the voyage as a potentially triumphant advance of civilization. Here civilization is chiefly associated with its presumed positive qualities: organized religion; cities; literacy; knowledge of, and power over, nature, as represented by the latest advances in science and technology; social order; civility; literature; and art. The chief focus of value, accordingly, lies to the east, identified at the outset with Rome and the other great capitals of Europe and, later, after the establishment of the first colonies, with the built environment along the eastern seaboard of North America. In this utilitarian interpretation of the myth, nature (the white on the map, empty space, untapped resources, land uninhabited save for the savages) is a "howling wilderness." Its manifest destiny is to be discovered, subdued, and settled—made useful—by arriving Europeans.

Here, then, is the genesis of what was to be the dominant version of the American ideology of space. The utilitarian bias was buttressed by the strong Protestant sense of the natural world as lawless, unredeemed, or satanic. The seventeenth-century New England Puritans, who were bent on building a model Christian community, a city on a hill for all the world to see, took seriously the biblical injunction to subdue the earth and exercise dominion over all its creatures. (In their lexicon, *nature* and *natural* referred to that which existed in a fallen state: for example, the state of the soul before receiving grace.) Their viewpoint exemplifies the extreme anthropocentrism that Lynn White, the distinguished historian of science, attributed to Judeo-Christian theology. In an influential essay, White argued that of all the great world religions, Christianity encourages least respect for the environment or, put differently, it lends most credibility to the idea that nature exists only to serve humanity.[5] The dominance of this utilitarian bias is reflected in the many accounts of North America by arriving Europeans that, far from describing the appearance of the natural landscape, merely consist of unadorned lists or inventories of forests, flora, fauna, minerals, and other resources of potential use to Europeans.[6]

John Locke, the philosopher who probably had the greatest influence on the men who founded the American republic, added economic specificity to this utilitarian concept of space. His famous statement, "In the beginning, all the world was America," often has been quoted out of context by American historians (including myself), with the misleading implication that Locke was calling attention to the general resemblance between the uncolonized state of North America and the prehistoric state of the world.[7] Locke's actual point in the chapter "Of Property" in his widely read *Second Treatise on Civil Government* (1690), however, is far more specific and revealing: namely, that incorporation into an economy, or commodity exchange, is a necessary precondition for imparting value to anything, including land:

> Where there is not something both lasting and scarce, and so valuable to be hoarded up, there men will not be apt to enlarge their possessions of land, were it never so rich, never so free for them to take; for I ask, what would a man value ten thousand or a hundred thousand acres of excellent land, ready cultivated in the middle of the inland parts of America, where he had no hopes of commerce with other parts of the world, to draw money to him by the sale of the product? It would not be worth the enclosing, and we should see him give up again to the wild common of nature whatever was more than would supply the conveniences of life to be had there for him and his family.
>
> Thus in the beginning all the world was America....[8]

Land in North America, according to Locke, is destined to remain worthless until it acquires the status of a commodity in a market or capitalist economy. With the image of America as boundless, scaleless space in mind, he was able to contemplate the possibility, unimaginable in Europe, that fertile, habitable land could be so abundant as to lack value. The importance of this commodity-exchange facet of the American ideology of space cannot be exaggerated. It is particularly revealing when we consider the state of the American landscape today, in the afterglow of the Reagan era. The principle of "letting the market decide" (with relatively few constraints) how we allocate and use the land was latent in the dominant American ideology of space from the beginning. We also are reminded that many of the delightful parks and landscape gardens we encounter in European cities survive from the era antedating the reign of the market and the commodification of land.

So much, then, for the first and most influential, or utilitarian, account of

American origins as a stage in the triumph of civilization over nature. As we will see, by the late eighteenth century this interpretation, identified with the highest values of European culture, was to be reformulated in the language of "progress." In the opposed, primitivist version of the myth—a second interpretation—the chief locus of value was the most distant, western edge of the mental map. Here the essential meaning and purpose of life in the New World is located as far away as possible, in space or time or both, from the great centers of European civilization. (In the primitivist version the most attractive aspects of nature are set in opposition to the negative attributes of civilization—political tyranny, economic oppression, war, injustice, constraint.) The desired destination of the transatlantic voyage thus is the pristine, unmodified state of nature associated with the "noble savages" of the frontier. Nature, in this view, is identified with freedom, spontaneity, authenticity; to recover the natural is to escape from the unhappy consequences of monarchical, aristocratic, and ecclesiastical oppression that constitute the dark underside of civilization.[9]

Unlike the utilitarian version of the myth, however, this primitivist version rarely has been taken seriously as a guide to life. To be sure, primitivism has inspired many works of art and expression, and in those aesthetic forms it has provided an imaginative basis for a telling, if often indirect, critique of organized society in general, and in particular of industrial capitalism and the heedless destruction of the countryside. No doubt the most tangible consequence of primitivism has been the motivation it provided for the conservation and preservation movements, the defense of public lands, and the establishment of national forests and parks. As we shall see, it also has helped to clarify the meaning of the third, intermediate or pastoral, version of the myth. The primitivist idea of America provides no basis for the life of a large population, however, and therefore has never been adopted by a significant social group. To most people, except for a minority of artists, writers, intellectuals, hermits, and wilderness preservationists, it has seemed a mere poetical vision or fantasy, not a live option or a feasible way of life.

The third, or pastoral, version of the myth has been favored by a much larger, if nonetheless somewhat dissident, minority of Americans. According to this viewpoint, the New World provided the first actual large-scale opportunity to realize the ancient dream of achieving genuine harmony between humankind and nature. Here the ideal locus of value and meaning is neither the overcivilization of Rome, Paris, or London, nor the savagery of the western frontier, but a "middle landscape" or "semiprimitivism," a *via media* neither urban nor wild, that combines the best features of each. This pastoral interpretation of the mental map is traceable to the idealization of the ancient Middle Eastern herdsman and to his role as a mediating, or what the anthropologist Victor Turner called a liminal (from the Latin *limin*, or "threshold"), figure, one whose calling required him to work in the borderland between civilization and nature.[10]

Thomas Jefferson consciously affirmed the applicability of this ancient pastoral ideal to American circumstances just before the Republic was founded. At that time, as I have argued elsewhere, he answered the question "Shall the new American republic develop manufacturers?" with an emphatic No! "Let our work-shops remain in Europe," he wrote in the 1780s. "It is better to carry provisions and materials to workmen there, than bring them to the provisions and materials, and with them their manners and principles."[11] Here Jefferson was specifically repudiating the primacy of economic criteria in choosing social policies. His characteristically pastoral goal for the material condition of the new republic was economic sufficiency, not the maximization of production or consumption. "The loss by the transportation of commodities across the Atlantic," he explained, "will be made up in happiness and permanence of government." Here he prefigured the deep conflict that has become ubiquitous since World War II: that between, on the one hand, those who give the highest priority to economic growth and economic criteria in shaping social policies, and, on the other, those committed to less tangible political, aesthetic, moral, environmental, or "quality of life" criteria in shaping social policies. Although Jefferson later changed his mind on the specific issue of manufactures, he did not abandon his vision of an ideal republic of the middle landscape.

THE VISUAL REPRESENTATION OF THE IDEOLOGY

By the 1830s, with the advent of the railroad and the marked acceleration in the rate of industrialization, a new set of images—and a new vocabulary—became available for representing the dominant ideology of American space. In the Jacksonian era its proponents began to depict the advance of European civilization in the New World as confirming evidence for the idea that history is in essence a narrative of human progress. *Progress*, in fact, became the code word for an all-encompassing view of life, one that extended and refigured the primary, or utilitarian, version of the myth of American origins; it thereby provided ideological support for a rapidly expanding capitalist economy. Now the transatlantic migration of Europeans was regarded as a particularly revealing chapter of modern history, and history was conceived as a record of the continuous, steady, cumulative, virtually preordained expansion of human knowledge about, and power over, nature. The many new improvements (a key word of the period, as in "internal improvements") made possible by advances in science and technology explained why most people were better off (had a "higher" standard of living) than their parents and why their children could expect a comparable improvement in their lot. The special circumstances of American life, the very idea of building a new nation in a virgin land, made the landscape a visible register of history and of progress.

A telling pictorial inscription of this belief system is Asher Durand's 1853 painting *Progress* (Fig. 86). At first sight this picture, with the framing trees at the left and the large body of placid water in the center, might be another conventional Claudian landscape. Unlike most landscapes of the period, however, this one depicts the industrial transformation of nature. (Durand himself had asserted that the greatness of landscape paintings depended on their success in celebrating the superiority of the works of God to the works of man.)[12] Durand situates the viewer to the west of this terrain, facing the rising sun

86. Asher B. Durand. *Progress*. 1853. Oil on canvas, 48 x 72". The Warner Collection of Gulf States Paper Corporation

and the oncoming march of civilization. At the center of the eastern horizon, from which the new power apparently emanates, the distant mountains and clouds are aglow in a kind of supernal light. On a peninsula in the middle distance on the right shore, Durand envisions a busy, thriving city of commerce and industry, with several plumes of smoke or steam rising from ships, locomotives, and factories. Closer to us, on the right side of the canvas, we see a train, its locomotive smoking, moving across a viaduct, a busy canal, and a wagon heading west along a dirt road—all serving to convey a sense of the inexorable, expansionary energy of progressive white European civilization.

The only possible note of discord in this optimistic prospect is introduced by the two Native Americans who stand on a promontory in the left foreground, gazing down on what must have been for them a dismaying exhibit of the white man's organized power and industry. The two "savages" stand amid unsightly vegetation: rotting stumps, twisted roots, jagged and tangled branches, and the skeletons of dead trees. This disorderly patch represents raw, unmodified, recalcitrant, death-dealing nature, or, to use a favorite New England Puritan epithet, the "hideous wilderness." Wild, hostile nature is the appropriate setting for these unfortunate "red men," often referred to at the time as "vanishing Americans" or an "extinct race" because progress foretold the inevitable "conquest" of the wilderness and its imminent transformation into a garden. In contrast to the display of the white man's power down in the valley, with its barely concealed genocidal implications, the Indians standing amid unmodified, unruly nature seem pathetically small, helpless, forlorn, bemused; they obviously are in retreat, and about to be pushed further back by the forces of progress—back, one imagines, all the way to the Pacific or, as it were, right out of the picture frame. Their presence evokes a pathos familiar to readers of Cooper, Bryant, or Whittier: a poignant sense of doom that is unfortunate but unavoidable, a doom that may, on reflection, be a consolingly small price to pay for the incalculable benefits humanity will derive from the future glory of civilization.

87. Currier & Ives. *Across the Continent—Westward the Course of Empire Takes Its Way.* 1868. Lithograph, 20⅛ x 27⅜". The Harry T. Peters Collection, Museum of the City of New York

Fanny Palmer made an even more obvious, almost diagrammatic statement of this progressive ideology of space in her popular 1868 lithograph, *Across the Continent: "Westward the Course of Empire Takes Its Way,"* published and widely distributed by Currier and Ives (Fig. 87). Here we look forward, across the plains toward the western mountains, and the straight diagonal formed by the right-of-way of the transcontinental railroad slices the entire scene in two. This boundary line serves the distorting purpose of myth; instead of dividing the terrain into southern and northern sectors, as the transcontinental railroad actually did, the diagonal enables Palmer to invest the picture with the ideological overtones of the east-west contrast. On the near, more easterly side of the tracks, therefore, is a frontier settlement, populated by energetic, civic-minded white adults, who are busy chopping down trees and dispatching wagon trains off to the West while their children file into a public school. The only people on the other, more westerly, side of the tracks, in the great expanse of unimproved land stretching towards the mountains, are "savages." The natives nearest to the settlement, in the foreground, are armed, but they are about to be enveloped by a plume of thick, dark smoke; it comes from a locomotive pulling a train of cars that also is headed toward the Pacific. The message hardly could be more explicit: progress, as represented by the powerful new technology, will overwhelm the natives and help to establish a new white European empire in North America.

At the other end of the spectrum of attitudes toward American space, Albert Bierstadt, a leading western landscapist, paints a primitivist vision of unimproved nature in *The Rocky Mountains: Lander's Peak* (1863) (Fig. 88). Here, in one of the most popular paintings of the day, Bierstadt strives to evoke a sense of wonder in the presence of nature's elevating grandeur, infinitude, or, in a word, sublimity. Although the compositional structure is Claudian, the locus of value is not, as it would be in a typical Claudian pastoral landscape, a harmonious blend of nature and civilization. The only evidence of a human presence is the obscurely rendered, technologically primitive encampment of the Native Americans in the shadowed foreground. Bierstadt saves the preternaturally intense light of the sun, which dominates the picture, for an almost garish celebration of the forms of untouched nature: the serene lake, the cataract, and the towering, awe-inducing mountains in the distance. This image of natural beauty, with its suggestion of infinite space, evokes feelings of reverent awe and fear that an earlier generation would have reserved for a more orthodox, supernatural divinity.

In his response to industrialization, Thomas Cole, known as the founder of the Hudson River school of landscape painting, exemplifies a quite different, pastoral, conception of American space. In his 1836 "Essay on American Scenery," he celebrated the beauty of the national terrain, but he also took the occasion to deplore the negligent way it was being transformed at a time when "a meager utilitarianism seems ready to absorb every feeling and sentiment, and what is sometimes called improvement in its march makes us fear that the bright and tender flowers of the imagination shall be crushed beneath its iron tramp."[13] The iron tramp Cole heard was of course, that of the iron horse, the nation's favorite exemplar of progress and a particular threat to one of his favorite scenes. In 1830 a railroad had bought a right-of-way on land overlooked by his Catskill retreat. By 1839 some twenty-six miles of track had been laid, and four years later Cole painted the scene, including an imagined smoking locomotive, in his *River in the Catskills* (Fig. 89).[14]

In view of Cole's expressed hostility to such alterations of the landscape, his depiction of the minuscule, inoffensive railroad is surprising. The "ravages of the axe are daily increasing," he had said in the 1836 essay. "The most noble scenes are made desolate, and oftentimes with a wantonness and barbarism scarcely credible in a civilized nation." Yet here the train seems to blend harmoniously with the rural scenery. To be sure, when historians have compared this work with Cole's 1837 painting of essentially the same vista, *View on the Catskill, Early Autumn* (Fig. 90), they have noted some differences that may be attributable to the artist's forebodings.

88. Albert Bierstadt. *The Rocky Mountains, Lander's Peak.* 1863. Oil on canvas, 73¼ x 120¾". The Metropolitan Museum of Art, Rogers Fund, 1907. (07.123)

89. Thomas Cole. *River in the Catskills.* 1843. Oil on canvas, 28¼ x 41¼". M. and M. Karolik Collection. Courtesy, Museum of Fine Arts, Boston

90. Thomas Cole. *View on the Catskill, Early Autumn.* 1837. Oil on canvas, 39 x 63". The Metropolitan Museum of Art, Gift in memory of Jonathan Sturges by his children, 1895

91. Claude Lorrain. *Landscape with Merchants.* c. 1630. Canvas, 38¼ x 56½". National Gallery of Art, Washington, Samuel H. Kress Collection

The earlier landscape, with its lovely images of running, wild (rather than iron) horses and of a woman in the foreground offering wildflowers to a child, has a distinctly elegiac touch. Of the two, it surely is closer in its compositional features to a typical painting by Claude like *Landscape with Merchants* (c. 1630) (Fig. 91). I am thinking especially of the repoussoir trees and the resulting sense of a framelike balance of vertical and horizontal lines. (Claude also represents the reconciliation of bourgeois society—the merchants—with the aesthetic order of nature.) As Barbara Novak has noted, Cole's 1843 painting betrays several possible signs of his altered feelings about the presence of the railroad: a greater horizontality (the absence of the usual tall trees); and the stumps, the fallen branches, and the man with the axe (all received icons of the beneficial transformation of nature in the progressive ideology of space) in the left foreground.[15]

Nevertheless, the fact remains that Cole's partly concealed, diminutive railroad hardly disturbs the rustic serenity of this scene. Nor does it effectively undercut the prevailing sense of confidence in the essential harmony between industry and landscape. Actually Cole's painting is one of many American landscapes of this period in which a minuscule but conspicuous, often centrally located railroad is made to blend seamlessly into a pastoral prospect.[16] Why did so many mid-century American painters produce work that ignored or denied the conflict—of which they, like Cole, surely were aware—between the new industrial technologies and the beauty of the landscape?

There are several possible answers. One has to do with the depth of their commitment to the form itself, which is to say, to the very concept of a landscape painting as an affirmation of pastoral harmony between society and nature; another has to do with the intimidating social power, the virtual hegemony, exercised by the national faith in progress. The wealthy patrons of landscape painting, including the railroad magnates who sponsored special journeys for artists, tended to be adherents of the progressive ideology. There also is reason to believe that Cole and several others more or less consciously adopted the strategy that Ralph Waldo Emerson had recommended in his 1842 essay "The Poet":

> For as it is dislocation and detachment from the life of God that makes things ugly, the poet [or painter] who re-attaches things to nature and the Whole— re-attaching even artificial things and violation of nature, to nature, by a deeper insight—disposes very easily of the most disagreeable facts. Readers of poetry see the factory-village and the railway, and fancy that the poetry of the landscape is broken up by these; for these works of art are not yet consecrated in their reading; but the poet sees them fall within the great Order not less than the beehive or the spider's geometric web. Nature adopts them very fast into her vital circles and the gliding train of cars she loves like her own.[17]

Cole, like Emerson, seems to have believed that art could provide, by means of a symbolic reconstruction of reality, an exemplary guide to social purpose. What poets or artists were able to represent of the subordination of power to purpose in words or in paint, society might emulate in fact—in the "real" world. If new technologies like the railroad threatened to destroy the beauty of American scenery, landscapes of pastoral reconciliation like Cole's 1843 landscape envisioned the possibility of quite another outcome.

The pastoral conception of American space, as exemplified by Jefferson, Emerson, and Cole, was in some measure a reaction to the dominance of the progressive view and to the fact of accelerating industrialization. In their effort to rescue American space from the harsher, more brutally utilitarian consequences of scientific and technological progress, a minority of disaffected or critical Americans endorsed the pastoral ideal of a middle landscape. Although this conception of space never replaced the dominant utilitarian conception, it was to provide a rationale for some of the most constructive thinking about and practice of architecture and landscape architecture, including the design of many parks and suburbs, and some of our most effective urban and regional planning.

THE FUSION OF THE PROGRESSIVE AND PASTORAL IDEALS

So far, then, I have distinguished three variants of the mid-nineteenth-century American ideology of space—the progressive, the primitivist, and the pastoral. Each version comports with a distinctive interpretation of the myth of national origins. It may be asked whether it makes sense, given the existence of these three variants, to speak of *the* ideology of American space, as if there were only one. I believe it does, although admittedly, the difference between the concept of a single ideology, embracing potentially conflicting modes of thought and behavior, and the concept of rival ideologies may prove to be a matter of emphasis more than of substance.

As noted earlier, in any case, the primitivist viewpoint surely did not provide a conceptual basis for a distinct ideology of space. Despite its imaginative appeal to artists, writers, and devotees of wilderness, only a tiny minority of Americans ever adopted primitivism as a guide to behavior. Even Henry Thoreau, who often has been mistaken for an advocate of a total hermetic withdrawal from organized society, was far from being a true primitivist. True, he insisted upon the indispensability of access to wilderness, but the chief locus of meaning and value in the world of *Walden* is the characteristic middle landscape of native pastoralism. The same can be said about most American thought and expression that withhold assent from the dominant progressive ideology. Although primitivist ideas have helped to shape our collective imaging of space—our shared mental map and our arts of representation —their direct influence on behavior, save for the creation of nature reserves and other measures for the preservation of wilderness, has been negligible.

What makes the notion of a single American ideology of space truly problematic, however, is the apparent contradiction between the progressive and pastoral ideals. In theory and in principle the two are ultimately irreconcilable, but in practice that logical contradiction has been relatively easy to disguise and ignore. Thus, a stock rhetorical strategy of the Jacksonian era was to valorize a technological innovation, like the building of a railroad to the West, as an example of improvement or progress and, at the same time, as a means of carrying Americans closer to the heart of unspoiled nature. Much the same dubious blend of the two ideals is still used nowadays as a rationale for, say, building superhighways into the northern New England ski country. The fact is that logical incoherence is not difficult to hide in the presence of collective fantasy and myth. This is especially true when the illogic is reinforced by material desires and rewards.

A more important reason for positing a single American ideology of space, however, is that the utilitarian outlook, as subsequently reformulated in the idiom of progress, has dominated our thinking in this realm from the beginning. To be sure, dissidents who were unmoved by the pieties of utility, commodification, possessive individualism, and progress often have adopted the pastoral conception of space as a hypothetical alternative. But in the event, pastoralism has not provided a serious, feasible alternative to the dominant mode of thought and behavior nurtured by the original European conception of American space. That conception, to repeat, included a sense of space in the New World as virtually limitless; as having no reason for being except utility to humanity; and as possessing worth only when incorporated into a market economy, which is to say, only when invested with exchange value. The result is that we always have treated land, and the resources upon and beneath the land, as if they were privately owned goods largely indistinguishable from cotton cloth, pork bellies, or any other marketable commodity.

According to this dominant ideology, the chief means of investing North American space with value was the European population's centrifugal, often warlike movement—a "conquest" or "annihilation" of space—from an eastern, established, built environment westward in the direction of nature. This seemingly preordained movement was, as the popular mid-century slogan had it, America's "manifest destiny." Today we continue to enact that centrifugal process. True, it no longer takes the form of a westward movement of population across the continent, but in the modern era Americans have participated in a massive movement out of central cities into the quasipastoral environment of suburbia. A certain continuity with the old myth of national origins is suggested by the distinct social character that process has had in England and America as compared with, say, Europe and South America. Whereas the more privileged members of the London and New York middle class have tended to move to the suburbs themselves, abandoning the urban core to relatively poor, powerless, and non-white groups, their counterparts in Paris, Vienna, or Rio de Janeiro have done just the opposite. Whether the ideology I have been describing chiefly accounts for this difference is not clear, but it surely has been a contributing factor.

The tendency to fuse pastoral and progressive values makes itself felt in the more explicit theories of American space formulated by certain of our most innovative planners and architects. One of their chief assumptions, in designing parks, parkways, and suburbs, has been that access to the natural—to open space, sunlight, lakes and ponds, vegetation, birds and animals—provides an effective remedy for the sensory and other deprivations and constraints of life in the industrial city. Frederick

Law Olmsted regarded both the urban park and suburbia as "strongly counteractive to the special enervating conditions of the town."[18] Olmsted's conviction that the successful park or suburb represents a "marriage" of town and country, a community in closer "harmony with nature," also makes itself felt in the thought and practice of, among others, Andrew Jackson Downing and Catherine Beecher.

A similar, if indirect or metaphoric, affinity with pastoralism is discernible in American architectural theory. I am thinking especially of the organicism that is traceable to Coleridge and German Romantic philosophy. The key to this theory is the distinction between "mechanic" and "organic" form; the form is mechanic when a predetermined pattern is imposed on the materials from without; the form is organic when it is innate, that is, when the form arises from within, as part of the object's development.[19] This organic principle of form, which rests on the likeness between the design process of art objects and the growth of organisms, was first Americanized by Horatio Greenough and Ralph Waldo Emerson; then applied with stunning originality to literary form by Henry Thoreau (in *Walden*) and Walt Whitman (in "Song of Myself"); and most effectively translated into the language of architecture by Louis Sullivan, Montgomery Schuyler, Frank Lloyd Wright, and Lewis Mumford. Here again, adherents of the doctrine conceived of buildings—and the process of designing buildings—according to the metaphor of organic growth. Thus the potential user's character and purpose, the building's intended function, are seen as the germinating entity, like the seed or DNA of the tree, from which the structure's ideal form should develop. As Sullivan famously put it, "Form follows function," or "What the people are within, the buildings express without."[20]

Lewis Mumford, a devoted heir and reinterpreter of this native aesthetic tradition, regarded organicism as a primary conceptual resource in controlling the forces of technological and economic progress. If properly understood and applied, Mumford argued, the organic principle will enable us to adapt technological power to those humane purposes he associates with the natural. For Mumford, as for Sullivan and Wright, organic form is an antitechnocratic principle of order, a principle that can and should guide the architect in subordinating the new architectural components (steel, glass, elevators, and so on) to the most inclusive sense of the building's or city's function. The principle thus would require the harmonious accommodation of each building to the site, each site to the city, each city to the region. As I have argued elsewhere,[21] the central idea in Mumford's view of the world is the control of the mechanic by the organic, as is implicit in his approving citation of Montgomery Schuyler's praise for the Brooklyn Bridge: "It is an organism of nature. There was no question in the mind of the designer of 'good taste' or of appearance. He learned the law that struck its curves, the law that fixed the strength of the relation of its parts, and he applied the law. His work is beautiful, as the work of a ship-builder is unfailingly beautiful in the forms and outlines in which he is only studying 'what the water likes' without a thought of beauty."[22]

Schuyler's statement exemplifies the most inspiring and useful expression of organicism. His organic principle is a native version of pastoral in the sense that its manifest aim, in the design of artifacts, buildings, and landscapes, is to subordinate technological means to the achievement of a more harmonious relation with nature, or "the natural." In this context the natural is conceived, first, as inherent in the materials, and second, as a more inclusive, even holistic, sense of the object's function or purpose. The same principles are the bases of Mumford's historically precocious and telling critique, in his seminal 1962 essay, "The Case Against 'Modern Architecture,'" of the abstract, disconnected sterility of much modernist building. That antiseptic style owes its origin, he argues, to "certain preoccupations about the nature of modern civilization," and especially to "the belief in mechanical progress," with its "assumption that human improvement would come about more rapidly, indeed almost automatically, through devoting all our energies to the expansion of scientific knowledge and to technological inventions."[23] He rejects a large part of architectural modernism as embodying the spirit of the machine rather than that of organic nature.

The backlash against architectural modernism, as expressed by Mumford, replays a deeply rooted American conflict of ideas. It can be traced to the nineteenth-century opposition between the dominant culture (with its patriarchal view that natural beauty is a lesser, soft, "feminine" concern and its uncritical commitment to technological progress) and the adversary culture (with its belief in the need for greater harmony between the man-made and the natural, as exemplified by the Jeffersonian ideal of a society of the middle landscape). The persistence and recurrence of this tension suggest that it is indeed possible to speak of a single ideology of space in the United States—one that embraces the recurrent opposition in discourse and practice between progressivism and pastoralism. At times that tension has been resolved, or it has seemed to be on the verge of resolution, within this or that sphere of the culture. One thinks, for example, of Olmsted's urban parks or Sullivan's tall, ornamented, steel-framed buildings, but in fact those resolutions have been relatively rare, partial, and temporary.

The nation's overall direction in its treatment of space has been set by the dominant utilitarian ideology of progress and its associated tenets: the maximizing of economic growth, trust in the operation of the market, the commodification of land, and the individualist ideal of "success" marked by upward social mobility and the ownership of a detached single-family home. As a nation, therefore, we have zigzagged in that progressive direction, with the pastoral ideal responsible for many of the deflections from a straight course. Pastoralism has inspired alternative practices, both positive and negative: innovations like our great system of national parks, and constraints on the unchecked operation of market forces like the Environmental Protection Agency. Nevertheless, the fact is that the pastoral conception of American space has not issued in a genuine alternative to the dominant ideology, and probably never will, for it rests on too many of the same fundamental assumptions. Hence, concurrent with the dominance of the progressive ideology, we witness the repeated acting out of the pastoral motive—the urge, in the face of the growing power and complexity of organized society, to move away from established urban centers in the direction of "nature." In American experience this centrifugal impulse often has combined the desire to escape from complexity with the desire to conquer, dominate, and commodify the environment.

THE OLD IDEOLOGY AND THE NEW AMERICAN TERRAIN

What sort of terrain is the American ideology of space now helping to create? If it can be said to embody our future goals, where is it leading us? If I had raised this question thirty years ago, when I published *The Machine in the Garden*, I doubtless would have pointed to suburbia, which I then regarded as a modern, if somewhat debased, effort to realize the pastoral ideal. The suburbs, on this view, reflect a widespread desire not uncharacteristic of pastoralism, to have it both ways: to enjoy the economic benefits of urban complexity while avoiding many of its disadvantages. This situation is made possible by modern transportation, especially the automobile and the daily commute; by the characteristic suburban pattern of class and racial segregation; and by such additional attractions of suburbia, not readily available in the urban core, as the single-family dwelling, a more complete separation of work and domesticity, and a simulacrum of genteel rusticity. Although the growth of suburbia has been an integral feature of the massive urbanization of the last two centuries, it simultaneously represents a negative reaction to the complexity and disorder of life in the central city; in that sense it may be described as another act of pastoral disengagement from social complexity by millions of Americans.

Until recently, I say, suburbia might have seemed the obvious terminus of the American treatment of space, but that is no longer so obvious. To be sure, the suburbs have continued to grow rapidly. Between 1950 and 1970, while the population of the central cities grew by ten million, that of the suburbs grew by eighty-five million. Nevertheless, in the last ten or fifteen years it has come to seem more likely that the characteristic future landscape of America is to be found elsewhere, beyond the suburbs, in one or more of the new kinds of settlement that are variously being called exurbia; technoburb; slurb; edge city; ruburbia; the citified or gentrified countryside; or the countrified city.

As this cacophonous inventory suggests, the settlements to which these names refer have appeared so recently that their essential character is a subject of extensive debate. My impression is that they fall into two categories. First, there are the new urban centers that have arisen along the suburban perimeter of, for example, Washington, D.C., Baltimore, Los Angeles, and Atlanta. These are citified cores with at least five million square feet of office space, more jobs than housing, and more people commuting in than out daily. According to one student of the subject, as many as fourteen such new high-rise cities are emerging in the Washington area alone.[24]

Second, there is a new kind of low-density-population growth that has appeared even more recently in the countryside at some distance from metropolitan areas. After a century and a half of decline, the population of rural America grew by eleven percent in the 1970s. This form of rural settlement, which I will call "ruburbia," does not fit any of our traditional categories of settlement: urban, suburban, town, rural. Ruburbia is being formed by the dispersal of industry, homes, and other buildings across two kinds of hitherto-underdeveloped terrain: the agriculturally least productive rural areas beyond the suburbs, and remote areas of sparsely settled states like Arkansas, New Hampshire, North Carolina, and North Dakota.[25]

For migrants to such places, the chief attraction seems to be that of jobs in the new high-tech industries. Single-family houses on relatively large plots of land close to open spaces and outdoor recreation also satisfy the needs of prospective workers in the new industries, the self-employed (working in the new electronic cottage industries), and the retired. These areas also offer escape from the crime and racial conflict, and the other assorted discomforts (smog, noise, traffic congestion) of the city, as well as escape from the many constraints, such as high rents and high taxes, that now typify both the suburbs and the cities. For the management of the characteristically high-tech, small-scale firms specializing in customized production that locate along rural freeways, the chief attractions seem to be plentiful, inexpensive land; low taxes; a more skilled, homogeneous, nonunion labor force; and fewer governmental regulations and restrictions.

A striking feature of ruburbia is the highly dispersed, decentralized, noncommunal pattern of settlement itself. In the counties where ruburbia has emerged, it is not unusual to find that many new industries have been established in the last ten years and that the population has increased markedly (as much as 300 or 400 percent between 1978 and 1988), but that there has been little if any corresponding growth in the size of towns or cities. Some new growth counties in North Carolina and Arizona have populations as high as 200,000 yet have no single city or town with more than 3,000 inhabitants.[26] The result is a new kind of decentralized community (if that is not an oxymoron), whose built core may consist of nothing more than a "strip," or cluster of shopping malls, and a few services located near a freeway intersection. The regional school and church often are located, more or less randomly, along one of the nearby secondary roads.

The cultural, political, and environmental character of this new kind of settlement is not yet clear, but some of the preliminary findings are disconcerting. Life in ruburbia is even more dependent upon the automobile and the long-distance commute (often by both husband and wife) than life in suburbia. The prevailing mindset here is privatism, with its atomized anti-city cultural life centering upon "family values," a reliance upon the electronic media, chiefly television, for contact beyond the family, and unconcern for the welfare of the increasingly non-white urban majority. The prevailing political ethos seems to be antiliberal, anti–government "interference" or "regulation," or, in short, Reaganism. The absence of an organized community means reliance on private water supplies and waste-disposal systems. The result is environmental degradation and the careless, wasteful use of land and other resources.

Ruburbia and the low-density continental sprawl it portends exhibit traits that have been encouraged by the utilitarian ideology of space from the beginning. It exemplifies our continuing propensity to obey centrifugal impulses like those that first populated this nation; our willingness to allow the operation of the market to make crucial choices about land use; our individualistic tolerance for uncoordinated, haphazard development; and, above all, our irrational yoking together of a desire for access to the unspoiled countryside and a persistent disregard for its long-term well-being and survival. It would be wrong to imply that the ideology is itself the driving force behind these new developments; rather, the ideology serves to validate the kind of behavior encouraged and rewarded by our economic system. "One need not be a Marxist to observe," writes Kenneth Jackson in summing up the influence of the economic system on suburbanization, "that outward residential growth in North America coincided with the rise of industrial capitalism and the separation of the population into extremes of wealth and poverty. The 'free enterprise' system provided incentives to land speculators, subdivision developers, building contractors, realtors, and lending institutions. When the economic system went into cyclical decline, as in the 1890s, 1930s, and 1970s, the construction of new housing and the movement of population into peripheral areas slowed."[27]

With this new pattern of unplanned, random settlement (ruburbia) in view, finally, let me return to an issue raised at the outset. Can there be any doubt that the prevailing American ideology of space has done more to shape the national terrain than the ideas and practices of our most gifted architects, landscape architects, and planners? However much we may cherish the work accomplished by men like Olmsted, Sullivan, Schuyler, Wright, and Mumford, not to mention the achievements of all the responsible teachers, practitioners, and critics whom they inspired, the fact remains that so far as the scope of their influence on the transformation of the American terrain is concerned, all their efforts put together hardly begin to compare with the results of the countless uncoordinated individual, corporate, and governmental decisions made in accordance with the reigning ideology of space. And when, in addition, we consider the speed with which we now are degrading the global environment, the need to repudiate that anachronistic ideology becomes all the more urgent.

1. According to the *Oxford English Dictionary*, the first recorded appearance of *landscape* in English, meaning "a picture representing natural inland scenery," was in 1603, just four years before the establishment of the first permanent English colony in Virginia. (That coincidence deserves careful examination.) The use of a corrupt form of the word, *landskip*, dates from 1598, and almost certainly is related to the vogue of landscape painting in Holland. See Henry V. S. Ogden and Margaret S. Ogden, *English Taste in Landscape in the Seventeenth Century* (Ann Arbor, 1955), pp. 5–6.

2. Peter Gould and Rodney White, *Mental Maps* (London, 1974).

3. "Just as for Freud the manifest meaning of behavior is distorted by its latent meaning, in myth the meaning is distorted by the concept." Roland Barthes, *Mythologies* (New York, 1972), p. 122.

4. I first heard this analysis of "Columbus discovered America" from Stokely Carmichael, a leader of the civil-rights movement, about 1965.

5. Lynn White, Jr., "The Historical Roots of our Ecologic Crisis," *Science* 155 (1967): 1203–7.

6. Such highly utilitarian responses to North America are examined in *Views of American Landscapes*, ed. Mick Gidley and Robert Lawson-Peebles (Cambridge, 1989).

7. See, e.g., Leo Marx, *The Machine in the Garden: Technology and the Pastoral Ideal in America* (New York, 1964), p. 120; Barbara Novak, *Nature and Culture: American Landscape and Painting 1825–75* (New York, 1980), p. 3.

8. John Locke, "An Essay Concerning the True Original, Extent, and End of Civil Government," *The English Philosophers from Bacon to Mill* (New York, 1939), p. 422.

9. To put it in the simplest formulaic terms, the eastern (advance of civilization) pole of this bipo-

lar construct is formed by contrasting the appealing aspects of civilization with the threatening aspects of nature, whereas the western (freedom of nature) pole is formed by reversing the terms and contrasting the negative aspects of civilization with the attractions of the natural.

10. For a useful summary of this view of pastoral origins, see David Halperin, *Before Pastoral: Theocritus and the Ancient Tradition of Bucolic Poetry* (New Haven, 1983), pp. 85–117; on the application of this view to American thought, see Leo Marx, "Pastoralism in America," in *Ideology and Classic American Literature*, ed. Sacvan Bercovitch and Myra Jehlen (Cambridge, 1986), pp. 36–69.

11. Thomas Jefferson, "Query XIX," in *Notes on the State of Virginia*, ed. William Peden (Chapel Hill, 1955); for a more detailed analysis of Jefferson's pastoralism, and of the widely held idea of America as a republic of the middle landscape, see Marx, *The Machine in the Garden.*

12. See Kenneth W. Maddox, "Asher B. Durand's *Progress*: The Advance of Civilization and the Vanishing American," in *The Railroad in American Art: Representations of Technological Change*, ed. Susan Danly and Leo Marx (Cambridge, Mass., 1988), pp. 51–69.

13. Thomas Cole, "Essay on American Scenery," in *The American Landscape: A Critical Anthology of Prose and Poetry*, ed. John Conron (New York, 1973), pp. 568–78.

14. Actually, the railroad never did operate with a steam locomotive. For the details, see Kenneth W. Maddox *The Railroad in the American Landscape*, ed. Susan Danly and Leo Marx (Wellesley, Mass., 1981), pp. 17–33.

15. Novak, *Nature and Culture*, pp. 162–36.

16. For a fuller discussion of these paintings, see Leo Marx, "The Railroad-in-the-Landscape: An Iconological Reading of a Theme in American Art," in *The Railroad in American Art*, pp. 183–208.

17. Ralph Waldo Emerson, *The Complete Essays and Other Writings* (New York, 1950), p. 312.

18. Frederick Law Olmsted, "Public Parks and the Enlargement of Towns," *American Social Science Association* (Cambridge, Mass., 1870), quoted by Robert Fishman, *Bourgeois Utopias: The Rise and Fall of Suburbia* (New York, 1987), pp. 127–28.

19. "Shakespeare's Judgement Equal to his Genius," in *The Selected Poetry and Prose of Samuel Taylor Coleridge*, ed. Donald A. Stauffer (New York, 1951), pp. 423–33.

20. For a lucid explanation of Sullivan's theory, see Lewis Mumford, *The Brown Decades: A Study of the Arts in America 1865–1895* (New York, 1971), pp. 64–75; for a recent critique of Sullivan's theory, see David S. Andrew, *Louis Sullivan: The Present Against the Past, and the Polemics of Modern Architecture* (New York, 1985).

21. "Lewis Mumford: Prophet of Organicism," in *Lewis Mumford: Public Intellectual*, ed. Agatha Hughes and Thomas Hughes (New York, 1990), pp. 164–80.

22. Quoted by Mumford, *The Brown Decades*, pp. 46–47.

23. Mumford, "The Case against Modern Architecture," reprinted in Donald L. Miller, *The Lewis Mumford Reader* (New York, 1986), pp. 74–75. My sense of Mumford's later career is that he became obsessed with what he saw as humanity's losing struggle with "mechanism," especially as manifested in the nuclear-arms race; his two-volume apocalyptic jeremiad, *The Myth of the Machine*, an admirable work in many ways, also is a testimonial to the difficulty of applying the organic principle to the operation of large institutions, and especially the state.

24. Joel Garreau, *The Emerging Cities of Washington*, Washington Post Reprint Series, March 8, 1987; June 14, 1987; Nov. 29–Dec. 1, 1987; and June 19–20, 1988.

25. John Herbers, *The New Heartland: America's Flight Beyond the Suburbs and How It Is Changing Our Future* (New York, 1986). See also William K. Stevens, "A Rural Landscape, But an Urban Boom," *New York Times*, August 8, 1988, p. 1. This is an account of more than five hundred rural counties in the United States whose population has grown, through the in-migration of largely affluent families from the suburbs, by almost fourteen percent in the 1980s in a process comparable to the gentrification of old urban neighborhoods.

26. A characteristic example of ruburbia is to be found in Nash County, North Carolina, whose 589 square miles contain 120 industries and no cities. Kenneth T. Jackson, *Crabgrass Frontier: The Suburbanization of the United States* (New York, 1985), p. 296.

27. Ibid., p. 296.

CAROLINE CONSTANT

From the Virgilian Dream to Chandigarh: Le Corbusier and the Modern Landscape

LE CORBUSIER'S CONTRIBUTION TO THE MODERN landscape has drawn little critical attention, since the landscape was not a primary concern of either the modern movement or his particular theoretical position.[1] Nevertheless, his design for the capital complex at Chandigarh may be the modern era's most convincing testimony to the integration of architecture and landscape. There he recovered a spirit of inquiry that has been pursued only intermittently since the eighteenth century, when architecture and landscape emerged as separate disciplines. Le Corbusier did not explicitly seek to reintegrate the two domains; indeed, his polemical theories tended to disrupt the traditional connections between them. Rather, his persistent desire to reconcile man, nature, and cosmos through architecture ultimately led to his broader concern for the designed landscape. This important aspect of Le Corbusier's work exemplifies a current within modernism that falls outside its polemical boundaries yet evolves out of its utopian aims.

Le Corbusier rarely wrote about landscape. Moreover, his interest in assimilating traditional landscape principles in a manner appropriate to the new age, evident in his early Purist buildings, is often belied by the images he used to publicize them. Such discrepancies between his polemics and his built work, often pointed out in criticism, have obscured the role of landscape in Le Corbusier's work.[2]

He ultimately achieved this reconciliation of architecture and landscape through his designs rather than his polemical writings. His attitude toward the landscape developed in no single, consistent line. Rather than start from a set of rules that invert historical principles, as he claimed of his architecture, Le Corbusier often appropriated historical landscape techniques directly, questioning them only in later projects. If his architecture derived from *a priori* theoretical concerns, his attitude toward the landscape evolved *a posteriori* from practice. Though his treatment of the landscape was initially eclectic and schematic, it evolved to encompass a symbolic dimension. Only after his architecture transcended its seeming negation of history, and his landscape its diagrammatic relationship to history, could the two domains meet in conceptual unity.

This essay is a revised version of an article originally published in *The Architectural Review*, London, in January 1987.

NATURE AS IDEAL

In Le Corbusier's writings, nature is a prevalent theme, often imbued with semireligious overtones. His understanding of nature was complex and often contradictory. Sometimes he invoked it as a force antithetical to the works of man, equivalent to chaos or the Romantic notion of the sublime; yet he understood nature in its essence as a system of which man is part and as an embodiment of order—an analogue of modern engineering, the beauty of which derives from adherence to natural laws: "The objects of nature and the results of calculation are clearly and cleanly formed; they are organized without ambiguity. It is because *we see clearly* that we can read, learn and feel their harmony."[3]

This dual interpretation of nature as original condition and emblem of rational order, is one of many polarities Le Corbusier sought to integrate within his architecture. The theme of nature was also central to his social aims. He considered it an agent for the moral regeneration of mankind, capable of rekindling humanitarian values lost to industrialized society: "Man is a product of nature. He has been created according to the laws of nature. If he is sufficiently aware of those laws, if he obeys them and harmonizes his life with the perpetual flux of nature, then he will obtain (for himself) a conscious sensation of harmony that will be beneficial to him."[4]

In evoking a state of consciousness that was simultaneously primordial and millennial, Le Corbusier infused modern rationality with a primeval *mythos*. He thereby sought to endow his architecture with universal and eternal validity: "There is no such thing as primitive man; there are primitive resources. The idea is constant, in full sway from the beginning."[5] This modernist conflation of a radical starting point with the quest for universal truths implied a return to nature and the natural landscape as essential points of departure.

For Le Corbusier, the source of man's alienation from human nature and from nature itself was the city. By bringing nature into the city, he hoped to relieve the ills of traditional urbanism without sacrificing its cultural possibilities. His utopian urban proposals dissolve the polarity of city and country, merging the density of the former with the "soleil, espace, verdure" of the latter. He sought to elevate the quality of modern life by providing a setting conducive to creative thought, encouraging both collective interaction and solitude through a combination of density and proximity to nature.[6] Yet his urban proposals with their Virgilian overtones fail to adequately conceptualize the designed landscape, which remains more diagrammatic than aesthetic, more eclectic than symbolic.[7]

Le Corbusier's interest in the natural landscape as integral to an architectural idea is evident in his early travel sketches.[8] He was particularly awed by the Acropolis (Fig. 92), which he claimed to have visited every day of his four-week stay in Athens. He extolled the way "the Acropolis extends its effect right to the horizon"[9]: "The Greeks on the Acropolis set up temples which are animated by a single thought, drawing around them the desolate

92. The Acropolis (fifth century B.C.)

landscape and gathering it into the composition. Thus, on every point of the horizon, the thought is single. It is on this account that there are no other architectural works on this scale of grandeur."[10] This image of the Acropolis remained embedded in his imagination, profoundly affecting the spatial and symbolic role of the landscape in his work.

An obsession with the horizon pervades his architecture, whether intensified through the geometric contrast of the Villa Savoye or through the more analogous plastic expression of Ronchamp. The horizon is a visible embodiment of the cosmological unity that Le Corbusier sought in architecture, as he reiterated shortly before his death: "We must rediscover man. We must rediscover the straight line wedding the axis of fundamental laws: biology, nature, cosmos. Inflexible straight line like the horizon of the sea."[11]

ARCHITECTURE AND NATURE

The search for a modern architectural language initially diverted Le Corbusier from these metaphysical aims. His theoretical principles, conceived in reaction to Beaux-Arts academicism, inverted the traditional relationship of building to landscape. Instead of using a rusticated base, thematically linking building and ground, Le Corbusier proposed to elevate buildings on *pilotis* to provide a continuous ground plane. The natural landscape, thereby isolated from the building volume, became an object for contemplation from within the architectural frame. He transferred the landscape as finite figure to the roof garden, domesticating nature in a room open to the sky.[12] Le Corbusier's dramatic roof gardens imbue his urban dwellings with the isolated quality of rural villas. They are compelling explorations into the designed landscape, demonstrating the quest for primordial values that led him to transcend his radical theoretical methods and ground his work in the more permanent symbolic dimension.

In his first significant garden, a roof terrace (Figs. 93, 94) overlooking the Champs-Elysées for Charles de Beistegui (1931), Le Corbusier was inspired by his eccentric client to use architectural forms to surreal ends.[13] Through this pictorial device, he expanded the expressive possibilities of the architectural landscape beyond the dialectical opposition of man-made and natural that characterizes his early Purist villas. On the penthouse roof he accentuated the rupture between garden and nature through formal manipulation: reflective glass paving stones set in a carpet of grass stand for water; hedge walls in mechanically operable trays act as draperies to control the view; and a fireplace in the parapet of the upper terrace transforms sky into ceiling, supported by columnar trees. The wall is a tilted ground plane elevating the horizon, on which the Arc de Triomphe appears as an isolated element in a continuous landscape. The uneasy equation of fireplace and urban monument suspends the ordinarily scalar understanding of space and enhances the sense of withdrawal from the space of the city, which is underscored by the periscope entombed on the lower terrace. While detachment from the urban condition was to remain a prevalent

93. Le Corbusier. Penthouse for Charles de Beistegui. 1930–31. Paris. Roof terrace

94. Le Corbusier. Penthouse for Charles de Beistegui. 1930–31. Paris. Roof garden for dining

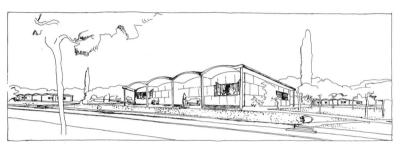

95. Le Corbusier. Marseille Block roof terrace. 1946–52. Marseille

96. Le Corbusier. Marseille Block roof terrace. 1946–52. Marseille

97. Le Corbusier. Maison Monol. 1920. Prototype

98. Le Corbusier. Maison de Week-End. 1934–35. La Celle Saint-Cloud

theme in his work, Le Corbusier later rejected such overt surrealist strategies, since the language of the Beistegui garden countered his aim of reintegrating man and nature.

Instead, on the roof of the Unité d'Habitation at Marseille (1946–52) (Figs. 95, 96) he evoked archaic values with primal natural forms, whose deliberate ambiguity amplifies the mythopoetic potential of the rooftop landscape. Totemic exhaust stacks evoke the presence of man, while irregular cooling towers recall nature. The ramped plane, understood simultaneously as ground and wall, is identified with the distant mountains, which he endowed with a similar ambiguity: though experienced as ground, from the Unité roof the mountains serve as a vertical backdrop against the sky. The parapet, like that of the Beistegui penthouse, blocks the city from view to become a substitute horizon, collapsing foreground and background. By visually eliminating the middle ground, Le Corbusier effected an isolation from the immediate environs to recover the spirit of integration with nature that he admired in the Acropolis.[14]

Le Corbusier's shift during the mid-1940s from an idealist preoccupation with prismatic solids contrasted with nature to a more poetic concern for integration with natural forms had foundations in his earlier work.[15] Of his three housing prototypes formulated by 1920, only the Maison Monol project (Fig. 97) with its traditional Catalonian vault, was firmly embedded in the earth.[16] Yet Le Corbusier began to exploit the Monol prototype only as integration with the landscape became important to his architectural ideas.

In the Maison de Weekend at La Celle Saint-Cloud (1934–35), Le Corbusier made a pivotal attempt to unite building and site by combining the Monol system with a warped plane of sod extending from garden to roof (Fig. 98). The warped ground plane derives from the ramp connecting roof terrace and ground that Le Corbusier first used in the Villa Savoye at Poissy (1929–31) to establish the conceptual and experiential unity of the *promenade architecturale*. While the warped ground plane of the Maison de Weekend remains isolated from the processional sequence, the theme provided an important starting point for three later public projects. For Harvard University's Carpenter Center for the Visual Arts (1959–64), Le Corbusier initially conceived a ramp descending from the roof as a landscape connecting gardens within the building.[17] In the Congress Hall at Strasbourg (1964), the ramp not only provides access to the building but also transforms the roof itself, dramatically merging building and site. Finally, in the church of Saint-Pierre in Firminy (1960–65), the warped ground plane achieves iconic significance (Fig. 99).

The church was commissioned in 1960 as the final component of his complex incorporating a sports stadium and cultural center outside an undistinguished industrial town in the undulating landscape of the Massif Central. The scarred site, originally a surface mine, had been used as a municipal dump for many years. The church's distinctive volume sustains multiple nuances of meaning. Formally, it is a synthesis of primary elements; the vertical transmutation from cube to pyramid to cone is terminated in a skylight cut on an oblique, suggesting a dome.[18] Symbolically it appears as an isolated rock, an appropriate allusion for a church dedicated to Saint Peter. Situated at the bottom of a scarred valley, the compelling form "asserts the presence of a temple on an inverted and imploded Acropolis."[19] The building appears in dynamic equilibrium with its site: the attenuated spiral promenade of the entry sequence is transposed within the building volume to become seating for the sanctuary; on the exterior, in counterpoint, the ground plane is excised to provide for vehicular entry. The profane geology of the site is transformed by this modest volume to a sacred dimension.

THE ROLE OF THE SITE

Although Le Corbusier claimed to base his architecture on a set of idealized assumptions, he always adjusted his formal principles to the particular circumstances of the site. His attitude toward the site is frequently misunderstood because of his insistence on a theoretical starting point, which he reinforced through careful manipulation of the photographic images illustrating his work.[20] He preferred closely cropped images to generalized overall views, and he often altered these to suit his aesthetic aims. Such propagandizing obscures the importance of the site as a challenge to his theoretical assumptions. Indeed, Le Corbusier advised architectural students that "the site is the nourishment offered by our eyes to our senses, to our intelligence, to our hearts. The site is the base of the architectural composition."[21]

In the exceptional case of his mother's house at Vevey (1925), Le Corbusier first evolved "a rigorous, functional, and efficient plan and then sought an appropriate site on Lake Geneva for its realization."[22] This procedure led to the critical displacement of the modest structure by its garden elements, which were scaled to the vast alpine landscape (Fig. 100). That the site be appropriate was also a condition for two projects realized in locations other than those for which they were designed, Villa Shodan (1956) and Maison des Jeunes (1960–65), and for the Firminy church, which he had contemplated building outside Bologna.[23] In 1961 he rejected the opportunity to design a church for La Chaux-de-Fonds because he found the site inappropriate to the symbolic program. In a letter to the pastor, Louis Secretan, he explained: "Had you said to me, 'Will you create a place open all the year, situated on the hilltops in the calm and the dignity, the nobleness of the beautiful Jura site?' the problem could have been considered. It was a problem of psychic nature, and, for me, of decisive value."[24]

More than any of his buildings, the pilgrimage chapel at Ronchamp (1950–54)

99. Le Corbusier. Église de Saint-Pierre. 1960–65. Firminy, France

100. Le Corbusier. House for his mother. 1925. Vevey, Switzerland

was inspired by the contemplative qualities of its natural setting. Built in the clearing (*rond champ*) on an ancient hilltop used in pre-Christian times for ritual sun worship, the chapel is, in Le Corbusier's words, "a vessel of intense concentration and meditation."[25] References to nature abound, from the abstract, geometric forms of the cistern to the alternative landscape of the roof, which he claimed was inspired by a crab shell. Le Corbusier rationalized his inspiration for the chapel's complex form: "One begins with the acoustics of the landscape, taking as a starting point the four horizons."[26] To interpret acoustical phenomena, he argued, was the privileged role of the artist, "a being sensitive to the things of the universe."[27]

If he first achieved such a fusion of architecture and nature in this religious building, it was probably because Le Corbusier endowed nature with a spiritual significance that to him surpassed religious values.[28] In the capital complex at Chandigarh (1951–65) he extended that fusion with nature to the fusion of architecture with a designed landscape. He accomplished this synthesis, influenced by the symbolically explicit model of the Mughal paradise garden, by transferring his mythopoetic treatment of the rooftop landscape back to the ground plane.

CHANDIGARH: THE DESIGNED LANDSCAPE

The need for a new capital city for the Punjab arose as a result of events following India's independence from British rule in 1947. In the partition that was a condition of independence, the state of Punjab was divided and its old capital, Lahore, became part of Muslim-ruled Pakistan. Chandigarh was created to fulfill practical, political, and spiritual aims: to satisfy the need for a new capital after partition, to accommodate resettlement of the west Punjab Hindus, and to fulfill the aspiration for a national identity following the prolonged period of colonial rule. Le Corbusier was called in as planning advisor and architect of the capital complex following the sudden death of Matthew Nowicki, his former collaborator and original architect of the capital. He was initially skeptical, since he was required to adopt the master plan conceived by the American planner, Albert Mayer, and he felt the chances for realization were slim. The progressive, utopian aspects of the project—as a symbol of Prime Minister Nehru's modern India—ultimately attracted Le Corbusier, affording him the opportunity to test his architectural ideas on an unprecedented scale.

At Chandigarh, he distinguished three scales of landscape: the pragmatic landscape of the residential city, the monumental landscape of the capital complex, and the more intensely symbolic landscape of the governor's palace. His master plan of 1952 (Fig. 101) retains the primary organizational features of Mayer's 1950 plan for the city (Fig. 102): broad boulevards dividing the city into housing and business sectors, with a separate government center at the head. Le Corbusier quickly transformed Mayer's organic layout into a geometric grid of boulevards contrasted with curved lateral streets and laced with irregular strips of public park. Despite the colonial associations of the design's monumental, axial qualities—reminiscent of Sir Edwin Lutyens's capital at New Delhi—Le Corbusier's plan corresponded to Nehru's aspirations for the city. Thus his revisions met with quick approval, allowing him to focus his attention on the more symbolically charged capital complex.

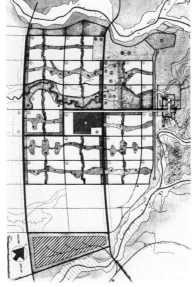

101. Le Corbusier. Plan for Chandigarh. 1952

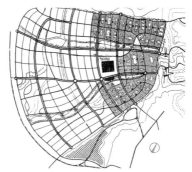

102. Albert Mayer. Plan for Chandigarh. 1950

The government center was set in a vast plain against the dramatic backdrop of the Himalayan foothills (Fig. 103). Le Corbusier separated it from the rest of the city by a roadway, a canal, and a series of artificial mounds, to effect in the flat landscape of the Punjab an isolation reminiscent of the Athenian Acropolis.[29] This separation from the more mundane sectors of the city, reiterated by the monumental government buildings, is accompanied by a corresponding synthesis with the landscape. The fusion is both spatial and symbolic: "The site united with the inexpressible, the imperceptible, the inexplicable.... Finally . . . I was able to erect an architecture which fulfills the day-to-day functions but which leads to jubilation."[30]

103. Le Corbusier. Model for Chandigarh

Le Corbusier's studies of boundaries for the capital complex reveal the historical origins of his spatial ideas. On the city side he proposed "a continuous *glacis* [consisting of] a horizontal embankment" (Fig. 104).[31] Viewed from the city, it resembles the outer ramparts of a Renaissance fortification, its folds and crevices intensifying both the separation and the continuity of natural and urban landscapes. From within, the embankment would operate much like his rooftop parapets, blocking the city from view while bringing the distant landscape into focus.[32] Elsewhere he proposed a ha-ha (Fig. 105) to preserve the unobstructed view of the Himalayas and exclude the grazing animals.[33]

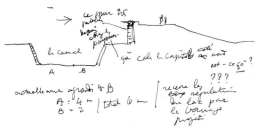

104. Le Corbusier. Chandigarh. Sketch of capital boundary

His initial delineation of the capital precinct was more radical (Fig. 106). First, he established corner posts or obelisks to mark its limits or boundaries and to demarcate 400- and 800-meter-square zones within.[34] Despite parallels drawn between the dimension of 800 meters and certain monumental distances in Paris, Le Corbusier's spatial order deviates sharply from that of the traditional city.[35] He associated the dimension of 400 meters with the mind rather than the eye: "Though the eye does not encompass a distance of 400 meters, the mind does conceive distances of 400 meters, 200 meters, and thence, the multiples of 800, 1200, etc., which automatically imply concepts of time."[36] The obelisks delimit overlapping squares in plan, derived from the Modulor and from traditional Mughal gardens, in which the square is equated with the ordered universe. The buildings are positioned within geometric fields. While the classical origins of the initial layout are explicit (Fig. 107), the modified symmetries of the final version increase the dynamism among the buildings and their integration with the broader landscape. Space, rather than object, is the primary datum.

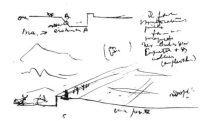

105. Le Corbusier. Chandigarh. Sketch of capital boundary

These boundary markers are abstract points on the ground plane, disconnected visually. Their meaning is revealed only in the conceptual overview of the plan: no buildings are to transgress the imaginary lines connecting these points.[37] The boundary between the landscape of the capital complex and the natural landscape is rendered imperceptible. The obelisks, while providing a modern counterpart to the ha-ha, also define precincts within the landscape—reinstating the garden within the domain of architecture. They enable Le Corbusier to resolve the inherent conflict between traditional notions of boundary and the modern spatial continuum. They have an experiential purpose as well: they provide a standard by which to measure the vastness of the Punjabi plain.

Le Corbusier's spatial vision was profoundly affected by modern aviation. The

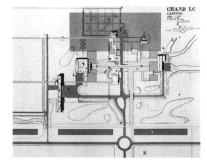

106. Le Corbusier. Chandigarh. Capital plan

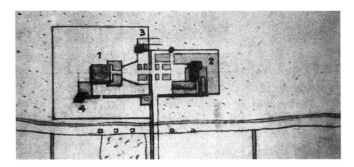

107. Le Corbusier. Chandigarh.
Capital plan. 1951

108. Le Corbusier. Chandigarh.
Secretariat and Assembly

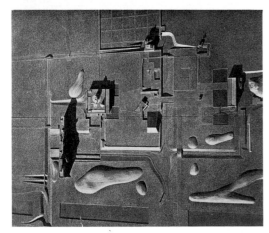

109. Le Corbusier. Chandigarh.
Monument to the Martyrs of the
Indian Partition

110. Le Corbusier. Chandigarh. Model
of the capital

airplane expanded perceptual possibilities, providing man with an experience hither-to impossible—the bird's-eye view—thus transcending the limitations of humanist perspective to achieve a new legibility that he associated with the cosmic: "But we have left the ground in an aeroplane and acquired the eyes of a bird. We see, in actuality, that which hitherto was only seen by the spirit. The whole spirit of our plans will be illuminated and amplified by this new point of view."[38] He was conscious of the difficulty in reconciling the spatial potential of the "fifth façade" viewed from above with the experiential implications of his plan[39]: "December 15, 1957. Moving through the space between the lake (the dam) and the Capital...I discover Asiatic space. My palaces 1,500 [meters] away fill the horizon better than at 650 meters. The scale is nobler and grander, from a distance [Fig. 108]...."[40]

He sought to transcend this difference by infusing modern spatiality with mythopoetic content. The vast pedestrian esplanade linking the Assembly and High Court (Fig. 109) was inspired in spirit and detail by airport runways,[41] while the reflecting pools to reduce the visual distance derive from Moghul precedents. The shifted ground plane, with its artificial mounds, reflecting pools, and sunken courts, represents a sacred landscape created *ex nihilo* (Fig. 110). Large earth mounds positioned to enhance the perceptual sequence allude to the distant mountains and contribute to the primal imagery. These landscape elements and the monuments intended to populate the esplanade (Fig. 111) suggest myriad nuances of meaning, as if to amplify their spatial significance.[42]

Throughout the capital complex, Le Corbusier used cosmic refer-ences to affirm the unity of nature and human consciousness. Many of its monuments and hieroglyphs cast in the concrete surfaces refer to the sun, its daily path, and its radiance.[43] Le Corbusier considered the sun a primal force ruling all life, an emblem of harmony between man and nature.[44] He invoked this theme in the Tower of Shadows, a lofty volume for meditation at the heart of the government complex, oriented to the path of the sun and the axis of the earth. In the adjoining Trench of Consideration, Le Corbusier inscribed a monumental inclined plane with the path of the sun and the play of two solstices, while he incised his symbols of proportional laws, the harmonic spiral and the Modulor, in the pedestrian plaza. He associated the Monument of the Open Hand

(Fig. 112), set to the east of the
Governor's Palace amid irregular
groves of sacred mango trees,
with the forces of nature; it was
designed to rotate with the
winds.[45]

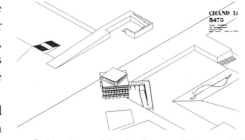

Le Corbusier often infused
such references to nature with
ritual intent. The ceremonial door of the Assembly building (Fig. 113) is
enameled with various cosmic symbols, including the sun in its diurnal revolution, the pyramid/mountain, and the tree of life. It is used only once a
year, on Republic Day, to admit the governor for the opening of Parliament,
when the skylight over the assembly hall was to cast a beam of sunlight on
the speaker's platform, in the spirit of the celestial observatories at Jaipur and
Delhi. On the Assembly rooftop (Fig. 114), the truncated tower and pyramid duplicate at a monumental scale the primal elements of the Ronchamp
cistern, while the elements intersecting the skylight symbolize the crescent
moon and the path of the sun. Le Corbusier elaborates: "This framework
will lend itself to possible solar festivals recalling to men, once a year, that
they are children of the sun (entirely forgotten in our unfettered civilization
crushed by absurdities, particularly in architecture and city planning)."[46] Through
such cosmic references, the Assembly roofscape is the psychological culmination of
the *promenade architecturale* rather than a substitute garden. Ritual and symbolic functions here supersede the purely visual qualities of Le Corbusier's earliest roof terraces;
it is a space of psychic as well as physical occupation, challenging the observer to
engage in its interpretation.

111. Le Corbusier. Chandigarh.
Esplanade monuments

112. Le Corbusier. Chandigarh.
Monument of the Open Hand

113. Le Corbusier. Chandigarh.
Assembly door

Le Corbusier's success at Chandigarh in uniting a mythopoetic conception of
space with a modern expression of the spatial continuum was ultimately limited. He
reflected on the unprecedented nature of the task: "There was anxiety and anguish
in taking decisions on that vast, limitless ground.... The problem was no longer one
of reasoning but of sensation. Chandigarh is not a city of lords, princes or kings
confined within walls, crowded in by neighbors. It was a matter of occupying a
plain. The geometrical event was, in truth, a sculpture of the intellect.... It was a
battle of space, fought within the mind. Arithmetic, texturique, geometrics: it
would all be there when the whole was finished."[47]

Indeed, as many critics have noted, Le Corbusier was unable to accommodate
the monumental scale that he associated with the aspirations of modern India to the
realities of perceptual experience. Furthermore, his vision of the capital was
significantly altered in execution. Le Corbusier's landscaping scheme was never completed, and the existing planting has not been adequately maintained.[48] Of the series
of monuments that he designed for the esplanade, only the Monument to the
Martyrs of the Indian Partition was realized during his lifetime.[49] Plans for the
Governor's Palace and adjoining garden to crown the complex were abandoned

because Nehru considered their inclusion with the government buildings unsuited to a democracy. These omissions significantly compromise the spatial and symbolic potential of the whole.

THE ARCHITECTURAL LANDSCAPE

For the Governor's Palace precinct, Le Corbusier proposed an architectural landscape to mediate the monumental scale of the government buildings and the more modest volume of the palace (Fig. 115). In his sketchbook Le Corbusier noted, "The garden will make the city," and, more emphatically, "Capital garden must be a Miracle!"[50] His use of a garden is particularly appropriate since the name Chandigarh (Hindi for "fortress of the war goddess") and the word *garden* derive from the same Indo-European root: *gher*, meaning "a place set apart, walled off."[51]

Instead of using traditional garden walls, Le Corbusier conceived a dramatic drop in the flat terrain to render the palace forecourt sacred. In this way he achieved the bounded quality of a garden without interrupting the spatial continuum. This transformation of the ground plane through changes in level and scale is reinforced by the formal imagery. Mock mountains are created by excising the ground plane, which also yields a totemic column, water course, and reflecting pool. Rather than mimicking architectural forms, as in the Beistegui roof terrace, Le Corbusier evoked natural forms and man himself in this garden.

The imagery is accessible to interpretation on many levels; its roots are culturally diverse. In an early sketch (Fig. 116) the garden and crowning Governor's Palace are evocative of an aircraft carrier. Like the cruise ship, the aircraft carrier was for Le Corbusier an important symbol of the modern age; both served as paradigms of the engineer's aesthetic and the autonomous communal structure. Unlike the cruise ship, the aircraft carrier is analogous to a landscape; it symbolizes the integration of nature and the machine.[52] On a more primitive level, the garden evokes the sacred landscape of an Egyptian temple complex; the stepped contour of the palace resembles a pyramid, symbolizing the axis of the universe and the cosmic mountain linking heaven and earth.[53] These diverse sources reflect Le Corbusier's desire to endow his work with universal significance, yet the spirit of this garden reflects its more immediate heritage: the sixteenth- and seventeenth-century Mughal gardens of India. In 1951 Le Corbusier visited two of these gardens, the seventeenth-century Pinjore gardens near Chandigarh (Fig. 117) and the Baradari gardens in Patiala. For the roof terrace of the Ahmedabad Museum (1951–56), he created an abstracted version of the Mughal garden, using a geometric arrangement of flowers, shrubs, and forty-five reflecting pools. For the Governor's Palace, Le Corbusier evoked the essence of the Mughal garden rather than reiterated its form.

The *charbagh*, or paradise garden, was the distinctive creation of nomadic Mughal tribes, built to serve in lieu of buildings as an open-air palace (Fig. 118). The *charbagh* (literally, "four gardens") was divided into four quadrants by water channels, representing the four rivers of life, and terraced to correspond to the Koran's description of paradise. At the Governor's Palace Le Corbusier transformed the geometric structure of the Mughal garden, adapting the formal precision of the

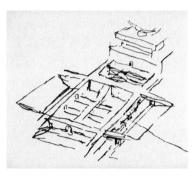

114. Le Corbusier. Chandigarh. Assembly roof

115. Le Corbusier. Chandigarh. Sketch of the Governor's Palace. 1952

116. Le Corbusier. Chandigarh. Sketch of the Governor's Palace

117. Pinjore Gardens, near Chandigarh. Seventeenth century

original to the ambiguities of modern spatial expression. Intersecting walkways at grade suggest the paradigmatic four divisions, displaced by shifting geometries based on the square and the golden section. In place of lush vegetation he substituted paved terraces, which he deemed more appropriate to the arid climate, yet he retained the traditional iconographic elements of the *charbagh*: terraced levels; water courses; mountains of paradise; and the cosmologically sacred tree, symbol of regeneration, immortality, and ascent to the heavens.

Mughal gardens were precincts for contemplation, sensual delight, and sedentary retreat from the intense heat rather than for appreciation through three-dimensional experience. Walkways were raised to allow irrigation of the planted areas and varied in height to align with the tops of plants (Fig. 119), thus creating the effect of a Persian carpet, whose patterns often reflected paradisal garden plans.[54] By keeping his causeways at grade while sinking the reflecting pools and terraced courts, Le Corbusier brought a modern spatiality to traditional Mughal motifs. The garden's contemplative qualities are revealed through the perceptual sequence. Upon descent to the lower levels, the man-made landscape supersedes the natural horizon and frames the palace, which in turn is preceded by its own reflection in the pool of water. This oscillation between foreground and background suggests a tension between traditional space, which is understood through perspective, and modernist space, which is collapsed and rendered ambiguous to engage the mind as well as the eye.

The approach sequence dramatizes the role of the Governor's Palace, which crowns the composition in volume and plan (Fig. 120). Its form recalls the silken awnings set on platforms that provided temporary enclosure in the earliest Mughal gardens. While the palace is the smallest building in the capital complex, it commands attention through its distinctive profile and integral relationship to the garden, capturing the essence of the Mughal *charbagh*. The direct connection of interior and exterior in the traditional garden is appropriated in the palace's free plan organization and its massing. The stepped terraces, alternating solid and void, also suggest the ritual levels of self-discovery on the Hindu path to unity with the divine.[55] These culminate on the roof in an upturned crescent, silhouetted against the Himalayan foothills, which serves as viewing platform, shading device, and trough to catch the monsoon rains. The singularity of this form contrasts with its deliberate ambiguity of meaning: it cradles the sky, simultaneously suggesting a crescent moon, mountain, and horns of the sacred ox, yet it also refers to Le Corbusier's favorite symbol of Chandigarh, the Open Hand. Just after he sent his final design for the palace to India, Le Corbusier spotted a similar form—a brick kiln atop a hill (Fig. 121)—in Bogota, confirming for him the universality of the gesture.[56]

The complex is steeped in a monumental tradition that links East and West. The garden, a haven from the hostile forces of nature, commonly symbolizes the creative potential of life and the reconciliation of man with the profusion of nature.

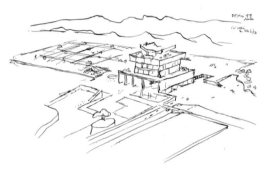

118. Lake Garden, Amber, India. Seventeenth century

119. Ram Bagh, Agra, India. Sixteenth century

120. Le Corbusier. Chandigarh. Sketch of the Governor's Palace

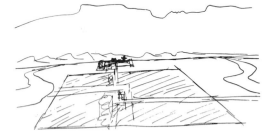

121. Brick kiln on hill. Bogota,
Colombia

122. Le Corbusier. Sketch of
Chandigarh. 1951

The form of the Mughal garden, derived from the mythological structure of the world, connotes the universe in microcosm. The crossing of the two major axes, creating the four-part subdivision, is a cosmic form associated with the Buddhist mandala; it is related to the ritually conceived pattern of ancient Indian towns as well as to the founding rites of the Roman town. In India the crossing of the major streets traditionally marked the elders' meeting place and the quarters of the highest caste, while in ancient Rome it was the site of the forum.[57] At Chandigarh Le Corbusier transformed this paradigmatic structure to relate three distinct scales of landscape: the garden of the Governor's Palace, the pedestrian plaza of the capital complex, and the organization of the city (Fig. 122).

By fusing Mughal symbols with primal imagery, imperial ritualistic space with classical architectural principles, Le Corbusier sought to conflate the traditional Indian concept of the sacred with a modern metaphysic, the cultural with the universal. He noted the congruence of his ideals with the aims of Hindu philosophy: "fraternity between the cosmos and living beings."[58] In addressing fundamental human concerns—the relationship of man to nature, and of architecture to landscape—he employed a degree of abstraction that transcends the iconographic roots of any particular element. Ultimately, the significance of the capital city rests not on its formal iconography, but on "the highly structured, ambiguous union of form and content"[59] that renders its meaning universal.

The significance of the Governor's Palace garden is both universal and particular: the garden unfolds as a microcosm of the Indian landscape. By separating out a discrete landscape from the general spatial continuum, Le Corbusier rendered meanings more intensely, while in the vast landscape of the capital city such symbolism is diffuse. The effect is reminiscent of Le Corbusier's description of the Acropolis: the architecture extends its influence to the horizon.

In a fitting final tribute, at his last rites the Greek architects deposited a portion of earth from the Acropolis on his grave, while those from India offered water from the Ganges.[60]

1. For peripheral but illuminating discussions of the landscape in Le Corbusier's urban theories, see Mary McLeod, "Le Corbusier and Algiers," *Oppositions* 19/20 (Winter/Spring 1980): 54–85; James Dunnett, "The Architecture of Silence," *The Architectural Review* 1064 (Oct. 1985): 69–75; Manfredo Tafuri, "Machine et Mémoire: The City in the Work of Le Corbusier," trans. Stephen Sartarelli, in *Le Corbusier: Urbanisme, Algiers and Other Buildings and Projects 1930–1933* (New York and London, and Paris: 1983), pp. xxxi–xlvi.

2. Indeed, in 1912, as architect of the Ateliers d'art réunis in La Chaux-de-Fonds, he included "architecte de jardins" among the services on his letterhead. Mary Patricia May Sekler, "Le Corbusier, Ruskin, the Tree, and the Open Hand," in *The Open Hand: Essays on Le Corbusier*, ed. Russell Walden (Cambridge, Mass., and London, 1982), p. 54.

3. Le Corbusier, *Towards a New Architecture*, trans. Frederick Etchells (New York, n.d.), p. 212. Sekler discusses the roots of Le Corbusier's attitude toward nature in "Le Corbusier, Ruskin," pp. 42–95,

and Christopher Green elaborates his responses to nature through painting and sculpture in "The Architect as Artist," in *Le Corbusier, Architect of the Century* (London, 1987), pp. 110–18.

4. Le Corbusier, *The Radiant City* (Paris, 1967), p. 83.

5. *Towards a New Architecture*, p. 70.

6. See Dunnett, "Architecture of Silence."

7. The plán of the Ville Contemporaine (1922), for example, is organized in a Beaux-Arts manner, with cultural facilities isolated in a *"jardin anglaise."* The entire ground plane is public, an idea influenced by Tony Garnier's *Cité Industrielle*, and the *maisons à redents* (set-back housing), borrowed from Hénard, are fragments of traditional courtyard blocks open to a communal landscape of classical French *parterres*, inspired by the Palais Royal and the Tuileries.

8. *Le Corbusier et Pierre Jeanneret: Oeuvre complète, 1910–1929* (Zurich, 1964), pp. 17–21.

9. *Towards a New Architecture*, p. 189.

10. Ibid., p. 204.

11. *Le Corbusier: Last Works* (New York and Washington, 1970), p. 177.

12. In the "Five Points of a New Architecture," initially published in 1927, Le Corbusier also proposed the horizontal strip window to express the independence of the façade from the structural grid of the free plan; where the traditional vertical window is related anthropomorphically to the human body, the strip window is analogous to the landscape itself. See Bruno Reichlin, "'Une petite maison' on Lake Leman: The Perret–Le Corbusier Controversy," *Lotus International* 60 (1988): 59–84. By denying the role of the window as frame, Reichlin argues, the strip window eliminates the real depth of the landscape to bestow a new objectivity on the image of nature it reveals.

13. For a brilliant analysis of the Beistegui penthouse, see Manfredo Tafuri, "Machine et Mémoire," pp. xxxi–xxxii.

14. He compares the Marseille Block to an Ionic temple: "The Modulor here smiles in the Greek, the Ionic fashion—smiling grace of mathematics, grace of proportion to the human scale." *Modulor II* (Cambridge, Mass., 1958), pp. 306–20.

15. In her seminal article, Mary McLeod relates this shift to Le Corbusier's plan for Algiers of the 1930s and his growing involvement with Syndicalism. See McLeod, "Le Corbusier and Algiers."

16. The Maison Monol is related to Gottfried Semper's little-noted second version of the primitive hut, based on the hearth and the wall.

17. "The spiral from the museum roof must become a track of gardens and dense rockeries set in the landscape and constituting landscape." *Le Corbusier Sketchbooks, Volume 4, 1957–1964* (New York and Cambridge, Mass., 1982), P59: 447.

18. Le Corbusier intended the skylight of the Firminy church, like the skylight conceived for the Assembly Hall at Chandigarh, to direct the sun's rays to illuminate the altar on Easter morning.

19. Anthony Eardley, "Grandeur Is in the Intention," *Le Corbusier's Firminy* (New York, 1981), p. 6.

20. Beatriz Colomina notes, for example, that in amending photographs of the Villa Schwob for publication, "Le Corbusier discarded everything that was picturesque and contextual in this house, concentrating on the formal qualities of the object itself." "Le Corbusier and Photography," *Assemblage* 4 (Oct. 1987): 12. Stanislaus von Moos, in an otherwise cogent analysis of Le Corbusier's work, argues: "He even considers the relationship of the project to the site to be of secondary importance. In fact, most of his projects were not bound to any particular location." *Le Corbusier: Elements of a Synthesis* (Cambridge, Mass., 1982), p. 299. For an excellent analysis of the formative influence of site, see Alan Colquhoun, "The Strategies of the Grands Travaux," *Assemblage* 4 (Oct. 1987): pp. 66–81. For the spatial implications of Le Corbusier's photographic images, see Thomas Schumacher, "Deep Space, Shallow Space," *The Architectural Review* 1079 (Jan. 1987): 37–42.

21. Le Corbusier, *Le Corbusier Talks with Students*, trans. Pierre Chase (New York, 1961), pp. 40–41.

22. *Oeuvre complète, 1910–1929*, p. 74.

23. The Villa Shodan (1951–56), originally commissioned by Surottam Hutheesin, was built on a new site in Ahmedabad without modification. See *Oeuvre complète, 1952–1957* (Zurich, 1957), p. 134. In Firminy, owing to conflicting municipal authorities, Le Corbusier was required to shift the Maison des

Jeunes (1960–65) to the opposite side of the sports stadium, which he also did without altering his original design. See *Oeuvre complète, 1957–1965* (Zurich, 1965), p. 130. In 1965, when realization of the Firminy church was in doubt, he negotiated to build the project in Bologna, subject to selection of an appropriate site, although none was ever agreed upon. See Martin Purdy, "Le Corbusier and the Theological Program," in *The Open Hand*, pp. 313–17.

24. Le Corbusier, letter to Louis Secretan, July 1961, archives of the Bibliothèque de La Chaux-de-Fonds, trans. Helen Walden, quoted by Martin Purdy, "Le Corbusier and the Theological Program," in *The Open Hand*, p. 291.

25. *Oeuvre complète, 1946–1952* (Zurich, 1953), p. 72.

26. Ibid.

27. *Modulor II*, p. 148.

28. Describing the pilgrimage chapel at Ronchamp, Le Corbusier explains: "The requirements of religion have had little effect on the design, the form was an answer to a psycho-physiology of the feelings." *Oeuvre complète, 1946–1952*, p. 72.

29. For critical analyses of the buildings at Chandigarh, see Peter Serenyi, "Timeless but of Its Time: Le Corbusier's Architecture in India," *Perspecta* 20 (1983): 91–118; and William J. R. Curtis, "Authenticity, Abstraction and the Ancient Sense: Le Corbusier's and Louis Kahn's Ideas of Parliament," ibid.: 181–94.

30. *Le Corbusier Sketchbooks, Volume 3, 1954–1957* (New York and Cambridge, Mass., 1982), H34: 190. See Tafuri, "Machine et Mémoire," for a different interpretation of the phenomenon of isolation in Le Corbusier's work.

31. *Le Corbusier Sketchbooks, Volume 2, 1950–1954* (New York and Cambridge, Mass., 1982), F26: 866.

32. *Le Corbusier Sketchbooks, Volume 4, 1957–1964* (New York and Cambridge, Mass., 1982), P60: 534.

33. *Sketchbooks 2*, G28: 951: "June 14, 1953/ it is absolutely necessary to close off the whole horizon of the Capital by *horizontal hills* /But on the side of the Himalayas it's admirable let the [farmlands] and the flocks run right up to a parapet. But watch out the goats will come gobble up everything." The ha-ha, according to Horace Walpole, was "the capital stroke, the leading step to all that has followed"; he credited its invention to William Kent, who "leapt the fence, and saw that all nature was a garden." Horace Walpole, *Anecdotes of Painting*, vol. 4 (1771), pp. 137–28, quoted in Isabel Chase, *Horace Walpole: Gardenist* (Princeton, 1943), p. 25.

34. See *Modulor II*, p. 214. Although the nature of these obelisks as built form was never resolved, Le Corbusier's repeated references to them in his sketchbooks attest to their critical role in the project. At different times he considered building them in metal, brick, and concrete: "Think of the obelisks/ view upon arrival crossing the river, before Chandigarh/ a brilliant metal/ + color/ stainless steel" (*Sketchbooks 2*, H30: 1042); "the Capital obelisks could be brick cones (matching the remaining walls) = recalling Muslim milestones in dark brick at Km. 61 on road from Delhi" (*Sketchbooks 3*, J38: 430). He ultimately differentiated them in size and material, according to the spaces they demarcate: "attention! the four obelisks ABCD/ large/ + the 4: 1.2.3.4./ small." (*Sketchbooks 3*, K41: 587); "rounded square hole/ like in the pylons of the Assembly portico/ the obelisks 400 metres" (*Sketchbooks 4*, P60: 538).

35. The dimension of 800 meters is the distance from the Louvre to the Place de la Concorde and from the Place de la Concorde to the Place Clemenceau. See *Oeuvre complète, 1946–1952*, p. 117.

36. *Modulor II*, p. 211. The residential sectors of Chandigarh measure 800 by 1,200 meters.

37. Since the Club House on Lake Sukhna (1958–64) violated this principle, Le Corbusier depressed the building three meters below grade to maintain an unimpeded view of the mountains from the capital complex. See *Last Works*, p. 78.

38. Le Corbusier and François de Pierrefeu, *The Home of Man*, trans. Clive Entwistle (London, 1948), p. 125. Fortuitously, the site for Chandigarh was selected by airplane reconnaissance. See Norma Evenson, *Chandigarh* (Berkeley and Los Angeles, 1966): p. 7.

39. See *Modulor II*, pp. 214–15; Le Corbusier, *Aircraft* (New York, 1935), text adjoining fig. 122. His sketchbooks are replete with notes on perceptual site considerations; see, e.g., *Sketchbooks 2*, E23: 638, 675, 677; F26: 866; G28: 951; H30: 1042.

40. *Sketchbooks 4*, M51: 13.

41. See *Sketchbooks 3*, J38: 140: "IMPORTANT Capital Esplanade make a serious pattern with compartmentalization in cement (Beirut airport)/ slab 3.66 x 7.7/ Simla Stone, flowers and bushes used flush with the paving or projecting: 43, 86, 113"; *Sketchbooks 4*, N56: 360: April 26, 1959, from Rome Airport, "Chandigarh esplanade courage of simplicity is needed." K43: 675: "L-C go to Orly to see for Chandigarh the various poured or prefabricated cement of the runways."

42. Le Corbusier credits Jane Drew with the suggestion that he include these symbols of his philosophy in the open plaza at Chandigarh. See *Oeuvre complète, 1946–1952*, p. 157. In his sketchbook he noted: "*The signs!* when the mind can conclude by a *sign* which henceforth will have something like an algebraic value, then thought takes a leap forward; it has liberated a space, an expanse from then on qualified (signified) by a *term* or mark instantly understandable by anyone." *Sketchbooks 2*, F27: 895.

43. Le Corbusier noted that *radieuse* (the name of his utopian urban proposal of 1935), a term with no suitable parallel in English, has "the attribute of consciousness." See *Le Corbusier Talks with Students*, p. 27. As hieroglyphs, Le Corbusier's personal signs are rendered at once primitive (hence comprehensible) and sacred.

44. "*The 24 hours of the solar cycle* constitute the measuring rod of all human activities; they are what gives our lives their scale and their perspective." Le Corbusier, *The Radiant City* (New York: 1967), p. 77.

45. "The Open Hand will turn on ball bearings like a weather-cock, not to show the incertitude of ideas but to indicate symbolically the direction of the wind (the state of affairs). A movement of the spirit in 1948 has taken in 1951 an eminent part in the composition of a capital in India." *Oeuvre complète, 1946–1952*, p. 155. For the symbolism of the Open Hand see Sekler, "Le Corbusier, Ruskin," pp. 69–83, and von Moos, *Le Corbusier: Elements*, pp. 291–93.

46. *Oeuvre complète, 1952–1957*, p. 94.

47. Le Corbusier, *Modulor II*, p. 215. By "texturique," he means "connection, arrangement of parts; ibid., p. 210.

48. *Oeuvre complète, 1952–1957*, pp. 108–13.

49. The Monument of the Open Hand and Trench of Consideration were inaugurated in 1985, and the Tower of Shadows was completed in 1987.

50. *Sketchbooks 2*, G28: 948 (1953) and *Sketchbooks 4*, M51: 39 (1957).

51. The name Chandigarh was borrowed from that of the nearest village, where there is a temple, erected centuries ago, in honor of the war goddess Chandi. *Last Works*, p. 52.

52. See *Aircraft*, ills. 14–18.

53. See Le Corbusier, *The City of Tomorrow* (London, 1929), p. 168. Le Corbusier visited Egypt in April 1952, on his return from Chandigarh.

54. These paths were occasionally elevated to the height of fruit trees; see Susan Jellicoe, "The Development of the Mughal Garden," in *The Islamic Garden*, ed. Elizabeth MacDougall and Richard Ettinghausen (Washington, D.C., 1976), p. 111.

55. See Alexander Gorlin, "An Analysis of the Governor's Palace of Chandigarh," *Oppositions* 19/20 (Winter/Spring 1980): 174. Gorlin's interpretation is flawed in its persistent references to Buddhism; Chandigarh is primarily a Hindu settlement.

56. *Sketchbooks 2*, E20: 431. He repeated this form at different scales on each of Chandigarh's public buildings: in the entry portico of the Assembly Building, over the door of the Secretariat, and in the topmost section of the High Court.

57. Norma Evenson, *Le Corbusier: The Machine and the Grand Design* (New York, 1969), pp. 13–14.

58. *Last Works*, p. 174; from *Sketchbooks 2*, E20: 448 (1951).

59. Robert Slutzky, "Aqueous Humor," *Oppositions* 19/20 (Winter/Spring 1980): 30.

60. *Last Works*, p. 188.

STEVEN R. KROG

Whither the Garden?

They always want to hear about . . . and I want to give them the experience itself so that they will be terrified and awaken.

—Jean Cocteau[1]

PERHAPS NEVER IN ITS HISTORY HAS THE PROFESSION of landscape architecture been more thoroughly confounded by self-doubt. To their credit, landscape architects have qualified themselves to deal competently with an extraordinarily wide range of environmental, planning, and design issues; and yet, along with this mobile center of gravity comes an imbalance of collective ideological will. Contemporary landscape architecture finds itself experiencing an intellectual interregnum, a disconnection from any continuum of reasoned ideas for the garden. Now, faced with a stylistically freewheeling last quarter of the twentieth century, landscape architecture seems prepared to do little more than reflect, or react to, cacophonous outside influences.

This has not always been the state of the profession, however. Of particular interest is the effervescent era that saw the advent of the modern garden—the 1920s and 1930s, especially in France. Consider the following developments:

123. André and Paul Véra. Garden designed for a house of the Vicomte de Noailles. 1926. Saint-Germain-en Laye, Yvelines, France. Photograph by Man Ray

• Suddenly in 1926 the traditionalists André and Paul Véra produce a small garden for the Vicomte de Noailles employing radical geometry and a mirrored fence. (The lone surviving record is a photograph by Man Ray [Fig. 123].)
• Pierre Legrain, master bookbinder, furniture designer, and creator of the original frame for *Les Demoiselles d'Avignon*, translates a Cubist motif into a provocative residential landscape (for the André Tachards at Saint-Cloud), which is at once politely complementary of its Tudoresque cottage, explosive in its disregard for symmetry and formal organizational rules, and subtle in its deviously creative cross-pollination of "traditional" landscape materials with harsh yet unmistakably modern forms and volumes (Fig. 124).
• Gabriel Guévrékian contributes to the Mallet-Stevens house for Noailles in Hyères an orderly terraced garden that adroitly molds a Cubist composition from the most French of garden traditions: symmetry, the parterre, and sculpture (Fig. 125).

• In California, Thomas Church's entry to the 1937 Contemporary Landscape Architecture Exhibit sponsored by the San Francisco Museum of Art anticipates the trend toward a fluid relationship between interior and exterior spaces with an exuberant residential project set in a twenty-five-foot-wide city lot (Fig. 126).

• Fletcher Steele, perhaps the most perceptive American critic of landscape design of the day, comments with reserved but approving enthusiasm on the concrete "trees" created by the Martel brothers for the 1925 Paris Exposition des Arts Décoratifs—an enthusiasm that undoubtedly piqued a professional audience firmly embracing the Country Place Era (Fig. 127).

The list of such accomplishments is longer than the record of the designers' thoughts, however, as if the pace of creation left no time for penning theories or manifestoes. When such writings did appear—for example, the pronouncements by Achille Duchêne at the Premier Congrès International des Architectes de Jardins in 1937 and the influential three-part series for *Architectural Record* by Garrett Eckbo, Dan Kiley, and James Rose in 1939–40—the emphasis had shifted away from garden design (Fig. 128). Cognizant of the social and environmental consequences of advancing urbanization, European and American landscape designers alike championed the cause of regional and recreation planning. With a utopian's fervor, Duchêne went so far as to proclaim, "The art of the garden [by which he meant private gardens for wealthy clients] is dead."

Just when it seemed imperative and opportune for a theory of modern landscape design to emerge, we instead were offered well-reasoned, but almost scientific, analyses of the importance of recreational facilities in industrial society, techniques for environmental planning, and calculations of the number of acres of parkland recommended per unit of population. While Duchêne's "social basis for design" paralleled and reinforced the egalitarian notions associated with early European modern architecture, his "death of the garden" proclamation proved hyperbolic. Published only one year after Duchêne's manifesto, Christopher Tunnard's *Gardens in the Modern Landscape* better outlined the future of mid-century landscape architecture and made extensive use of residential projects as noteworthy examples of the progressive landscape. (Interestingly, the enfants terribles Eckbo, Kiley, and Rose subsequently went on to join Church, Steele, and Tunnard in producing masterful private gardens.) Engulfed by the wave of modern architecture, Tunnard wrote of an indisputable need to reform the garden in accordance with changing lifestyles, the discoveries of modern science, the requirements of modern architecture, and other influences. He quoted approvingly from the writings of Le Corbusier and Loos, "The styles are a lie," and he derided the continued use in the garden of ornaments that "have ceased to mean anything and…have become too familiar to evoke in the spectator more than a casual polite interest."[2] Tunnard countered the prevailing

124. Pierre Legrain. Hedgerow with serrated bedline, in the garden of the Tachard House. c. 1926

125. Gabriel Guévrékian. Garden terrace for the Vicomte de Noailles's villa. 1925. Hyères, France. The sculpture is by Jacques Lipchitz

126. Thomas Church, landscape architect, and William Wurster, architect. Model for California residential project, 1937

127. Robert Mallet-Stevens, architect, Jean and Joël Martel, sculptors. Garden with concrete trees at the Exposition des Arts Décoratifs et Industriels Modernes. 1925. Paris

128. Model of a garden designed by James Rose. c. 1938

Beaux-Arts approach to garden design by promoting what he carefully referred to as three new design "techniques": "functionalism," the "oriental influence," and "modern art."

Tunnard's exhortations, like Steele's reports from Europe, were coldly greeted by most American landscape architects, who, preoccupied with bolstering the status of their nascent discipline among competing professions, found themselves uncomfortable with the unpredictable and experimental proclivities of the modern movement. Norman T. Newton's misinterpretation of modernism's intentions was a widely held opinion:

> The conscious effort to "go modern" by creating dizzy patterns and weird plant forms which may appear beautiful to some observers, and the use of a pretentious symbolism to which some have referred as a source of emotion, may yet have an undiscovered appeal to the senses rather than to the thought-process, but at best they seem to be purely extraneous intellectual experiments. We must direct our efforts toward a more nearly complete understanding of the essentials of our design, to the function and purpose of things, to the beauty latent in them, and to the merit of the results. The landscape architect must devote his energies to the application of changeless principles to our changing modes of living; the question of "modern" or "not modern" will take care of itself.[3]

Stymied by a conservative professional constituency and interrupted by World War II, the further development of a theory of landscape design appropriate to the twentieth century foundered. (The 1960s would provide morally and environmentally based dictums for how to think about the landscape, in the form of Lawrence Halprin's *RSVP Cycles* and Ian McHarg's *Design with Nature*, though neither tells us what those landscapes should look like.) As lucidly composed as they may be, appreciative and insightful commentary (Steele), enthusiastic speculation (Tunnard), provocation (Eckbo), and humor (Rose) do not comprise an operational design theory.

With the best of intentions, landscape architecture has appropriated the images of modern art and oriental gardens but—out of ignorance, convenience, or deliberation—failed to comprehend the ideas that generated those images. Of the early modern American landscape architects, only James Rose, for example, seems to have realized that the "oriental influence" invoked by Tunnard demands of the designer and the client the commitment to a way of life and is not simply a peculiar fashion of arranging rocks and azaleas. Of modern art's formative imperatives—the antimaterial philosophies of Mondrian and Kandinsky, utopian social ideologies, psychoanalysis—we find little mention and even less comprehension in the writings of the early modern landscape architects.

Tunnard's techniques proved persuasive, however. Coupled with the post–World War II mass distribution through *Sunset Magazine* and similar publications of photographs of the California lifestyle-cum-landscape as demonstrated by the work of Church and others, they were able to dominate the design vocabulary of landscape architecture for more than four decades, doing service to this day.

One result has been the ill-conceived notion that techniques such as Tunnard's are formulaic and can be relied upon to resolve aesthetic issues that are now far removed from those confronting Tunnard's day. As Hilton Kramer explains, "If history is any guide—and in these matters it usually is—we can be reasonably certain that every aesthetic crisis in art involves some sort of *crisis of belief*, and aesthetic solutions . . . are likely to be unavailing as long as this deeper crisis persists." He continues: "To attempt to surmount this crisis of belief by invoking the appeals of [stylistic invention] . . . is to offer little more than aesthetic palliatives for a problem that aesthetics alone is unequipped to deal with."[4] The soul of Tunnard's book was an authentic and deeply felt 1938 crisis of belief regarding the way gardens were failing to respond to changing times. While the crisis was real and immediate, its resolution was, by necessity, specific to an era in the throes of startling modernization. Tunnard's techniques provided important, but only cursory, relief.

Today's crisis of belief may perhaps be stated simply as follows: In an age of nearly infinite pluralism, how are standards of quality to be set for art? This mood is rampant in much of the world of music, dance, painting, theater, architecture, and the other arts, but it is not endemic to those spheres alone. Landscape architects now find themselves in the unfamiliar position of sharing the artist's anxiety. Some might say the company is appreciated, if not the crisis. Landscape architects, too, question what might be "appropriate" for landscape design and suspect that the employment of some sort of illusion or allusion, fashion or formula, might be the means by which their own work will remain contemporary and marketable; but just as Kramer castigates switching of artistic political parties, so would I warn against aesthetic panaceas for landscape architecture. Self-conscious striving for effect may be momentarily exhilarating, but it is only Prismacolor deep.

What have we today? An abundance of storefront design religions: historicism, contextualism, perspective trickery, environmental symbology, and plagiarism, among others. Comments made by Roger Kimball in his review of architect Robert Stern's PBS series *Pride of Place* concerning the now popular invocation of mythology apply equally to landscape architecture:

> Mr. Stern would have us believe that postmodernist architecture helped put our culture back in touch with the dimension of myth, tradition and "dreaming" that the rationalistic imperatives of modernism abjured. One hears such talk about "the recovery of myth" and the like a good deal these days, of course, though in truth it is rarely more than a rhetorical gesture. As Jacques Maritain has pointed out, myths in the sense Mr. Stern intends "have no force except through the faith man has in them. It is essential to them to be believed in." But postmodernism's attachment to myth is purely superficial; it toys with myth the way it toys with historical ornamentation, arbitrarily appropriating first this, then that element or motif. At bottom it remains as firmly rooted in the mod-

ern, technological world as the strictest Miesian, all the while refusing to acknowledge the implications of this contradiction. Never is there any question of belief, of authenticity; "myth" for postmodernism, like "history," is little more than a kind of costume, a kind of mask it dons in order to disguise its essentially modernist underpinnings and to achieve an aura of tradition.[5]

The mythological narrative has been recast in the contemporary garden as well,[6] and little fault can be found in such a fascination with tales created by the ancients to assuage their fears of the unknown. They are, after all, part of the foundation of Western culture. To the extent that they might suggest physical relationships of a fundamental nature, they are of some utility. To place much importance upon the reading of the garden design as a text, however, seems problematic. A strong case could probably be made that almost every garden embodies some story, literary or otherwise, but can the plot or the moral be deciphered in the absence of an accompanying text? If a designer wishes to employ such a strategy, must we be able to ferret out the clues, as if engaged in some intellectual or horticultural scavenger hunt? Is a garden the best vehicle for telling a story?[7]

Except in extraordinary situations, the mythological petition for the modern garden seems naïve and overreaching. A Buddhist friend comments this way: "From the time a shaman stood in front of a cave painting and recited the myth or tale that inspired it, words have been a necessary part of art. But it was not the myth or tale that inspired the painting, it was a vision that inspired the painting. The myth or tale was his attempt to re-create that vision. What remains today are the myths and the tales, sometimes the paintings, and very rarely, so rarely that it is almost not worth mentioning—the vision itself."[8]

Of Tunnard's original "techniques," a vaguely defined "art" retains the most visible seat in the pantheon of design ideologies. Yet today, the call for "art" is a taunt or a dare—"Shock me!" "Entertain me!"—with treacherous consequences awaiting the artist who assumes these objectives. Consider the competition: Julian Schnabel successfully markets paintings composed of broken dinner plates and deer antlers; Eric Fischel paints teenagers masturbating in suburban backyards; and Anselm Kiefer creates foreboding images mindful of the Holocaust. Kramer's admonition bears repeating: "That the culture [Picasso] set out to attack and transform proved to be more resilient in its response to this assault than anyone at the time had reason to expect; that it showed itself capable of absorbing such assaults and profitting from them—this, I should have thought, would now, in the next to last decade of the twentieth century, have become an acknowledged datum of critical intelligence."[9]

Contemporary claims of "subversiveness" by landscape designers should most likely be viewed as exaggeration or misinformation.[10] The audience for today's new landscapes clamors for the bizarre—is immune to being shocked. Of what value, then, is alleged subversiveness without a vision of the future that promises more than an endless parade of colorful juxtapositions and pattern-making? As Jean Cocteau wryly noted, "To be up-to-date is to be quickly out-of-date."[11]

If there is reason for optimism regarding the efforts of today's landscape architects, it lies with the resurgence of interest in designs that are, as Annie Dillard says of the best literature, "in the service of an idea."[12] These ideas, which fall into several broad categories, garner our attention if not our unqualified support.

The most comprehensive of these notions, one that serves as a corollary for all others, is, as expressed by George Hargreaves, that "landscape architecture expresses how our culture meets nature."[13] Such a charge places considerable responsibility on the landscape architect's shoulders—responsibility that most designers would not shirk, even though it is unclear for what they are being held accountable. As with most generalizations, this one leaves the definitions of its terms open to interpretation: which "culture" and which "nature"? If the built work of Hargreaves and others is accepted as evidence, it appears that the "culture" in question is that of middle-class urban and suburban America, and the "nature" that of the artificial, designed variety. It seems to me that urban parks and pedestrian plazas, suburban residences, and corporate office complexes—mainstays of contemporary landscape architecture—have more to say about politics, real estate, and economics than about nature, but, then, perhaps that is Hargreaves's point. This approach to design is inherently limited by its self-imposed emphasis on reflecting the prevailing attitudes and concerns of its ambient culture. What is the designer to do if those beliefs are superficial, banal, or misinformed? Is not one purpose of art to provide insights that workaday society is not able to engender? Elucidating accepted attitudes may comfort the landscape architect striving to make his work "accessible" to the public. Although it competes for the common-denominator role once reserved for "functionalism," this approach seems an unlikely arena for substantive achievement.

Another increasingly ubiquitous generator of landscape designs is the fascination with addressing site-related natural processes (drainage, wind, topography, geology, the seasons, etc.) in such a way that these processes are magnified and made evident, usually to remind the projects' users of the ever-present forces of nature that the pace and conveniences of modern living have caused them to overlook or forget. One successful example is Doug Hollis's *Sound Garden* at the National Oceanic and Atmospheric Administration in Seattle, Washington (Fig. 129). Other forms these didactic landscapes have taken include Hargreaves's fissured lawn at Charleston Place in Mountain View, California, and Noguchi's *California Scenario*, which, like many such projects, exhibit a tentativeness and obviousness that one hopes may soon disappear as these experiments mature. To date, preoccupation with the mechanics of manipulating the natural processes and events under examination supersedes the experiential qualities of the resulting work. To be sure, the landscape is capable of serving an educational function, and is rightfully so used. Is this approach fertile ground for the artistic landscape? Perhaps designers should heed Dillard's advice: "[Art] is not a mirror, not a window, not a document, not a surgical tool. It is an artifact and an achievement; it is at once an exploratory craft and the planet it attains."[14] The venerable Woodland Cemetery in Stockholm comes to mind.

As landscape architects' interests and expertise have widened, their work has become a stage set for technological innovation. Lasers, fiber optics, hydraulic

129. Doug Hollis. *Sound Garden*. 1982–83. Seattle, Washington. The wind vanes emit tones

design, and other devices have advanced the garden to the brink of the twenty-first century, as demonstrated by Peter Walker's mist-emitting stone mound for IBM Corporation in Texas and Michael Van Valkenburgh's *Ice-Vine Garden* on Martha's Vineyard. The technology-supported garden is aided by the fact that, in an era when elementary-school children study computers, few visitors are mystified or overly impressed by their means of execution. The Water Organ at the Villa d'Este they are not. We are reminded that, as always has been true, the art of engineering complements the art of landscape architecture.

What is one to make of these so-called avant-garde landscapes? How valuable or important are their fundamental ideas? Are we witnessing the advent of a new era in landscape design?

Regrettably, many contemporary landscapes are strident and pleading, like advertising. And maybe that is just what they are intended to be—for their owners and designers. Some seem so anxious to please and entertain that, lest we might miss something, they broadcast the final score before the first inning is played. Considering the ardent striving and industrious amassing of disparate forms, images, and colors, I am perplexed by how few demands these landscapes make (and astonished and embarrassed by how naïve most are, relative to art of substance): spatial and graphic one-liners, they are amusing and discardable, demanding little from the audience and delivering the equivalent in return. This is the triumph of attitude over insight and authenticity—seemingly all the proof Roland Barthes would need to substantiate his claim that what distinguishes so-called advanced societies from those of the past is their consumption of images rather than beliefs. Landscape architecture desperately needed the jolt of the Bagel and Necco gardens, and Tiffany and Harlequin plazas. One cannot but admire the open-mindedness that was a prerequisite for the creation of these places. Just don't ask me to make any towering claim for the depth of the thinking. I appreciate fireworks, but fireworks dissipate so quickly.

Since gardening and the landscape have become topical among a broadening audience over the past decade, it might have been expected that landscape design (and designers) would compete for attention alongside other forms of art, architecture, and entertainment, but this turn of events is no less disappointing. That landscape architects are quoted in weekly news magazines does not necessarily mean that the landscapes discussed will be found of lasting importance. In an applicable observation regarding art, Kenworth Moffett noted:

> [The] most fashionable of fashionable art always makes a big assertion and is offered as a candidate for "important" or "serious" art, but it inevitably becomes a period piece when things get sorted out. A period piece is mainly of sentimental appeal and charm. It has "historical interest." At the opposite pole from the period piece is the masterpiece, the great work by the great artist. No one would ever call a great Rembrandt or a great Cézanne a period piece, but we experience the typical pictures of Rosa Bonheur, Bouguereau, and Alma Tadema, salon stars of the late nineteenth century, primarily as period pieces. *They don't transcend their time, but succumb to it* [italics added], and we're amused.

But as art, as personal expression, a Bouguereau is banal and obvious. Indeed, its sheer obviousness is exactly what made it so popular in its time, and what makes it "camp" today.[15]

Upon examination, the interests of contemporary landscape architecture bear a striking similarity to those expressed fifty years ago by Tunnard and his early modern colleagues: both include strategies for dealing with societal changes; respect for new attitudes toward nature and the environment; the application of new technologies; the denigration of identifiable styles of design. Indeed, rather than being a harbinger of a new beginning, the much heralded avant-garde of the late twentieth century is instead a much-delayed ending—of the original early twentieth-century modernist landscape architecture.

If Arthur Danto's enumeration of the seeds of modernism is correct,[16] landscape architecture could be said to have commenced its reentry into the modernist period when, in the late 1970s and early 1980s, two particular characteristics appeared. First, adherents of the new ideology began to vigorously and publicly define landscape architecture *as* art. Producing work that they claimed could not be viewed as a continuation of its immediate predecessors, they often contended that they could distinguish between landscapes that were "art" and those that were not. Second, landscape architecture began to exhibit a self-consciousness whereby it become the subject of its own work: gardens about gardens. The degree to which such imperatives are reiterative of early modern landscape architecture is made apparent by a review of the writings of Joseph Hudnut[17] and of Tunnard, who in the foreword to *Gardens in the Modern Landscape* succinctly identified the still-operative principal aspirations of twentieth-century landscape design: "I believe that if we can gain a clearer picture of *what a garden is, or should be* [italics added], we shall be better equipped to evolve a technique of planning which will play a part in satisfying the complex needs of modern society."[18] Many of today's neo-modern gardens could have comfortably substituted for those by Jean Canneel-Claes and Gabriel Guévrékian illustrated in Tunnard's book.

Assertions of what something is or is not are of course philosophical in nature. It is therefore distressing to find conspicuously absent from the neo-modernists' contentions the fulcrum for any such debate: a firm theoretical basis for the claims made. For a second time within fifty years, this profession stands ready to make sweeping declarations of intent without first building an intellectual foundation.

Though it is a truism that in art, practice produces theory, not the reverse, one might still ask why landscape architecture has not deemed critical appraisal of both its immediate and its distant history to be essential to the design process. Reasons abound. In the decades following World War II, believing they had learned the lesson of modernism and that the lesson licensed the disregard of history, landscape architects indulged in a seldom-impressive blend of functional problem-solving and geometric revelry. The post-1970s neo-modernists abhorred the suggestion that they owed anything to anyone and have only recently acknowledged their debt to the early modernists.[19] In 1925 José Ortega y Gasset had already observed that this posture is characteristic of modernism: "[Modern art] cannot be understood unless this negative mood of mocking aggressiveness is taken into account.... Successive styles contain an ever increasing dose of derision and disparagement until in our day the new art consists almost exclusively of protests against the old. The vigor of the assault stands in inverse proportion to the distance."[20]

The garden's return to modernism occurs at a fortuitous moment fraught with danger for its proponents. Moffett notes with approval the burgeoning audience for art, while he laments that audience's thirst for "easy excitement and obvious kinds of activity and diversity . . . that move quickly";[21] so might we respond with dismay to the increasing production of flamboyant neo-modern landscapes (created to supply a ready market) that, subject to minimal critical examination by their designers or anyone else, do disservice to their designers, users, and the work itself. In contrast to this dearth of criticism stands the tradition of critical landscape-design ideology that can be found in the writings of such pre-twentieth-century theorists as Alexander Pope, William Shenstone, Horace Walpole, Humphry Repton, Andrew Jackson Downing, and others. Martha Schwartz's suggestion that "when [landscape design] gets more interesting, we'll have more criticism"[22] begs the question. There is no inherent equivalency between criticism and its subject. Indeed, informed and illuminating criticism might be said to be of greatest value when the subject body of work is least successful.

Landscape architecture's discomfort with these matters is understandable. Compressing half a century of modernist experimentation into a decade or two is bound to elicit confusion and anxiety. The question is whether the concerns generating these emotions might not be better resolved by conceding the modernist roots of contemporary design and intelligently responding to modernism's interrogatives. The uneasiness about the future of landscape design now being voiced in professional journals by practitioners and academics is indicative of a discipline at a cusp: modernism has not yet been consigned to history, and already there are cries for a new landscape. Although we may be captivated by modernism's insistence on exploring and defining the essence of, and qualifications for, art, and anxious to map an avenue for a new landscape, neither choice will be available to a profession seemingly content to neglect its history, except as a storehouse of plunderable images, and to disregard the importance of critical appraisal.

Landscape architects are doubly cursed. First, in the absence of a critical mechanism for confronting the past, a progressive future remains elusive. Second, as intellectually satisfying as it may be that landscape architecture has once again picked up the lost trail of modernism, those designers harboring hope that the fashionable products of neo-modernism are their salvation will discover that this hybrid landscape architecture will no more conclusively decipher the modernism riddle than have its counterparts in the sister arts. Many of the ideas these projects purport to engage, though not entirely without merit, border on the simpleminded or the meretricious. Even if landscape architecture were to suddenly rise to the challenges of modernism, it would find that those questions operate, as Danto says, "in the unhistorical atmosphere of philosophy,"[23] suggesting that their resolution is not immediately at hand. Landscape architecture ultimately must resign itself to the fact that the nature of its artfulness is undefinable and that the pursuit of the understanding of that nature will not constitute the core of whatever the new landscape will be.

130. Robert Irwin. *Wave Hill Garden.* 1987. Installation at Wave Hill, Bronx, New York

It is not necessary for the new garden to turn away from modernism, which is now a legacy like so many others; but it is my sense that landscape architecture and its clients will be better served by less self-consciousness. Consider, for example, Luis Barragán's proposal that, in light of the environmental, social, psychological, and political chaos that is the twentieth century, it is the duty of every garden to offer a place of serenity. This, it seems to me, is one of the few truly provocative charges issued by a landscape architect in twenty-five years—one that makes intellectual rather than stylistic demands.

If landscape architecture wishes to be ranked among the serious arts, it might begin by taking itself more seriously. In *The Writing Life*, Annie Dillard points out that "writing sentences is difficult whatever the subject. It is no less difficult to write sentences in a recipe than sentences in *Moby Dick*. So you might as well write *Moby Dick*." She also recommends that authors write as if the "audience consist[ed] solely of terminal patients.... What could you say to a dying person that would not enrage by its triviality?"[24] The comparison to garden design is slightly stretched, but the sentiments retain their potency. The garden has been a magical place since the Creation; why has it been so casually debased? One reason is that great gardens are tortuously difficult to make; that this fact has been used by designers to justify poor performance, is another. Although no census exists, it seems likely that the number of great gardens is far smaller than that of great paintings and other works of art.

The body of works indicating that the contemporary landscape is equal to the highest challenges is small. Examples include artist Robert Irwin's sensitive enlivening of the gardens at Wave Hill, Bronx, New York, with his 1987 exhibition (Fig. 130). Irwin's measured intervention in the garden—gentle prodding that coaxed visitors to look anew at the garden, lawns, adjacent Hudson River, and distant New Jersey Palisades—might provide one clue about how to bring life back to an art of garden design awash in coercive preconceptions.[25]

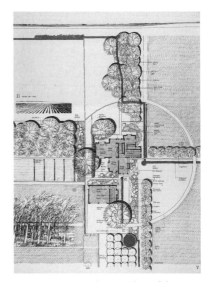

131. Terence Harkness. Plan of the agrarian *East Central Illinois Garden* (unbuilt). 1986

Among the work of landscape architects, that of Terence Harkness is of particular interest. In the unbuilt *East Central Illinois Garden*, Harkness explores a specific cultural and physical environment as the source for a residential landscape (Fig. 131). It attempts to offer a forum for examining one's perception of, and response to, an everyday contemporary place. The exploration involves memory and the meaning embodied in the regional landscape. Harkness has set for himself two tasks. In the general sense, he wishes to determine if an "unsentimental dialogue can be created between the viewer, the site, the landscape, and the region." In particular, he asks if

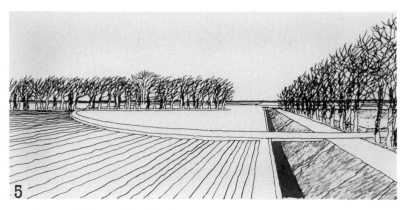

132. Terence Harkness. *East Central Illinois Garden* (unbuilt). 1986. Sketch of drainage channel and hedgerow

"the essential experience of East Central Illinois [can] be evoked within the man-made frame of a garden."[26] He wishes to reveal the uniqueness of this specific landscape and, in doing so, to heighten the viewer's awareness of common experience. But his is not a lecture on the environment nor a story with a moral. This is a garden composed of the non-gardenesque—farm fields, drainage channels, hedgerows, and farmstead. Where else could one discover that early-morning frost on a field of soybean stubble can look like an eighty-acre Japanese raked sand garden (Fig. 132)? The experience is like when someone points out to you the key figures in a previously unfathomable Cubist painting; never again can you fail to recognize them.

Equally important, the project succeeds even if Harkness's self-imposed goals are set aside. The garden has a richness and a variety that elude categorization—qualities conspicuously absent from more photogenic, attention-grasping projects. Unlike most neo-modern landscapes that stand adamantly frozen in time (or at least try to), the *East Central Illinois Garden* welcomes the vagaries of change as inevitable and central to life and the landscape. I note in Harkness's garden something akin to the discovery that prompts the need, as Rilke said of Cézanne, to paint "here it is" rather than "I love this here."[27] Gardens like those of Barragán, Harkness, and Irwin remind us that the landscape *is* capable of revealing some sense of what this life is about. They function in the arena of ideas, not that of technique or cleverness. Finding a place in landscape design for this inquiry is a tall order—which may be why so much contemporary work is but fashionable decoration, willing and anxious to be adopted by the moneyed consumers of design objects while simultaneously claiming a place among the "avant-garde." No one seems to have noticed that this dual identity is a supreme contradiction in terms.

In his durable *Landscape Architecture* (1961), John Simonds concluded that "to be valid the form [of the plan] must take its shape from the planned experience, rather than the experience from the preconceived form."[28] Strictly applied, however, this approach implies that the artist has knowledge of some sort of answer and only needs to discover what it looks like. But art is not the answer to a question, and the artist retains no control over the audience's response to a work. Indeed, what we frequently value most in art is its capacity to support a multiplicity of experience and response. A garden experience may be planned by the designer, but the visitor will have his own way with the place.

Rilke observed that a "work of art is good if it has sprung from necessity. In this nature of its origin lies the judgment of it: there is no other."[29] This "necessity" emerges from a designer's intimate knowledge and understanding of a place and its people, the project brief, and of himself, not from the information gathered by an eye kept on the audience. It is a quality that accompanies passion—publicly displayed or privately held. It does no commerce with "intentions," styles, or reputations. Tellingly,

Harkness writes that his garden expresses his "enduring affection for the beauty and character of a particular place."[30] The lesson is that nothing lies outside the realm of art; that only your truest understanding will suffice; and that, while your discoveries may be culturally biased, they cannot be the product of willful manufacture.

1. Jean Cocteau, quoted in Ned Rorem, "Cocteau and Music," in *Jean Cocteau and the French Scene* (New York, 1984), p. 172.

2. Christopher Tunnard, *Gardens in the Modern Landscape* (London, 1938).

3. Norman T. Newton, "Modern Trends—What Are They?" *Landscape Architecture* 22, no. 4 (July 1932): 303.

4. Hilton Kramer, "The Crisis in Abstract Art," *Atlantic*, Oct. 1986, p. 98.

5. Roger Kimball, "Making a Spectacle of Architecture on PBS," *The New Criterion*, May 1986, p. 32.

6. See discussion of the work of Pamela Burton in: W. L. Douglas, S. R. Frey, N. K. Johnson, S. Littlefield, M. Van Valkenburgh, *Garden Design* (New York, 1984), p. 176.

7. In contrast, see the description of the symbolic content of the gardens and architecture of the Villa Lante in: Reuben M. Rainey, "The Garden as Myth: The Villa Lante at Bagnaia," *Union Seminary Quarterly Review*, 37, nos. 1 and 2 (Fall/Winter 1981–82).

8. Letter, Gerald Eule to the author, n.d.

9. Hilton Kramer, "The 'Primitivism' Conundrum," *The New Criterion*, Dec. 1984, p. 6.

10. See remarks by Martha Schwartz, *Landscape Architecture* 80, no. 1 (Jan. 1990): 54.

11. Quoted in Rorem, *Jean Cocteau and the French Scene,* p.172.

12. Annie Dillard, *Living by Fiction* (New York, 1982), p. 106.

13. George Hargreaves, quoted in *Progressive Architecture*, July 1989, p. 13.

14. Dillard, *Living by Fiction*, p. 25.

15. Kenworth Moffett, "Abstract Art and Middlebrow Modern," *Partisan Review*, no. 2, 1983.

16. Arthur Danto, "Narratives of the End of Art, *Grand Street* 8, no. 3 (Spring 1989).

17. Joseph Hudnut, "Space and the Modern Garden," *Bulletin of The Garden Club of America*, no. 9 (May 1940).

18. Tunnard, *Gardens in the Modern Landscape*, p. 5.

19. See remarks by Peter Walker in *Landscape Architecture*, 80, no. 1 (Jan. 1990): 124.

20. José Ortega y Gasset, *The Dehumanization of Art*, trans. Helene Weyl (Princeton, N.J., 1948), pp. 43–44.

21. Moffett, "Abstract Art," p. 261.

22. Martha Schwartz, quoted in *Landscape Architecture* 80, no. 1 (Jan. 1990): 59.

23. Danto, "Narratives," p. 180.

24. Annie Dillard, *The Writing Life* (New York, 1989), pp. 71, 68.

25. See author's review of the exhibition in *Landscape Architecture* 78, no. 1: 22–28.

26. Terence Harkness, "Landscape Design and the Common Landscape," unpublished manuscript, n.d., p. 2.

27. Rainer Maria Rilke, *Letters on Cézanne*, trans. Joel Agee (New York, 1985), p. 51.

28. John Ormsbee Simonds, *Landscape Architecture* (New York, 1961), p. 225.

29. Rainer Maria Rilke, *Letters to a Young Poet*, trans. M. D. Herter Norton (New York, 1954), p. 20.

30. Harkness, "Landscape Design," p. 2.

MARC TREIB

Sources of Significance: The Garden in Our Time

Tʜʀᴏᴜɢʜᴏᴜᴛ ʜɪsᴛᴏʀʏ, the garden has served two primary purposes: as a zone of modulated and intensified sensual experience; and as a vehicle for expressing symbolic, political, and religious ideas beyond the realm of its tangible materials (Fig. 133). The world's people share no common definition of the garden. In our culture, however, the notion of at least partially defined limits and some amount of vegetation are basic to the idea of the garden. Without a sense of limits, we have a field or a park; without vegetation, a court or a yard.

In the past, the garden often presented desirable environmental qualities missing from the quotidian lives of the people. In dry climates, it was rich with vegetation and flush with water. In forested areas, it might be primarily a cleared precinct.[1] Thus, the zone of the garden offered an alternative, a form that embodied an aspiration for physical need, or social or metaphysical striving. Whether overtly or covertly, the aspirations were embedded in its form. In seventeenth-century France, the organization of the garden extended to the horizon using vegetation and water, and beyond the horizon through psychological implication. In eighteenth-century England, on the other hand, park and landscape became so intertwined that one could hardly discern where the one ended and the other began. Although differing in their degree of formality, both garden types were, of course, landscapes highly contrived; both reflected attitudes toward nature and its perfecting, political governance, and a host of other factors addressed in their design.

The consummation of this striving for perfection is to reflect a paradise on earth. A garden paradise must reward scrutiny, and to provoke that scrutiny both a subject and sufficient details must be provided. Subject and details pervade places like the Patio de los Naranjos in Seville (Fig. 134), with its almost magical elevation of a pragmatic irrigation system into a reflection of cosmic order, and that Saiho-ji in Kyōto (Fig. 135), whose eerie irregular contrivance implodes upon itself and the suggestion of paradise within its walled enclosure. In this garden, the meandering path and the pond it circumscribes conjure a sense of the Western paradise, where the Amida Buddha awaits the

133. Ashikaga Yoshimasa. Ginkaku-ji. c. 1480. Kyōto, Japan

134. Patio de los Naranjos. Sixteenth century. Seville, Spain

enlightenment of all sentient beings.[2] A belief system saturates both these gardens with a power that far surpasses the limits of the physical means of their realization.

135. Muso Kokoshi. Saiho-ji. 1339 (renovation). Kyōto, Japan

The perfection of the garden can be manifest as much in what is omitted as what is included. The justifiable fame of Zen dry gardens such as Ryoan-ji or Daisen-in derives from the mystery created by understatement and absence—phenomena that parallel the dramatic and mysterious gap between the evocation of the novel and the specificity of the film. One *asks* of the viewer; the other tells. Both modes are valid in making a garden.[3]

In the past, when power structures were relatively centralized and clearly defined, and cultures more insulated, the garden could be granted a form by decree. We possess no such luxury today. Typically—as we have done with so many aspects of primary living experience—we have reduced the essence of past garden types to a mere wisp of their prior meaning and greatness. The English park flavors, rather than informs, suburbia: the profundity of the Japanese contemplative space or the garden of classical antiquity has been trivialized as a "classical" or "Asian" "touch for your home." We might well ask, then, just where to turn for sources of significance in today's world.

Although archaicism may have a viable place in the creation of sculpture, I believe that the creation of neo-Stonehenges or solar alignments as sources of significance in gardens is rather limited. We live in a postindustrial society, and I do not believe that we can go back "home" again. In borrowing primitive forms without their systems of significance, by wrenching them from their settings and their societies, we risk confusing syntax for semantics. Nor do I think that yet another iteration of the picturesque clump or the classically derived landscape presents us with a viable model; in the process, we can acquire only the representation of a representation, compounding the entropic process and the dissolution of meaning.

At the close of the 1930s, the French architect Jean-Charles Moreux dismissed the idea of a garden art based on contemporary garden movements. "Some attempts have been made to introduce unusual gardens in the 'cubist' sense," he wrote, "but to my mind they are as out-of-date as a fabric or an ornament designed on cubist lines.... In reality there are only two forms of garden," he continued, "the formal garden, which is the point of contact between house and nature, for it is a product of them both; and the landscape garden, which is an imitation of nature. The general rule will always be: to use both common sense and imagination, and this applies to all gardens the world over."[4] Period. According to Moreux, there are neither modern gardens nor not-modern gardens, only the formal and the informal. Common sense and imagination—the extremes of praxis and poetics—are both necessary. But he, too, concerned himself only with syntax.

It would seem that the garden must concern how we are as a people today, the lives we live and the means by which we live them. The garden can thus serve as both a lens and a mirror. As a lens, it allows us to focus on *where* we live and build. We should develop forms and utilize planting and hard materials that address the

136. Isamu Noguchi. *California Scenario*. 1982. Costa Mesa, California

place, our land, our climate, our relation to the sun, and how we experience the passing of the seasons on a particular site. The vineyard offers us one example: a territory in which land contour and agricultural yield, orientation and order, merge into a landscape aesthetic. As a mirror, on the other hand, the garden reflects upon us as human beings, our relationships to nature, to other human beings, and to ourselves as individuals. It reminds us where we have come from and provokes us to action or silence—both necessary in today's world (Fig. 136).

Recently, I had the opportunity to visit Stonypath, or Little Sparta, the home and garden in Scotland of the poet-sculptor Ian Hamilton Finlay.[5] I have been an admirer of Mr. Finlay's for many years, since I first came across his concrete poetry in the late 1960s. Now he has made his poetry truly concrete. There is little formal order to the layout of the garden, and yet it feels comfortable within the well-worn path of the English landscape tradition. In place of the folly and the spatial marker, Finlay has peppered his landscape with words and ideas and feelings given palpable form. The horror of war is transmogrified into the ornament, as an aircraft carrier becomes a birdbath in a section of the garden intended to recall the mock naval battle (*naumachia*) and the Villa d'Este at Tivoli. He seeks the single species in his admonition "Bring back the birch" and the fleeting moment in a series of sundials. There is even humor in the watering can, where Gertrude Stein meets Gertrude Jekyll. Around its girth endlessly runs the text "a rose is a rose is a rose." But it is the Gertrude known for her herbaceous border plantings, rather than Gertrude the poet, who receives the credit for its creation.

Finlay exhorts us to "See Poussin, Hear Lorrain," and with his help, indeed we do. Trees receive architectural bases and inscriptions; each is a collaborative work between the poet and the calligrapher, craftsman, or artist that manifests a perfection of graphic form and material. Upon the *object* in the landscape is the *word*. The word tints, taints, directs, instructs—but it remains continually gentle (Fig. 137).

Separating the garden of the house from the garden of the pond is a simple wire fence. It is made for animals more than for humans, but even fences like these have to be dealt with by human bipeds. We face a dilemma: how to traverse the boundary. Finlay frames the conceptual situation: thesis, fence; antithesis, gate. From these opposites—with some help from the Hegelian dialectic—he forges a formal synthesis: a stile (Fig. 138).

We know *our* thesis—our history—well. We have formulated many antitheses: both the perfection of the planned garden and the happenstance of the city and functioning landscape (Fig. 139). A literary landscape such as Ian Hamilton Finlay's is but one of a number of possible models for our own garden. Now we should return to the site—return again to ourselves, singly and collectively—to forge a new synthesis, to design a garden that soothes, or stimulates, or motivates us today.

137. Ian Hamilton Finlay. *Michelet.* 1960s on. Little Sparta, Dunsyre, Scotland

138. Ian Hamilton Finlay. *Hegel's Stile.* 1960s on. Little Sparta, Dunsyre, Scotland

139. Kew Gardens, England. 1972

1. The garden as paradise thus reflects a culture's idea of heaven, often conceived in opposition to the less desirable conditions of daily life. This theme is developed by Yi Fu Tuan in *Topophilia: A Study of Environmental Perception, Attitudes and Values* (Englewood Cliffs, 1974).

2. See Marc Treib, "Reduction, Elaboration and Yūgen: The garden of Saiho-ji," *Journal of Garden History* 9, no. 2, Apr.–June 1989).

3. The condition and aesthetics of removal are discussed in Marc Treib, "The Presence of Absence: Places by Extraction," *Places* 4, no. 3 (1987).

4. *Gardens and Gardening. 1939*, ed. by F. A. Mercer (London and New York, 1939), p. 17. I am grateful to Dorothée Imbert for bringing this quotation to my attention. The argument is not Moreux's alone, but a familiar theme in the dialectic of landscape styles. Compare this to Reginald Blomfield, arguing at the turn of the century for a more formal sensibility in the English garden in order to bring architecture and garden into greater accord:

> The question at issue is a very simple one. Is the garden to be considered in relation to the house, and as an integral part of a design which depends for its success on the combined effect of house and garden; or is the house to be ignored in dealing with the garden? The latter is the position of the landscape gardened in fact....The formal treatment of gardens ought, perhaps, to be called the architectural treatment of gardens, for it consists in the extension of the principles of design which govern the house to the grounds around it. (Reginald Blomfield, *The Formal Garden in England*, London, 1985 [first published in 1892], pp. 1–2.)

5. Although numerous articles have been published on Stonypath and Ian Hamilton Finlay's work, including several excellent studies by Stephen Bann, the most comprehensive treatment appears in Yves Abrioux, *Ian Hamilton Finlay: A Visual Primer* (Edinburgh, 1985). This book includes introductory notes and commentaries by Stephen Bann.

JOHN BEARDSLEY

Earthworks:
The Landscape after Modernism

For a time in this century, it appeared that American art had forgotten its covenant with landscape. In the nineteenth century, little mattered more. Not only was art then dominated by the image of landscape: more important, art was central to a process of national self-definition in which some of our prevailing cultural attitudes (political, theological, economic) were derived from, or inscribed upon, the landscape. All that America was, or could be, was in the landscape, it seemed, a point that nineteenth-century painting contrived to make plain. In our own century, by comparison, little has mattered less. The landscape did not entirely disappear from art; the subject continued to be of importance to certain photographers, especially, and was looked to as a source by those engaged in abstraction. But its explicit image was forsaken, even repudiated, by those we have come to venerate as modern. Its virtues turned to liabilities; its nationalist overtones, in particular, must have seemed parochial to a generation at once more cosmopolitan and more concerned with the primacy of the individual imagination. For the most part, landscape and modernity proved, in fundamental ways, to be mutually embarrassing.

It may prove, in hindsight, that nothing signaled the end of the modern era in art so much as the restoration of landscape to an important position among artists of a particularly venturesome character in the latter half of the 1960s. Why such a change took place will be a recurring theme in this essay, although I am as concerned with consequences as with causes. Suffice it to say at the outset that the restoration of landscape in the late 1960s can be traced to broad cultural forces as well as to those originating in the art world: it was then that we began reckoning with the awful repercussions of industrial progress, which for the most part we had previously only been celebrating. Consequently, landscape was very much on people's minds—although artists would never achieve a unified or unambiguous position on ecological matters. In addition, there was a feeling among certain artists that paintings, especially, were economically overvalued (still a trenchant notion, as matters in this regard by now have become truly obscene) and superfluous. They would find their antidote to the commodity status of art in environmental projects, now commonly known as earthworks, in which art and site were inextricably linked. Landscape was not simply the subject of this art, but also its locus and raw material.

"The position of art as malleable barter-exchange item falters as the cumulative economic structure gluts," the sculptor Michael Heizer wrote in 1969. "The museum and collections are stuffed, the floors are sagging, but the real space still exists."[1] Real space for Heizer, a Californian by birth, was to be found principally in the deserts of the American West. Heizer began working in the earthworks idiom in 1967, although nothing survives of many of his initial pieces: trenches, motorcycle drawings, dispersals of soil and pigment from the backs of moving trucks, and in 1969, a series called *Displaced/Replaced Mass*, in which granite boulders were brought from high in the Sierra Nevada and toppled into depressions cut into the Nevada desert. In late 1969 and early 1970 came the enormous and still-extant *Double Negative* (Fig. 140), consisting of two cuts, each thirty feet wide and fifty feet deep, made in opposite sides of a scallop in the escarpment of the Mormon Mesa near Overton, Nevada. From end to end, the piece measured some 1,500 feet in length and displaced 240,000 tons of earth.

On the face of it, *Double Negative* achieved Heizer's objectives: it would never become a portable commodity like other works of art. In a more profound sense, it also declared its independence from traditional sculpture: it was not a solid mass or even a constructed form. It was composed of space; in this sense it was more architecture than sculpture. Paradoxically, however, it achieved this independence while still employing the reductive, geometric vocabulary that had characterized the Minimalist sculpture of the mid-1960s. This would also be the case with Heizer's next large-scale work in the Nevada desert, *Complex One/City* (1972–76). The first of a group of geometrically configured earth-and-concrete structures planned for a site in central Nevada, *Complex One/City* (Fig. 141) is an elongated trapezoidal mastaba with a group of linear concrete elements positioned in front of or cantilevered from it. From the front—the west—these elements read as a continuous band that frames the mound; from any other perspective, they break up into shifting alignments. Here again was something close to architecture in the idiom of contemporaneous sculpture.

Heizer has always bristled at the suggestion that his work has anything to do with landscape. "I don't care about landscape," he says. "I'm a sculptor. Real estate is dirt, and dirt is material."[2] He points out that *Complex One/City* will ultimately be one side of an enclosed precinct that will shut out all views of the surrounding desert. Inasmuch as *Complex One/City* has obvious external references, they are admittedly to pre-Columbian and Egyptian ceremonial architecture rather than to the tradition of American landscape painting or design. In electing to work in the western deserts, however, Heizer unavoidably triggered associations with the American landscape tradition—a fact he has, on occasion, acknowledged. He has said that he found in the western landscape "that kind of unraped, peaceful, religious space artists have always tried to put into their work."[3] These associations prove to be the most potent aspect of *Double Negative*. It is a consecrated space, in which one experiences sensations of great distance, aloneness, and silence that inescapably recall the sublime.

140. Michael Heizer. *Double Negative*. 1969–70. Two cuts in a mesa displacing 240,000 tons of earth, 50 x 30 x 1,500'. Near Overton, Nevada

141. Michael Heizer. *Complex One/City*. 1972–76. Concrete, granite, and earth, 24 x 140 x 110'. Central Nevada

142. Walter de Maria. *The Lightning Field*. 1974–77. Four hundred stainless-steel poles (approximately 20' high) in a rectangular grid, overall dimensions: 1 mile x 1 kilometer. Commissioned and maintained for public visiting by the Dia Center for the Arts. Near Quemado, Mexico

143. Ian Hamilton Finlay. *Stonypath*. Begun 1967. Lanarks, Scotland

This effect is even more evident in Walter De Maria's *The Lightning Field* (Fig. 142), built between 1974 and 1977 in the desert of western New Mexico. De Maria, another Californian, had executed his first western work—two parallel chalk lines, each a mile long, drawn on the Mojave Desert—in the company of Heizer in 1968. His subsequent work, *The Lightning Field*, would aspire to even greater dimensions. It is composed of a rectangular grid of 400 stainless-steel poles spaced 220 feet apart, with 16 rows of 25 poles stretching a mile on an east-west axis and, correspondingly, 25 rows of 16 poles reaching just over a kilometer on a north-south one. Despite fluctuations in the surface of the ground, the poles are placed in such a way that their tips form a plane at an average height of approximately twenty feet.

Like *Double Negative*, *The Lightning Field* addresses itself to space and employs a reductive, geometric vocabulary, but it does so in a way that also evokes the sublime. It literally delineates an awe-inspiring area; by the succession of poles, it implies an infinite extension of this grid. Moreover, De Maria restricts the number of people who can visit *The Lightning Field* at any one time in order to intensify the feeling of solitude experienced at the site. "Isolation is the essence of Land Art," he has said succinctly.[4] De Maria adds to this mix the implications of power and of danger, among the most forceful attributes of the sublime. The steel poles sometimes attract lightning, and although one is not always literally at risk on *The Lightning Field*, there is always the suggestion of this potentially lethal power.

Like Heizer, then, De Maria sought a clear alternative to previous art—"a quantum leap," as he put it, beyond the succession of styles that characterized art history.[5] But, again like Heizer, he found history difficult to escape. Not only did his vocabulary link him to recent geometric abstraction, but his work also reached back across modernism to the landscape art of the eighteenth and nineteenth centuries. Bridging this chasm has been a more deliberate goal for other artists, however, especially James Pierce, on this side of the Atlantic, and Ian Hamilton Finlay, on the other. Pierce and Finlay are not typically considered in the context of the earthworks movement, but they began their work in the landscape at virtually the same time as those now identified as earth artists and seem an equally important counterpoint: while Heizer and De Maria were looking for a way beyond modernism, however ambiguously, Finlay and Pierce were suggesting a way back from it.

In 1967 Finlay, with his wife, Susan, began work in Lanarkshire, Scotland, on a poet's garden—known as Stonypath or Little Sparta (Fig. 143)—in the tradition of Alexander Pope or William Shenstone. Over the next two decades, they transformed four acres of moorland and ponds into a sequence of gardens containing a variety of inscriptions that make reference to the traditions of landscape in art and literature, and to political history, especially the French Revolution. At the same time, they have converted two rough agricultural buildings into garden temples, which, together with numerous architectural fragments in the garden, reveal Finlay's effort to reactivate the classical tradition and its meditations on wisdom, power, and virtue.

Finlay is one of the few recent British artists to intervene in the landscape in any way approaching the scale of contemporary American work; most others take a more modest, even reverential approach, which is conditioned, one assumes, by the smaller scale and more domesticated character of the British landscape. Finlay does not hesitate, because he identifies with what he describes as "the Neoplatonic idea of improved or Ideal Nature, as opposed to the modern view, which is of 'nature' itself as being the ideal (and more ideal the more it is untouched by the human intellect)."[6] He is also emboldened because, as he puts it, "Certain gardens are described as retreats when they are really attacks."[7] Finlay's garden is a deliberate and highly literate assault on contemporary culture, which he perceives as willfully ignorant. In this context, the many references to the French Revolution—for which Neoclassicism was almost an official idiom—suggest the extent to which Finlay thinks culture needs to be reformulated.

144. Ian Hamilton Finlay. *Stonypath*. Begun 1967. Lanarks, Scotland. Plaque bears inscription: *Et in Arcadia Ego*. After Guercino

Stonypath is thus intended as a series of provocations. To this end, Finlay has deployed a number of objects and inscriptions around the garden that recapitulate and attempt to reinvigorate Western intellectual history. These objects, as he puts it, "are works in themselves, as well as references, and (importantly) elements in larger compositions which include the plants." Some refer to art history: a patch of marsh is signed with Albrecht Dürer's monogram (an evocation of Dürer's watercolor *Das Grosse Rasenstück* [*The Great Piece of Turf*]); a block of stone bears the legend *See Poussin/Hear Lorrain*, inviting us to contemplate the landscape as these artists might have depicted it. References to the more general tradition of pastoralism in literature and art abound: the lovers Angelica and Medoro are invoked on the tree plaque, while on another (Fig. 144) the inscription *Et in Arcadia Ego* surmounts the death's-head insignia of the German SS-Panzer division, in a provocative updating of a painting by Guercino. Finlay is here returning moralism to the pastoral theme, reminding us of the original meaning of the phrase—that death rules even in Arcadia—but he is also linking the modern image of death with the Nazi war machine. In numerous other instances in Finlay's work, twentieth-century images of warfare and death appear: aircraft carriers, tanks, the lightning-bolt insignia of the Nazi storm troopers. All suggest the problematic relationship between power and terror, and bring the negative aspects of the sublime to life in contemporary terms.

While the references in Finlay's garden are deliberately wide-ranging, those in Pierce's are more specifically linked to the tradition of the picturesque. Since the summer of 1970, Pierce has been at work on a farm in central Maine creating a seventeen-acre "garden of history," a landscape in the tradition of eighteenth-century Britain. Like the typical picturesque park, Pierce's landscape is composed of contrasting areas of open meadow and dense plantings—in this case, stands of evergreen and birch. Meadow and forest meet along an irregular contour; in the distance is the obligatory body of water—here, the Kennebec River. What links Pierce's garden more specifically with the picturesque landscape, however, is his incorporation of latter-day "follies," elements that arouse associations with the ancient, the remote, or the unfamiliar.

In the main, the first of the elements that Pierce added to his garden of history

145. James Pierce. *Triangular Redoubt*. 1971. Earth; 5' high, length of each side: 65'. Pratt Farm, Clinton, Maine

146. James Pierce. Left: *Burial Mound*. 1971. Earth; 4' high, 4' in diameter. Right: *Stone Ship*. 1975. Earth; 40 x 12'. Pratt Farm, Clinton, Maine

147. James Pierce. Foreground: *Turf Maze*. 1972–74. Earth; 120' on a side. Center: *Observatory*. 1974. Upper right: *Motte*. 1975. Earth; 8' high, 20' in diameter. Pratt Farm, Clinton, Maine

in the early 1970s were forts and burial monuments. *Triangular Redoubt* (Fig. 145) was built at one edge of the central meadow, *Circular Redoubt* at the other, and *Motte*, a spiral mount, on a hill to one side. Built in the manner of crude eighteenth-century fortifications, the different redoubts allude to the fact that the Kennebec was, for a time, the boundary between French and British settlements in North America. The burial markers are also of several sorts (Fig. 146): a mound that suggests American Indian prototypes, a Viking "ship burial," a shaman's tomb. In the midst of making these defensive and mortuary forms Pierce created the more ambiguous *Turf Maze* (Fig. 147), cut into the ground in the manner of ancient mazes. It is an allegory, as Pierce tells it, of penance and redemption, of insemination and birth.

Turf Maze anticipated suggestively procreative elements that would be added to the garden in the latter half of the 1970s. Among them were *Earthwoman*, inspired by the dorsal view of the Venus of Willendorf, and *Suntreeman*, an ithyphallic figure that is half-human and half-vegetable. Near this suggestion of Adam and Eve was coiled *Stone Serpent*. More recently, Pierce has reverted to historically evocative forms: an eighteenth-century warship by the river; and a wagon reminiscent of the earliest known representation of a wheeled vehicle (found on a cylinder seal in the Middle East) by a road that runs past the farm. These forms are not direct copies of their prototypes: they are allusions to an all-but-forgotten history. Pierce's landscape thus might be read as an indictment of contemporary culture, like Finlay's, but with its suggestion of conflict, death, and regeneration, its emphasis seems more personal and psychological than polemical.

Whether deliberately or inadvertently revealed, the present relationship to history proved to be one of the central issues in earth art. Robert Smithson would recognize this, too, but would make a conscious effort to refute history entirely. Looking around him in 1967, he found the landscape so altered from its traditional form that he struggled, in a series of essays, to develop a new vocabulary for describing it. On "A Tour of the Monuments of Passaic, New Jersey," he identified pumping derricks, unfinished highway construction, and sewer pipes as the significant components of the contemporary landscape. He described them in terms like "zero panorama," "ruins in reverse," and "monumental vacancies."[8] What he saw was a landscape of blandness, of change and decay, of increasing randomness and disorder. He wrote in another essay in 1968: "The abysmal problem of gardens somehow involves a fall from somewhere or something. The certainty of the absolute garden will never be regained."[9] For Smithson, the compelling landscape was postindustrial and postlapsarian. It was one that gave evidence of a series of natural cataclysms and human interventions, rather than one that aspired to perfection.

Nevertheless, none of this was cause for despair. For one thing, Smithson observed, "processes of heavy construction have a devastating kind of primordial grandeur." For another, one might make of disruption a positive artistic challenge. "A bleached and fractured world surrounds the artist," he wrote. "To organize this mess of corrosion into patterns, grids, and subdivisions is an aesthetic process that has scarcely been touched."[10] Smithson began this aesthetic process in landscapes that were obviously disrupted or degraded. His most familiar work, the 1970 *Spiral Jetty* (Fig. 148) was built in the virtually lifeless environment of the Great Salt Lake, where an arid climate fosters little vegetation and the extreme salinity of the lake prohibits all but one life form: colonies of algae that turn the water pink. Moreover, the site was but a mile up the shore from an abandoned oil-drilling operation, marked by dilapidated shacks and rusting equipment. "A great pleasure arose from seeing all those incoherent structures," Smithson wrote. "This site gave evidence of a succession of man-made systems mired in abandoned hopes."[11]

This entropic imagery appears in *Spiral Jetty*, which collapses in upon itself; but the spiral also derives from Smithson's reading of the local topography, which he described as like "an immobile cyclone." Moreover, it resembled the structure of the salt crystals that formed on the rocks as the lake water receded. Not even Smithson could evade historical references entirely: he likened the spiral to Indian legends that said the Great Salt Lake was connected to the ocean by an enormous whirlpool.

Smithson chose as the site for his next work a landscape even more disrupted, this time entirely by human action. During 1971, in a virtually depleted sand quarry in the Netherlands, he executed *Broken Circle* and *Spiral Hill*: the former, a curved jetty and canal forming a nearly complete circle on the edge of the quarry pond, the latter, an earthen mount on a slope above it. Smithson was inspired by this experience to pursue the use of his work in land-reclamation schemes in the United States. "Across the country," he wrote, "there are many mining areas, disused quarries, and polluted lakes and rivers. One practical solution for the utilization of such devastated places would be land and water recycling in terms of 'earth art.'"[12] He circulated his proposals to mining companies in Ohio and Colorado, but despite some expressions of interest, nothing had come of them at the time he was killed while planning what would become his final work, the *Amarillo Ramp* (1973).

Nevertheless, Smithson's effort to address and even to help restore the postindustrial landscape would prove his most potent legacy. His ideas gave rise, at least in part, to a number of projects in and around Seattle in the late 1970s, including the reclamation of an approximately four-acre gravel pit by Robert Morris and the restoration of an eroded streambed and the construction of storm-water retention basins for the city of Kent, Washington, by Herbert Bayer. More recently, Smithson's colleague and wife, Nancy Holt—creator of the monumental *Sun Tunnels* (1973–76) in the Utah desert—has been asked to design a public park to be created on the fifty-seven-acre site of a landfill in the New Jersey Meadowlands. In addition, Michael Heizer was called in to participate in the reclamation of a 200-acre surface coal mine in central Illinois. Heizer's contribution to the effort consisted of five *Effigy Tumuli Sculptures* (completed 1985), massive earthen forms in the abstracted shapes of a water strider, a frog (Fig. 149), a catfish, a turtle, and a snake that are

148. Robert Smithson. *Spiral Jetty*. 1970. Black basalt, limestone rocks, and earth, 1,500 x 15'. Great Salt Lake, Utah. Estate of Robert Smithson

149. Michael Heizer. *Effigy Tumuli Sculptures; Frog Effigy*. 1985. 17½' high x 340' long. Buffalo Rock State Park, Ottawa, Illinois

150. Nancy Holt. *Dark Star Park*.
1979–84. Overall approximately two-
thirds of an acre. Rosslyn, Arlington
County, Virginia. View through
entrance tunnel

151. Andrew Leicester. *Cincinnati
Gateway Sculpture*. 1988. Sawyer Point
Park, Cincinnati, Ohio

reminiscent of prehistoric Indian mounds of the upper Midwest. Heizer insists that his work had nothing to do with reclamation, that it was simply an opportunity to work at a large scale. Nevertheless, his effigies have a decidedly incantatory character, as if he were luring life back to the previously toxic and despoiled site.

The legacy of the earthworks movement goes deeper than the notion of land reclamation, however. The suggestion that art could derive aspects of its form, material, and content from the topographical and cultural context in which it is made contributed to the emergence of a phenomenon known as sited or site-specific sculpture. The earthworks movement cannot alone account for sited sculpture—the phenomenon was implicit in earlier landscape projects of artists as diverse as Isamu Noguchi and Richard Serra. It was chiefly earth art, however, that precipitated the widespread engagement with landscape that is still a significant force among artists today. More important, site-generated art—sometimes looking like a cross between sculpture and architecture, sometimes a hybrid of sculpture and landscape architecture—plays an increasingly prominent role in the contemporary public space. The *Vietnam Veterans Memorial* in Washington, D.C., for example, surely the most significant public monument of the past two decades, is inconceivable without the example of recent environmental sculpture. Its simple form, dug into the ground, its attenuated horizontal axes, and its symbolic alignments with the other memorials on the Mall all recall the precedent of earth art, although not earth art alone.

Maya Lin, designer of the *Vietnam Veterans Memorial*, is but one of the many artists now remaking the public landscape—especially the urban public landscape—in the wake of the earthworks episode. Some, like Siah Armajani and Scott Burton, who collaborated with the architect Cesar Pelli and the landscape architect Paul Friedberg on the design of the North Cove precinct at Battery Park City in New York, have striven for a functional landscape that is without an artistic signature. Others, such as Nancy Holt, have tried to reconcile their personal artistic vocabularies with the requirements of public leisure and utility, as at her *Dark Star Park* in Rosslyn, Virginia (Fig. 150). Still others—Andrew Leicester is perhaps the best example—try to make their landscapes reveal as much as possible about the history of the site in which they are working. For his *Cincinnati Gateway Sculpture* at the new Sawyer Point Park on the Ohio River (Fig. 151), for example, Leicester packed his landscape with maps, canal locks, flood markers, bridge towers, smokestacks, sculpted fish and pigs—images all drawn from his reading of the history of the Cincinnati riverfront.

Even apart from the legacy of sited sculpture and reclamation, however, earth art can be said to have reinvigorated the landscape tradition in American art. Reaching both forward from and back over the ellipsis of the modern era, earth art has returned landscape to a position of importance in American art. The covenant has been recalled, and reformulated: art is now striving to reshape the landscape itself in some beneficial way. It is once more acknowledging the power of landscape to shape our cultural values and to address both our problems and our possibilities.

1. Michael Heizer, "The Art of Michael Heizer," *Artforum* 8 (Dec. 1969): 34.

2. Michael Heizer, conversation with the author, April 1989.

3. Quoted in Howard Junker, "The New Sculpture: Getting Down to the Nitty Gritty," *Saturday Evening Post* (Nov. 2, 1968): 42.

4. Walter De Maria, "The Lightning Field," *Artforum* 18 (April 1980): 52.

5. Walter De Maria, as quoted in Calvin Tomkins, *The Scene: Reports on Post-Modern Art* (New York, 1976), p. 131.

6. Unless otherwise noted, quotations from Ian Hamilton Finlay are from correspondence with the author.

7. Ian Hamilton Finlay, "Unconnected Sentences on Gardening," in Yves Abrioux, *Ian Hamilton Finlay: A Visual Primer* (Edinburgh, 1985), p. 38.

8. Robert Smithson, "A Tour of the Monuments of Passaic, New Jersey," in *The Writings of Robert Smithson*, ed. Nancy Holt (New York, 1979), pp. 52–57.

9. Robert Smithson, "A Sedimentation of the Mind: Earth Projects," in *Writings*, pp. 85, 91.

10. Ibid., pp. 82, 83.

11. Robert Smithson, "The Spiral Jetty," in *Writings*, p. 111.

12. Robert Smithson, "Untitled," in ibid., p. 220.

GALEN CRANZ

Four Models of Municipal Park Design in the United States

FOUR MODELS HAVE GUIDED AMERICAN thought about park design. The underlying principles we use to shape our world are social and cultural, whether we work at the scale of architecture or landscape, and in that spirit, I am going to summarize the four kinds of parks that have served as models for solving social problems, starting in the nineteenth century and moving quickly into the twentieth.

PLEASURE GROUND: 1850–1900

I chose this image (Fig. 152) for the cover of my book *The Politics of Park Design: A History of Urban Parks* (1982) because it subverts one of the clichés about the nineteenth-century pleasure ground: the notion that it was for passive recreation while the contemporary park is for active recreation. In my opinion, that is a self-serving comparison made today to rationalize our parks' not being as rich and complex as the pleasure ground, which was intended for both active play and contemplative experience. The nineteenth-century model was the result of a public movement originating in the 1850s, when citizens decided that they had better try to do something about the high rates of disease afflicting the cities, particularly in the summer. Transcendentalists had also agitated to save cities from the problems of density and growth. Only in response to cholera epidemics, however, were legislators convinced to purchase land with public money for the creation of parks. Previously, small squares, commons, or intersecting bits of land that were not useful for other purposes had been donated to cities, but never before had municipal governments decided to create open space.

These new parks were usually located on the periphery of cities, because that was the cheapest land. Originally, Central Park was to be located on the waterfront of the Lower East Side near tenements on a site called Jones Woods, but for political and economic reasons that plan was abandoned in favor of a Central Park that

152. Lawn tennis. c. 1880s. South Side Park, Chicago

was central to nothing except the geographic center of the island. In fact, the first building built on the periphery of the park was nicknamed the Dakota because it was so far away that it might as well have been in the Dakotas. The choice of this remote location was a compromise between public-health officials and property owners. Doctors then believed that the quality of air around trees defeated disease. They were still following the medieval view that disease was caused by miasmic vapors. (Pine trees, in particular, were thought to produce a smell that would stop these diseases.) Public-health officials, on the one hand, wanted to stop disease by creating a public park, while land and commercial interests, on the other, did not want to take valuable docking land—Jones Woods—off the free market. Central Park was the compromise, but the land value around Central Park rose so quickly that land developers and real-estate interests became the chief promoters of these pleasure grounds in cities, starting right next door in Brooklyn and moving all the way cross-country. Invariably, the parks were sited on undesirable land, as in San Francisco, where Golden Gate Park was created on shifting sand dunes.

153. *Bird's-Eye View of Golden Gate Park/San Francisco/1892*

All pleasure grounds used curvilinear circulation to create meadows (Fig. 153), because the pastoral was thought to be the perfect compromise between the awesomeness of pure wilderness, which Frederick Law Olmsted thought overwhelming, and the congestion, confinement, and finitude of the city. The pasture represented both nature and culture, neither pure wilderness nor pure artifice. It was felt that architecture ought to play a minimal role, trees ought to be native so that intellectual attention would not be stimulated by the novelty of exotic species. By using native trees, a designer could modulate space and get people to move through space without the benefit of signs. Signs were to be avoided because they exercised overused "left-brain" functions. Olmsted did not have the convenience of the left-hemisphere, right-hemisphere concept in his day, but I think it applies fairly to his thinking about landscape experience. He felt that the city provided too much linear and finite experience of cause and effect, so he did not want to stimulate that part of the brain. He wanted instead what he called a class of countervailing conditions: that is, he wanted the user to appreciate music, color, and movement through space, all of which we now view as linked to the right side of the brain. This goal dictated native materials, so that one's intellectual powers would not be stimulated; no flowers, because they imply the hand of man, unless in naturalistic bands or at the base of buildings, which are already artificial; still and placid water, to promote serenity instead of running brooks, which would be too exciting; and a confusion between sky and water, so that their merger would suggest infinity (Fig. 154).

154. Landscape in Jackson Park, Chicago. c. 1880s

REFORM PARK: 1890–1930

At the turn of the century, policymakers recognized that unless the working classes could visit parks, the instruction encoded in them was useless. Therefore, they

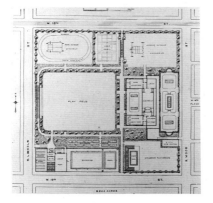

155. Harrison Park, Chicago. 1944. Plan

156. Indoor recreation. c. 1915.
Seward Park

157. Outdoor gymnasium and
playground. c. 1915. Stanford Park.
Chicago South Park District
Annual Report

158. Advertisement for playground
equipment. 1965

decided to locate parks close to workers in the tenement districts.
The new parks were reduced in size, and the pastoral illusion was
abandoned. The plans were symmetrical rather than asymmetrical;
trees were no longer used to modulate space, but simply to decorate
edges (Fig. 155); and for the first time, interior recreation was considered a virtue. Up to this point, the pleasure ground had been
considered an antidote, among other things, to factory life, which
was confined indoors and exercised only what programmers called
the small-muscle groups. Moving an arm up and down would be
too much like factory work, so pleasure-ground programmers wanted to encourage sports that would use the whole body.

    This period saw the most radical changes in the history of
municipal-park design in the United States. A photograph from 1915
(Fig. 156) shows a group of all girls, all the same age, engaged in the
same activity with the same piece of equipment, indoors, under
supervision. One new idea of the time was that spontaneous play
could no longer be trusted; people needed supervision. That notion
came partly from developmental psychology, which posited that
humans have distinct needs at different developmental phases.
Therefore, the needs of boys, of girls, and of each age group were all
thought to be different, and consequently age and sex segregation
was introduced. Play equipment was introduced, because this was the time when
psychologists recognized that the physical developmental needs of children were different from those of adults. This is in sharp contrast to the pleasure-ground ideal of
the family (or of other so-called natural groups, religious and ethnic) using the parks
spontaneously. The reform park introduced a division of recreation very much like
the division of labor characteristic of the whole industrial order. The designers of
this park type made no effort to obscure its physical boundaries: they used no berms,
no pastoral illusions whatsoever (Fig. 157).

RECREATION FACILITY: 1930–65

In the 1930s another shift occurred, when Robert Moses became Commissioner of
Parks for New York City. He repudiated prior attitudes toward parks when he
wrote, "We will make no more absurd claims as to the superior importance and
value of the service we are called upon to render...." This statement marks what I
would call the end of ideology. Moses argued that planners should no longer use
parks as a way to solve urban problems. The previous two models had been very
heavily endowed with social agendas, whereas this one saw the park as "just for the
fun of it" (Fig. 158). Instrumental justifications for parks and recreation were no
longer offered. The new justification was fun, an end in itself, because people want
it. It was a market mentality: if there's a demand, supply it.

    When people do not have ideals and when they do not have a clear idea of what
problems they are solving, there are unfortunate consequences for form, which
becomes extremely banal. I call this period the era of the recreation facility, and a

look at any stadium-and-parking-lot gives a clue as to why the word *facility* is so frequently used in this period: the park as we traditionally understand it, associated with greenery, is no longer essential. Parks departments came to administer any kind of environment that attracted large numbers of people for recreational purposes. Spectator sports became very important. Instead of the reform park's complex playground that was almost a settlement house, the recreation era produced blacktop, cyclone fence, and basketball hoops, and emphasized maintenance.

OPEN-SPACE SYSTEM: AFTER 1965

Our own period in park design began in 1965. I selected this date because that was when John Lindsay ran for mayor of New York City and produced a white paper on parks, making them a plank in his political platform. Once again policymakers decided that parks could be used as an agent of social reform. An important conceptual shift in this period has been that we care less about recreational designations and more about the potential of any space to provide us with recreational experience. However, the change in actual spaces is less important than the change in perception. When we change our perceptual lens, suddenly everything is different: for example, walking down the street can entail a recreational experience, and I think the fine art of the day has helped us to move toward that perception. In the late 1960s in Chicago I visited a kinetic sculpture exhibit at the Museum of Contemporary Art. As I pulled a lever on one piece, another lever moved, and when I walked by another piece, it blinked. Afterward, out in the street, red and green lights blinked to regulate my walking; next, I pulled open a lever on a blue metal box and put an envelope in it. The message was that daily life, if one looks at it the right way, has an aesthetic component. Open-space planners have picked up on this perspective. Previously rejected plots of land, like the underapproach to a bridge, have been transformed for recreational purposes by, for example, the building of tennis courts. In the previous era, planning standards were established regarding how much square footage of park and recreation space a district needed per thousand of population, and so forth. All of this has been abandoned in the open-space era, and replaced by a "get it where you can" attitude.

159. Playground. 1967. Twenty-ninth Street and Second Avenue, New York City

Two formal contributions have emerged during this period: the adventure playground for children (Fig. 159) and the vest-pocket park for middle-class shoppers and office workers. The playground has been denatured; certainly all the adventure was taken out of the adventure playground when it crossed the Atlantic Ocean from Scandinavia and England, and was reduced to low-maintenance, abstract forms at best meant to stimulate children's imagination. Whether or not they do is an empirical question that has not been researched. The vest-pocket park, as exemplified by Paley Park in Manhattan (Fig. 160), marks a major departure from the old recreation-facility standards, because that site was not even a fragment of a block, just the footprint of a single building. Despite its size, Paley Park successfully created a feeling of oasis.

160. Zion & Breen. Paley Park. 1965–68. Three East Fifty-third Street, New York City

Jung and the Art of Landscape:
A Personal Experience

JUNG WAS ONLY A NAME TO ME WHEN I first realized that the subconscious[1] could be enlisted, as in all art, to reinforce the conscious and the tangible in landscape design (Fig. 164). Paul Klee was my mentor. Was it possible to sublimate a technically correct but otherwise insignificant design by inserting within it an invisible idea that only the subconscious could comprehend? The first trials, during the six years 1957–63, were concerned only with what can be described as the upper layer of the subconscious. The process is simple. You first prepare a design in the normal way, you find it uninspiring, you place the drawing at a distance and preferably upside down, and you gradually become aware that it suggests a shape foreign but friendly to any idea of your own. In this shadowy shape you hope to discern some form that aspires to the perfection we call beauty (in the first three examples that follow are concealed animal forms, humans as symbolism, and allegory). You now reorganize the details of your design to conform (but not recognizably so) to the abstract idea within. Tell no one, if you can, for this is a message from one subconscious to another, and the intellect spoils such things.

THE WATER GARDENS, HEMEL HEMPSTEAD (1957)

Having been commissioned to plan the new town of Hemel Hempstead north of London in 1947, I was appointed ten years later to design the town park (Fig. 165) along a narrow green strip through which meandered the River Gade. On one side was the service road to the town high street and on the other, a series of car parks broken by a public flower garden. The strong lines of a straight canal seemed needed to organize the scattered environment: upstream, the canal would emerge from the natural river and, downstream, would culminate in a lake. Pedestrian bridges would connect one side to the other.

The design was technically orthodox, but stillborn. How to bring it to life and thus win the affection of the people? It was then, with Paul Klee as inspiration, that I first had the idea of concealing a ghost within the visible. As seen from a distance, the design suggested an abstract serpent. So, if London had the Serpentine, could not Hemel Hempstead have one also? Smaller, certainly, but much more expressive. Thereafter, all detail was subordinated to this single idea: the tail flipping round the artificial hill; the soft underbelly with its subtle curve; the bridges that fasten the flower garden like a howdah on its back; the huge head with the single fountain eye and watery mouth.

164. Sir Geoffrey Jellicoe. *A post-Jungian diagram of the landscape-subconscious.* Drawing, Pen and ink on vellum, image: 4¾ x 4"; sheet size: approximately 10½ x 6½"

165. Sir Geoffrey Jellicoe. *Water Gardens.* Hemel Hempstead. 1957. Photocopy, hand-colored in blue pencil, 8½ x 11". Original, pen and ink and blue pencil

The town loved the gardens from the start, unaware of the animal within. Then, recently, came a proposal to impinge on the lake for road widening. To rational man the scale of protest seemed unjustified, and only now have I revealed to a deputation what I conceived to be the root cause. Even rational man will pause before chipping at a much-loved civic monster and work of art, however deeply embedded in the subconscious.

THE HARWELL HILLS (1960)

The story of Harwell Hills is one of a light-hearted frolic into the expression of a deep-rooted and sinister idea. While evolving the design (Fig. 166), I sat next to Henry Moore at meetings of the Royal Fine Arts Commission in London, and I remember how he encouraged the concept of modeling the land as sculpture on a gigantic scale. Basically, the fun was to find out whether one could play upon the subconscious emotions through association of ideas. This attempt is described in the following extract from *The Guelph Lectures*:

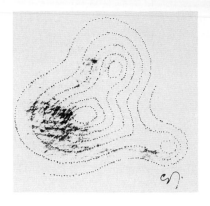

166. Sir Geoffrey Jellicoe. *Three Hills* above Rutherford Laboratories, Harwell, Berkshire. 1960. Photocopy, 8½ x 11". Original, pen and ink

> Harwell's subterranean laboratories are concerned with high-energy research. Above them was a huge waste heap of excavated chalk which was to be remodelled to fit the existing landscape at the foot of the Berkshire Downs. The scientists will tell you that the splitting of the atom leads to infinity or (as one scientist said) to God. Be this as it may, the project was named "Nimrod," the mighty hunter and scourge of mankind. As if to act as guardians of this underground monster, three hills were placed upon it and named Zeus, father of gods and man; Themis, one of his wives, divine justice, daughter of heaven and earth, goddess of law, justice, and order; and their daughter Klotho, one of the fates who determine the life and death of man. The assurance was that so long as Klotho remained constant, the future of man was safe. But this was not to be . . . for shortly before start of work a telephone call stated that the small hill, Klotho, would impede certain rays emanating from Nimrod and so Klotho returned to Themis' womb and only the two hills of Zeus and Themis were made. The fate of man still hangs in the balance.[2]

THE KENNEDY MEMORIAL (1964)

A memorial in England to a president of the United States following an assassination at the height of his power is a great dramatic idea. The essential monument of the Kennedy Memorial (Fig. 167) was to be an "acre" of land, given in perpetuity to the United States, taken out of primitive meadowland on the slopes overlooking the flat fields of historic Runnymede. Any commemorative and descriptive feature was to be subsidiary to the existing *genius loci*.

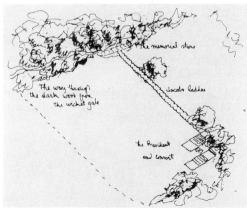

167. Sir Geoffrey Jellicoe. The Kennedy Memorial overlooking Runnymede. 1964. Photocopy, 8½ x 11". Original, pen and ink

The commission was a challenge: how to insert into the landscape, without disrupting the *genius loci*, an idea grander than the landscape itself, and at a cost of only three per cent of the funds raised for scholarships in the Kennedy Trust?

I recollect that I had arrived at an agreeable composition of approach, memorial stone, and seats of contemplation before I became aware that I was instinctively groping for something of far more importance.

The path sequence was one of continuous movement, suggesting the three phases of human experience: life, death, and spirit. A likeness to the allegory of Bunyan's *Pilgrim's Progress* became clear. I would now place a similar idea into the modest landscape, recognizable to the visitor only through the subconscious. I calculated that full awareness of a sublime experience would not surface immediately. Such was the idea, and now it only remained to interpret this idea into every detail of reality: the wicket gate, the granite sets as pilgrims moving upward through the dark wood, the catafalque borne on the shoulders of the populace, the path like Jacob's ladder leading to seats symbolizing the President and his First Lady in repose and perpetual contemplation.

The memorial was inaugurated by Queen Elizabeth in the presence of Mrs. Kennedy and a multitude in the fields below, on May 17, 1965.

The design of the Kennedy Memorial was of such significance that after completion I turned for the first time to the writings of Carl Jung to confirm that the path I was following was not a figment of my own imagination. It was not. Jung states clearly that the subconscious ("feeling," or instinct) lives a life of its own, independent of the conscious (the intellect); that each, operating separately, can be ineffectual and even chaotic; that opposition of one to another can be catastrophic; but that in unison they can create the great works of civilization.

Until retirement from an active practice some twenty years later, I had neither the time nor the inclination to do more than ruminate on the abstruse theories of the subconscious. Then came a number of commissions from sympathetic clients that enabled me to put theory into practice on a truly heroic scale: Sutton Place in Surrey, Shute House in the west country, and the Moody Historical Gardens in Texas.

168. Sir Geoffrey Jellicoe. Diagram showing Creation, the Good Life, and Aspiration at Sutton Place, Surrey. 1980. Photocopy, hand-colored in blue pencil, 8½ x 11". Original, pen and ink and blue pencil

SUTTON PLACE, SURREY (1980)

Built in 1521 in a transitional style between medieval and Renaissance, Sutton Place is the finest existing mansion of its period in England. Here Henry VIII first met Anne Boleyn. Of the original landscape there exists the line of the axial approach, a walled kitchen garden, and the remnants of a hunting park. New gardens made in 1905 extended the existing axis through the house and, with the garden beyond, created a cross-axis. The property was acquired by Stanley Seeger in 1979, and a great landscape in modern terms was commissioned the following year (Fig. 168).

Since the ethos of place was so strong, the existing classical framework was preserved and further extended. As if in response to the modern paintings now in the mansion, however, the interstices of the overall pattern were filled with gardens of the present-day psyche: a secret garden as a springboard for the imagination, a Magritte surrealist garden as an entry to the subconscious, and others. These were the pleasure gardens within a very much larger reconstructed landscape.

An intimation that something more profound was stirring deep in the subconscious was first aroused by the wider composition's extremities, spaced nearly half a mile apart. In the design, at one such extremity, the largest Henry Moore sculpture in the world was to be situated on a small knoll beside the fish-shaped lake and overlooked by two artificial hills representing man and woman; the biological forms were approved by the sculptor in studio and on site.[3] At the other extremity was a gigantic Carrara-marble "wall" by Ben Nicholson—also his most monumental work. Both these gargantuan features were out of scale with the mansion and its domestic gardens, and yet were fitting. Why should this be so?

Here, in fact, inserting itself without my conscious knowledge and consent, was a great allegory of man's place on the planet, suggesting creation from water, the pleasures of life itself, and, finally, human aspiration and the future. I remember that when this idea first surfaced I was surprised and strangely excited.

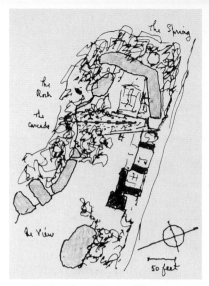

169. Sir Geoffrey Jellicoe. *Water and Rock (Yin and Yang)* at Shute House, Wiltshire. Begun 1970. Photocopy, hand-colored in blue pencil, 8½ x 11". Original, pen and ink and blue pencil

SHUTE HOUSE, WILTSHIRE (BEGUN 1970)

The project for Shute House (Fig. 169), still in the making, is in every respect complementary to Sutton Place. The estate is small by comparison: three acres of gardens and a meadow. Instead of a single splendid historic moment of architecture set in a pleasant landscape, Shute represents a medley of dates: Roman, medieval, Palladian, Victorian, and modern. With a perpetual spring at its highest point, it lies in a beautiful landscape that is one of the birthplaces of the English school of landscape gardening.

Shute has been the laboratory of ideas from which the extraordinary Moody Historical Gardens were to emerge. The owners, Michael and Anne Tree, have been pioneers, with myself as executive, in an instinctive search for what I now recognize to be a fundamental Jungian archetype: the hard and the soft (the *yang* and the *yin*), the matrix that unifies the diversities of the visible world.

The landscape before alteration, like the house, was a complex of romantic charm. Water from the spring flowed downward through dense woodlands, along the way feeding water shapes made at different dates for different purposes, and finally flowing into a partially obscured scene of distant downs, along which ran an ancient way across southern England. There was never any doubt that it was the thought, presence, action, and sound of water that was holding together the competing ideas that had been introduced into the woodlands—ideas remotely associated with Islam, Greece, the Middle Ages, the primeval, and other times and cultures. It was not until the summer of 1988, when the view was opened up and an abstract design of further pools introduced, that a unity of earth and sky became apparent. At the time of writing, a crystalline rock is on order to complement the water and so complete the idea of the *yang* and the *yin*.

THE MOODY HISTORICAL GARDENS, GALVESTON, TEXAS

With two such different experiences of the subconscious, I was well placed for a combination of the two for the proposed historical gardens of the Moody Foundation (Fig. 170). While astronauts at the nearby Houston Space Center will be experiencing space and time outward and upward, at the gardens we shall be doing

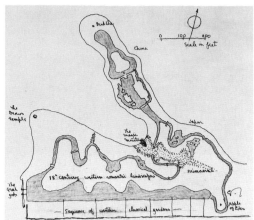

170. Sir Geoffrey Jellicoe. The Moody Historical Gardens, Galveston, Texas. Begun c. 1988. Pen and ink and blue pencil, with traces of graphite, on vellum, image: 7 x 8"; sheet size: approximately 12½ x 11¼"

so inward and downward. We shall penetrate the superficial delights of this our material world, pass through the weird worlds of the different levels of the subconscious, and, in reaching our own goal, touch on the immensely greater realities of Jung's belief in the ultimate unity of all existence.[4] The first of the following two quotes is from Jung and establishes the way; the second is from my own *Landscape of Civilisation*, a description of the Moody Gardens that are to come:

> All the most powerful ideas in history go back to archetypes. This is particularly true of religious ideas, but the central concepts of science, philosophy and ethics are no exception to this rule. In their present form they are remnants of archetypal ideas, created by consciously applying and adapting these ideas to reality. For it is the function of consciousness not only to recognise and assimilate the external world through the gateway of the senses but to translate into visible reality the world within us.[5]

The Moody Historical Gardens are intended to be both "a translation into visible reality of the world within us" and "an expression of the ultimate unity of all existence." Although not specifically mentioned by Jung, it is argued here that landscape cultures can also be traced to a single archetype or essence. In the Moody Gardens the source is the water (in China the *yin*) and the corollary is the magic mountain (the *yang*). Together they are an abstract idea which unifies the disparate objects of the visible world.[6]

Beneath the visible world of the gardens will be at least three levels of the subconscious. The uppermost layer will be composed of those emotions arising from the association of ideas that I first tried at Hemel Hempstead, such as the mountain divide or the waters of Buddha. The middle layer will be formed by a triangle of religions symbolized by Eden, the Greek gods, and Buddha, now in harmony as part of a single idea. The deepest level will be the magic mountain and the water upon which you, the voyager, will pass unharmed through thirty thousand years of time and half a globe in space.

---

1. I use the term *subconscious* instead of the more orthodox *unconscious*, which seems to me to suggest oblivion. The subconscious is very active indeed.

2. Geoffrey Jellicoe, *The Guelph Lectures in Landscape Design* (Guelph, 1983).

3. The sculpture was offered at cost by Henry Moore, who died during the negotiations. It never came to Sutton Place; it had been cast in West Germany and was subsequently acquired by the city of Berlin. Sutton Place itself was resold in 1984.

4. Anthony Storr, *Jung: Selected Writings* (London, 1983).

5. *The Collected Works of C. J. Jung,* ed. Adler, Gerard, et al., trans. R. F. Hill (Princeton, 1968).

6. Geoffrey Jellicoe, *The Landscape of Civilisation, as Experienced in the Moody Gardens* (Northiam, East Sussex, 1988).

JOHN B. JACKSON

The Past and Future Park

LIKE MOST AMERICANS, I expect to find in every city, every town, even in every village in the country, an outdoor recreation area or what is usually called a park; and I am seldom disappointed. No matter how new and unfinished a town may be, or however old and poor, I know that it will contain, wedged in among the crowded blocks of buildings, a rectangular space with grass and trees and meandering paths, and perhaps a bandstand or a flagpole. Some of them, like Central Park in New York or Golden Gate Park in San Francisco, are so famous or so beautiful that I would go out of my way to see them, but the average small-town park has a different kind of appeal. All the basic elements are there—the trees, the grass, the pathways—but it is so quiet, so naked, so lacking in vitality, that I wonder who uses it, and why. It is like what an archetype would be: a specimen of the original, timeless Ur-park as it might have appeared in the Bronze Age, or even earlier.

But the truth is, the urban park is a newcomer to the landscape. In terms of greenery and design, no such space existed in ancient Greece or in Rome, and it first appeared in European towns not much before two centuries ago. Medieval towns had, of course, a number of public spaces (which, in accordance with vernacular practice, could be used for a succession of functions): the marketplace, the parvis in front of the church, the graveyard next to it, the place for processions, and that for executions. But no open space in the town was ever set aside—let alone designed—for such a vague purpose as recreation.

Rich and powerful families had their own orchards and gardens, hidden behind walls, stocked with rare plants from Asia or America, and adorned with the statues, specimens of topiary art, and fountains that played tricks on unwary visitors. Expert gardeners were called in to make a formal composition of flower beds and walks and flights of steps, and the garden was often the scene of elaborate social events. In time, the owners were persuaded to allow certain reliable elements in the town to come and admire their gardens. They consented to this not simply out of vanity—for a garden showed how rich a man was and what good taste he had—but also out of philanthropy. They believed that the working class, for all its shortcomings, could be morally improved through exposure to beauty and order and a display of good manners. They were overoptimistic, but the condescending point of view persisted among members of the establishment up to about a century ago.

The men who designed the gardens, eager to please their patrons, suggested that one way to educate the common people was to make broad, straight avenues leading out of the garden—flanked by uniform trees and statues of famous men and occasional Latin inscriptions promoting piety and respect for the law. The straightness of the avenues had the advantage of making them easy to police, and of offering an impressive view of the palace or castle or mansion—the symbol of authority.

As a place where all citizens could spend their leisure walking to and from beneath the trees, the *allée* at once became popular. At certain afternoon hours, the world of fashion made its appearance in carriages or on horseback, and all elements benefited from access to what was soon to be called the park. It was there that garden came together with city, greenery with architecture and social forms. Indeed, the *allée* in a more urbanized guise has survived to this day in many cities: Pall Mall, the Cours-la-Reine, and the Unter den Linden are familiar examples.

The formal garden itself, the museumlike collection of curiosities, did not fare so well, and in the early eighteenth century it began to suffer from neglect. No doubt the rise of a prosperous and educated middle class, particularly in England, accounted for the change. The geometrical garden, identified with the French aristocracy, failed to offer privacy and intimacy or a chance for the amateur gardener to try his hand. Writers like Alexander Pope and Joseph Addison ridiculed the prevalence of straight rows of identical plants and the shaping of box to look like lions or dragons. Travelers back from Italy had much to say about picturesque ruins and the pleasing disorder in the Italian landscape. From paintings they had learned that the landscape was more than a collection of isolated structures and spaces; that it was a composition, which even included light and shadow and the remoter background of sky. It is now considered old-fashioned (though it is still usual) to perceive the landscape in painterly terms, but in its day this reaction was very novel. It marked an awareness of the wider environment, of nature in all its forms and colors. Those who stayed at home in England found pleasure in discovering winding lanes bordered by hedges and wildflowers, the unplanned grouping of trees in the countryside, and many among the more prosperous English began to think of owning their own place in the country. Merchants and lawyers bought up small farms and woodlands, and even whole villages, with the idea of making more money in specialized or commercial farming, thereby becoming owners of estates, members of the gentry. At the same time, they had visions of creating their own personal landscape, generous in scale, adorned with lakes and groves of artfully planted trees and distant views; they, too, had seen paintings. A delightful feature of such an estate would be that, despite its openness and simplicity, it was entirely private and removed from the local workaday world: an oasis of rustic beauty.

Out of these various impulses and memories and aspirations there evolved in the middle decades of the eighteenth century a new kind of garden or park, sometimes called the picturesque landscape garden or the Romantic garden. Though originating in England, it became fashionable in France and Germany and, eventually, in nineteenth-century America. In the beginning it, too, had its absurdities— ruins and Chinese pagodas and dark caves where some venerable hermit might have lived—but it soon evolved its own standards of correctness and good taste, and the older classical garden was either forgotten or transformed in accordance with the new style. Generally speaking, it is the style of landscape design that we all instinctively accept. It belongs in countries that have a moist climate, good soil, varied topography, and a firm belief in the value of privacy and outdoor living. Whether it is adapted to great cities and to urban poverty is a question we are beginning to ask.

Nevertheless, the Romantic style of landscape has always had a good press. It has been approved by art historians and by the general public, and for good reason: it has taught us how to design magnificent outdoor spaces as well as the smallest family garden. It has taught us how to achieve beauty with the simplest and commonest of means, the landforms and vegetation everywhere surrounding us, and it has brought us closer to nature and made us more at home in wilderness and mountains than our ancestors. I am one of those who believe that our current guilt-ridden worship of the environment is a sign of moral and cultural disarray, and I doubt if it lasts. But the Romantic school of design is not entirely to blame for our exaggerations, and scholars are correct in saying that it has had an immense influence not only on what we now call landscape architecture, but on architecture and urban planning as well.

Critics have a tendency to dwell on the production aspect of art—on the artist and his skill, and what he tried to convey—but a garden is more than a work of art, a product. It has a practical value, and how the consumer uses it has to be included in the critical verdict. I think it can be said that the privately owned picturesque landscape was almost perfectly adjusted to the needs of a certain fortunate class of consumers: the ones with money enough to want it and acquire it. It provided solitude; beauty; the uninterrupted, essentially passive, spectator experience of nature; a sense of ownership; and, above all, the ability to exclude, tactfully but effectively, all outsiders and contact with the urban world. How the sensitive visitor was supposed to react to this landscape is the theme of much polite eighteenth-century literature: he is alone or accompanied by his beloved and wanders without apparent destination in search of the several emotional treats that the garden provides, such as melancholy, awe, terror, and sense of oneness with nature. Unlike the Baroque garden, with its well-defined axis leading to the palace, or the religious sanctuary focused on the shrine, the picturesque garden had no dominant feature to draw people together—at most, an oval lawn. Architecture failed to play one of its traditional roles: the owner's residence, when not located in a secluded domestic area of the garden, sought to blend with the natural setting. "The effect of introducing buildings amongst artificially established rocks and cascades as part of the landscape," Peter Collins writes, "was merely the first step towards establishing the general idea that rural architecture ought essentially to be thought of as making natural scenery more 'picturesque,' i.e., more like a landscape painting."[1] Architects adopted Gothic architecture (A. J. Downing and his landscaped gardens) or the rustic appearance of peasant farmhouses (the *hameau* of Marie Antoinette). As Collins observed, the gradual abandonment of architectural symmetry in the Romantic garden had the effect of producing a more flexible interior layout and of making the country house, whatever its scale or size, more habitable and less conspicuous. In the late eighteenth century, the country house or villa, thanks largely to its landscaped setting, developed into a distinct house type, while the building with a public or official status—insofar as its presence suggested the intrusion of the city—was discouraged. In one German Romantic garden of the period a temple to Mercury, proposed as a suitably classical touch, was rejected: Mercury was the god of commerce.

Do we need to be reminded that the picturesque garden culture of two centuries ago flourishes in many of our more prosperous suburbs and resorts? It has been refined and simplified: the man of the family now goes to work in the city, instead of reading Rousseau and Byron in the garden, and the once-common experience of the sublime has been replaced by gloomy thoughts about styrofoam in packaging and the fate of the blue whale. But they come to much the same thing: nature is all-important in human affairs.

It is much more difficult to explain the proliferation of the picturesque landscape in precisely the environment its designers once feared and avoided: the city. By and large, almost all of our parkways and larger city parks are modernized versions of the Romantic park, with winding paths, varied landforms, pastoral lawns and lakes and groves of beautiful trees, and isolation from the urban setting. In fact, many of the finest specimens of the style are to be found in the heart of cities in America and Europe.

The story of how the Romantic garden or park came to be chosen as the official establishment public park has been neglected by historians of landscape architecture—perhaps because they are unaware that there was, and still is, a vernacular tradition in the design of places for predominantly working-class recreation. In seventeenth-century England the public had access to many aristocratic gardens, and, though used in farming, many country paths and lanes leading through beautiful scenery were open to all. The practice seems to have been common throughout prerevolutionary Europe: in Germany a number of towns were known for their attractive and well-maintained country walks, each with a recreational destination. Popular, or *volks*, gardens were created near Vienna and Berlin and other cities. Though they still had a definitely geometrical layout with radiating *allées*, they included a lively assortment of popular attractions: tents and booths where refreshments could be bought, merry-go-rounds, shooting galleries, bowling alleys, and dance music played by a military band. In 1836 Dickens wrote a vivid account of how working-class Londoners spent their Sundays, setting out at an early hour and walking to where they found a coach or a steamer to take them to such places as Greenwich and Richmond. There they picnicked, walked through the nearby fields, played cricket, and celebrated in the many taverns before going home. Paris had its *guinguettes*, or taverns with gardens where there was wine and music, and in pre–Central Park days (and undoubtedly later) New Yorkers frequented vernacular resorts in Hoboken and Long Island and along the beaches. Reading between the lines of descriptions appearing in papers and magazines, we discover that these resorts were rarely visited by the more fastidious citizens, for they were crowded and boisterous and sometimes violent. Nevertheless, they possessed a valuable quality largely absent from the carefully designed "natural" spaces of the city park, which eventually took their place: because of their location in a working, often farming environment, they offered the spectacle of interaction between work and play, between the private and the public realms, between producer and consumer, between urban and rural ways of life. The vernacular resort, on one day of the week, was a kind of marketplace for the exchange of ideas and information, the exchange of goods and services: a reincarnation of the traditional street, which was gradually disappearing under the impact of the industrial city. In a sense those extramural places of recreation were the last remnants of the old vernacular culture: they had their own kind of music, their own kind of sports and games, their own kind of food, and their own code of manners.

The last decades of the eighteenth century saw the emergence in city after city of the picturesque park, open to the public; and each came to represent the power of three distinct social forces: the urge to improve the living conditions of factory workers in crowded industrial centers; the urge to bring all classes in close contact with the moral and physical benefits of a "natural" environment; and the urge to improve the real-estate values of areas surrounding the new parks. Birkenhead Park near Liverpool (which so inspired Frederick Law Olmsted) was in large part a real-estate development venture, as were Regent's Park and Hyde Park—and so, for that matter, was Central Park, as Olmsted acknowledged. It should be clearly recognized that over the last two centuries the large public park has helped accomplish three objectives: the park is a source of health and pleasure, it is a work of art, and it has had a powerful influence on the evolution of the city. We are more and more aware of the fact that its role is changing, however, and that the resurgence of the vernacular resort, thanks to the automobile, has diminished its overall importance in the lives of many urban Americans.

Of late, the Olmsted tradition has been the subject of reappraisal: while his work as a landscape architect and urbanist is almost universally admired, his social philosophy has been criticized because of its elitism, its antiurban tone, and its overemphasis on the moral impact of the natural environment; but, most important, because his definition of the park called for the fragmentation of society, for the solitary experience (or at least for the family experience), and for a passive relationship between the individual and his or her environment. Roger Starr has formulated this last objection in a telling paragraph: "Most people recognize…that the non-human world is a battleground for survival, and that if it can be said to set forth any example of morality, it does so by providing an escape from those human vices connected with speech: hypocrisy, lying, group hatred, envy. It is a long list. What the park offers is a relief from the constant buzz of the city, and the stony messages implicit in its buildings. The park offers speechlessness." Starr comments on Olmsted's emphasis on the "tranquility" of the park; "The word…suggests not merely silence but peace, the absence of contention.…The park designer, like the poet [Wordsworth in "Upon Westminster Bridge"], saw in the silent speechlessness of stone and buildings a moral orderliness that the weekday city could not provide."[2]

What we now see is the proliferation of ad hoc public spaces where the interaction and confrontation of the marketplace prevail: the flea market, the competitive sports event, the commercial street in the blue-collar part of town temporarily transformed into a fairgrounds, the parking lot transformed into spaces for games and spectacles, and the popularity of those small downtown spaces that William H. Whyte has so effectively studied, where the presence of others is the main source of pleasure and stimulation.[3] The park as a total experience for all classes of citizens is gradually becoming merely one space out of many, now serving an invaluable function primarily for children, older people, and the dedicated student of nature, while the more mobile, more gregarious elements seek recreation in shopping malls, in the street, on the open road, and in sports arenas. Do they find it? Not as often as they should; and those ad hoc spaces are the ones to which the designer—the landscape architect or developer or architect—should give form and meaning.

1. Peter Collins, *Changing Ideals in Modern Architecture* (London, 1965), p. 50.

2. Roger Starr, "The Motive behind Olmsted's Park," in *The Public Face of Architecture*, ed. Nathan Glazer and Mark Lilla (New York, 1987), pp. 271–72.

3. See William H. Whyte, *The Social Life of Small Urban Spaces* (Washington, D.C., 1980) and idem, *City* (New York, 1989).

PAUL GROTH

Vernacular Parks

DESIGN PROFESSIONALS usually see urban parks as official places: special areas reserved for finding aesthetic and spiritual refreshment, and for learning the ruling interpretations of nature and society. The Mall in Washington, D.C., and its adjacent museums constitute an obvious example. Other official parks—such as the inevitable History Park collection of pioneer cabins rudely collected at the edge of a mid-sized city or the arrows pointing tourists toward the booster's view of downtown—lead visitors and local citizens alike to preplanned conclusions. Even though such parks may not be high style, in their form they still suggest clear rules of behavior.

If we look at ordinary American environments, however, we can find a very different and very vibrant urban park tradition, one that we might call the vernacular park. The vernacular park is ad hoc: it is not focused on a correct visual style, on the adulation of certain types of geological or botanical specimens, or on a prescription for specific activities. It is not particularly urban or wild, but simply removed from one's normal environment. Like other vernacular landscapes, it is not focused on the future or on abstract ideas, but instead on the present and the everyday. People develop vernacular parks where official order is beginning to crumble—in underused areas of the city or out on the urban fringe. An uncharacteristically permanent but ubiquitous form of a vernacular park is the speedboat dock. Vernacular parks often exist *within* official parks: for instance, a dirt road behind the levee of an otherwise official urban park.

Children innately create and use vernacular parks largely invisible to the adult population. For the eight-year-old with a model boat or raft to float or pull with a string, the chains of mud puddles along the side of a road form a public recreation space that can stretch for several blocks. Children of all classes and ethnic backgrounds create and use vernacular parks, but the adults who do so typically come from the lower half of the socioeconomic spectrum. They are recent urban migrants, racial or ethnic minorities, or young adults: people whom the official population might disparagingly categorize as working-class, lowbrow, redneck, or merely adolescent. They often have access to a car—most often a used car.

For these people, the vernacular park is not the covertly transformed nature of official parks, but brazenly commodified nature. The experience of nature goes hand in hand with buying, collecting, and using nature. An exuberant example of this

171. Entrance to gift shop at the Reptile Center, near Luray, Virginia, 1988

172. Official sign in Humboldt Redwoods State Park, near Myers Flat, California, 1983

173. A vernacular area, Humboldt Redwoods State Park, near Myers Flat, California, 1983

commodification is the Reptile Center gift shop near the Luray Caverns in Virginia's Shenandoah Valley (Fig. 171). Lowbrow entrepreneurs often run vernacular parks as a business; a brightly colored sign directing motorists to buy tickets at a gift shop is typical. How different are the announcements in the official park, where small, tasteful signs might merely label the park and credit its benefactor or denote its memorial status (and thus falsely appear to be value-free). In California's Humboldt Redwoods State Park, for instance, islands of official tall redwoods are discreetly denoted with woodsy log signs (Fig. 172). California viewers of a sign saying "Fannie K. Haas Grove" will automatically connect the trees and the park with the prominence of the Haas family, well known as part of the Levi Strauss fortune and of San Francisco's urban leadership. However, stretching between the official groves of Humboldt redwoods are long areas of private land. In these areas entrepreneurs have erected a vernacular redwoods park, consisting of coffee shops, redwood-burl emporiums, dubious museums, and other tourist attractions all related somehow to the adjacent trees (Fig. 173). Both the official and the vernacular are important and authentic parts of Humboldt Redwoods Park. In both zones nature is commodified. At only one of them, however, can visitors buy redwood burls to take home and make into coffee tables. To the official eye, parkland trinkets are offensive; yet, since Americans are constantly taught to buy material possessions for their membership in society, why should they not decide to buy into nature as well?

Interviews and surveys in Jackson State Forest (reported in 1988 by Marcia McNalley and Randy Hester for the California Department of Forestry and Fire Protection) show that the vernacular park is not a sacred realm, but a scenic backdrop for ordinary and everyday activities, many of which ignore nature altogether. Hester and McNalley found that park users felt automobiles, trucks, loud radios, or a motorboat (in the case of water) were usually considered essential; park use could mean such mundane activities as fixing an automobile transmission or watching television. Throughout the United States, vernacular park use for teenagers can consist of having a drinking party or just hanging out. The nearer a vernacular park area is to the center of the city, the more likely its daytime social promenade will include waxing one's car in the shade while potential admirers cruise by on the nearby road.

The easy juxtaposition of everyday activities with a naturalistic background reveals an attitude among those users that does not separate culture from nature—at least not nearly so much as do the people who design official parks. A few years ago a billboard at the entrance to Glacier National Park announced that an auto tape tour would permit visitors to "Hear Glacier National Park Come to Life!" Nature, in this format, was clearly something outside the car, separate from humans and separate from culture. In the vernacular park, however, nature is not only outside the car, but also inside the car. Any intervening educational programs of plaques, brochures, or tours are commercial. In the vernacular park, wilder nature is simply there, usually in the background and admittedly compromised on occasion by erosion, litter, or vandalism. Everyday activities are also there, scenically a bit better off than at home. In their own minds, vernacular users are not desacralizing the park. For them, it was never particularly sacred in the first place.

As a lesson for official parks in the United States, the vernacular tradition reminds us that wherever park use thrives, there the automobile usually thrives, too. To tap into the potential vitality of the vernacular park, landscape architects and planners may need to stifle their professional urge to eliminate cars or to hide them in the background. In popular vernacular parks, seemingly random parking along the roadside and among the trees blurs the conceptual boundaries between road, parking lot, and park. Inside even Yosemite National Park (as official a park as one could find), the parking lots are dramatic in and of themselves and often see more pleasurable social activity than the hiking trails. Along the vernacular zone of Humboldt Redwoods Park, the predictable roadside attraction of a drive-through tree and drive-on log also prove that parks *can* embrace automobiles and their occupants (Fig. 174).

Vernacular and official parks may be inherently contradictory; if so, we must insure that park programs are pluralistic enough to allow both traditions. We must also find ways to mitigate the ecological damage of the vernacular traditions without undermining them with official control. We might, for instance, find ourselves designing shelters for waxing cars as well as shelters for picnic tables. If indeed we are to make a park for the future, perhaps we ought to start with the parking lot.

174. Sign inviting automobile use in Humboldt Redwoods State Park, near Myers Flat, California, 1983

BIBLIOGRAPHY

Compiled by C. Allan Brown

BOOKS

1. Ambasz, Emilio. *The Architecture of Luis Barragán*. New York, The Museum of Modern Art, 1976.

2. Archer, B. J. and Anthony Vidler. *Follies: Architecture for the Late Twentieth Century Landscape*. New York, Rizzoli, 1983.

3. Balmori, Diana, et al. *Beatrix Farrand's American Landscapes: Her Gardens and Campuses*. Sagaponack, New York, Sagapress, 1985.

4. Bardi, P. M. *The Tropical Gardens of Burle Marx*. New York, Reinhold, 1964.

5. Barzilay, Marianne. *L'Invention du parc: Parc de La Villette*. Paris, Graphite Editions, 1984.

6. Baumann, Ernst. *Neue Garten, New Gardens*. Zurich, Girsberger, 1955.

7. Beardsley, John. *Earthworks and Beyond: Contemporary Art in the Landscape*. New York, Abbeville, 1984.

8. Boesinger, Willy. *Richard Neutra*. Zurich, Girsberger, 1955.

9. Brattleboro Museum and Art Center. *Built Landscapes: Gardens in the Northeast*. Brattleboro, Vermont, 1984.

10. Brown, Jane. *The English Garden in Our Time: From Gertrude Jekyll to Geoffrey Jellicoe*. Woodbridge, Antique Collectors Club, 1986.

11. Bye, A. E. *Art into Landscape, Landscape into Art*. Mesa, Arizona, PDA Publishers, 1983.

12. Byrd, Warren T., Jr. and Reuben M. Rainey. *The Work of Dan Kiley: A Dialogue on Design Theory*. Charlottesville, University of Virginia, 1983.

13. Byrd, Warren T., Jr. *The Work of Garrett Eckbo: Landscapes for Living*. Charlottesville, University of Virginia, 1987.

14. Church, Thomas. *Gardens Are for People*. New York, Reinhold, 1955.

15. Collins, Peter. *Changing Ideals in Modern Architecture, 1750–1950*. London, Faber and Faber, 1965.

16. Colvin, Brenda. *Land and Landscape*. London, J. Murray, 1970.

17. Cranz, Galen. *The Politics of Park Design: A History of Urban Parks in America*. Cambridge, Mass., MIT Press, 1982.

18. Creese, Walter L. *The Crowning of the American Landscape: Eight Great Spaces and Their Buildings*. Princeton, Princeton University, 1985.

19. Crowe, Sylvia, ed. *Shaping Tomorrow's Landscape*. Amsterdam, Djambatan, 1964.

20. Cutler, Phoebe. *The Public Landscape of the New Deal*. New Haven, Yale University, 1985.

21. Eckbo, Garrett. *Landscape for Living*. New York, Architectural Record, 1950.

22. Fairbrother, Nan. *New Lives, New Landscapes*. New York, Knopf, 1970.

23. Greber, Jacques. *Jardins modernes: Exposition internationale de 1937*. Paris, Éditions d'Art Charles Moreau, 1937.

24. Gromort, Georges. *L'Art des jardins*. Paris, Vincent Fréal, 1934.

25. Hackett, Brian. *Man, Society and Environment*. London, Marshall, 1950.

26. Halprin, Lawrence. *The RSVP Cycles: Creative Processes in the Human Environment*. New York, Braziller, 1970.

27. Hines, Thomas S. *Richard Neutra and the Search for Modern Architecture*. New York, Oxford University, 1982.

28. Holmdahl, Gustav. *Gunnar Asplund, Architect*. Stockholm, Tidskriften Byggmastaren, 1950.

29. International Federation of Landscape Architects World Congress. *Landscape Towards 2000: Conservation or Desolation?* London, RIBA, 1979.

30. Jackson, J. B. *Discovering the Vernacular Landscape*. New Haven, Yale University, 1984.

31. Jackson, Kenneth T. *Crabgrass Frontier: The Suburbanization of the United States*. New York, Oxford University, 1985.

32. Jellicoe, Geoffrey. *The Guelph Lectures on Landscape Design*. Guelph, University of Guelph, 1983.

33. Jellicoe, Geoffrey and Susan Jellicoe. *The Landscape of Man*. New York, Viking, 1975.

34. Jellicoe, Geoffrey and Susan Jellicoe. *Modern Private Gardens*. London, Abelard-Schuman, 1968.

35. Karson, Robin S. *Fletcher Steele, Landscape Architect*. New York, Abrams, 1989.

36. Kassler, Elizabeth B. *Modern Gardens and the Landscape*. New York, The Museum of Modern Art, 1964.

37. Kepes, Gyorgy. *The New Landscape in Art and Science*. Chicago, Paul Theobald, 1956.

38. Le Corbusier. *Towards a New Architecture*. New York, Payson and Clarke, 1927.

39. McGuire, Diane and Lois Fern, eds. *Beatrix Jones Farrand: Fifty Years of American Landscape Architecture*. Washington, D.C., Dumbarton Oaks, 1982.

40. McHarg, Ian. *Design with Nature*. Garden City, N.Y., Natural History Press, 1969.

41. Mindlin, Henrique E. *Modern Architecture in Brazil*. New York, Reinhold, 1956.

42. Moholy-Nagy, László. *The New Vision*. New York, Wittenborn, 1946.

43. Motto, Flavio. *Roberto Burle Marx*. São Paolo, Nobel, 1984.

44. Pean, Prosper. *Le Nouveau Jardiniste moderne*. Paris, Librairie de la Construction Moderne, 1929.

45. Pool, Mary Jane, ed. *Twentieth-Century Decorating, Architecture and Gardens: Eighty Years of Ideas and Pleasure from House and Garden*. New York, Holt, Rinehart and Winston, 1980.

46. *The Princeton Journal, Volume Two: Landscape*. Princeton, Princeton Architectural Press, 1985.

47. *Process Architecture* [series], No. 4, "Lawrence Halprin" (1978); No. 33, "Landscape Design: The Works of Dan Kiley" (1982); No. 46, "Landscape Design in Japan: Current Issues and Some Ideas" (1984); No. 59, "Creative Environment: Japanese Landscape" (1985); No. 61, "Landscape Design: New Wave in California" (1985); No. 78, "Pocket Park" (1988); No. 82, "M. Paul Friedburg: Landscape Design" (1989); No. 85, "Peter Walker: Landscape as Art" (1989).

48. Richard, Winfried. *Vom Naturideal zum Kulturideal: Ideologie und Praxis der Gartenkunst im deutschen Kaiserreich*. Berlin, Technische Universitat, 1984.

49. Rose, James C. *Creative Gardens*. New York, Reinhold, 1958.

50. San Francisco Museum of Modern Art. *Contemporary Landscape Architecture and Its Sources*. San Francisco, 1937.

51. San Francisco Museum of Modern Art. *Lawrence Halprin: Changing Places*. San Francisco, 1986.

52. Shepheard, Peter. *Modern Gardens*. London, Architectural Press, 1953.

53. Simonds, John Ormsbee. *Landscape Architecture: The Shaping of Man's Natural Environment*. New York, McGraw-Hill, 1961.

54. Smith College Museum of Art. *Landscape Architects from the Cambridge School*. Northampton, Mass., 1984.

55. Snow, Marc. *Modern American Gardens Designed by James Rose*. New York, Reinhold, 1967.

56. Solomon, Barbara Stauffacher. *Green Architecture and the Agrarian Garden*. New York, Rizzoli, 1988.

57. Sorenson, Carl T. *The Origin of Garden Art*. Copenhagen, Danish Architecture Press, 1963.

58. Tafuri, Manfredo and Francesco Dal Co. *Modern Architecture*. New York, Abrams, 1979.

59. Tishler, William H., ed. *American Landscape Architecture: Designers and Places*. Washington, D.C., Preservation Press, 1989.

60. Tunnard, Christopher. *Gardens in the Modern Landscape*. London, Architectural Press, 1938.

61. Tunnard, Christopher. *Man-made America: Chaos or Control?* New Haven, Yale University, 1963.

62. Van Valkenburgh, Michael. *Transforming the American Garden: Twelve New Landscape Designs*. Cambridge, Mass., Harvard University Graduate School of Design, 1986.

63. Wright, Frank Lloyd. *An Organic Architecture: The Architecture of Democracy*. Cambridge, Mass., MIT Press, 1939.

64. Wright, Frank Lloyd. *The Future of Architecture*. New York, Bramhall, 1953.

65. Wright, Frank Lloyd. *Modern Architecture*. Princeton, Princeton University, 1931.

66. Zagari, Franco. *L'Architettura del giardino contemporaneo*. Milan, A. Mondadori, 1988.

ARTICLES

1. Bottomley, M. E. "Landscape Design in a Modern Manner," *Landscape Architecture* 37 (January 1947): 43–49.
2. DeForest, Lockwood. "Opportunity Knocks!" *Landscape Architecture* 36 (October 1945): 10.
3. Dill, Malcolm H. "To What Extent Can Landscape Architecture 'Go Modern'?" *Landscape Architecture* 22 (July 1932): 289–92.
4. Earle, George F. "Is There a 'Modern' Style of Landscape Architecture?" *Landscape Architecture* 47 (January 1957): 341–43.
5. Eckbo, Garrett. "Is Landscape Architecture?" *Landscape Architecture* 73 (May–June 1983): 64–65.
6. Eckbo, Garrett. "Outdoors and In: Gardens as Living Space," *Magazine of Art* 34 (October 1941): 422–27.
7. Eckbo, Garrett. "Small Gardens in the City: A Study of Their Design Possibilities," *Pencil Points* 18 (September 1937): 573–86.
8. Garris, Laurie. "The Changing Landscape," *Arts and Architecture* 3 (1985) 4:56–59.
9. Geddes, Robert. "The Common Ground," *Landscape Architecture* 73 (May–June 1983): 66–67.
10. Griswold, Ralph E. "To What Extent Has Landscape Architecture Been Modern since the Renaissance?" *Landscape Architecture* 22 (July 1932): 296–99.
11. Groening, Gert and Joachim Wilschke-Bulmahn. "Changes in the Philosophy of Garden Architecture in the Twentieth Century and Their Impact upon the Social and Spatial Environment," *Journal of Garden History* 9 (April–June 1989): 53–70.
12. Jones, E. Fay. "The Generative Idea," *Landscape Architecture* 73 (May–June 1983): 68–69.
13. Kiley, Dan. "Nature: The Source of All Design," *Landscape Architecture* 53 (January 1963): 127.
14. Krog, Steven R. "Creative Risk-Taking," *Landscape Architecture* 73 (May–June 1983): 70–76.
15. Krog, Steven R. "Is It Art?" *Landscape Architecture* 71 (May 1981): 373–76.
16. Krog, Steven R. "The Language of Modern," *Landscape Architecture* 75 (March–April 1985): 56–59.
17. Meyer, Elizabeth K. "The Modern Framework," *Landscape Architecture* 73 (May–June 1983): 50–53.
18. "New American Landscape" (seven-article anthology), *Progressive Architecture* 70 (July 1989).
19. "New Styles in Gardening: Will Landscape Architecture Reflect the Modernistic Tendencies Seen in Other Arts?" *House Beautiful* (March 1929).
20. Newton, Norman T. "Modern Trends: What Are They?" *Landscape Architecture* 22 (July 1932): 302-303.
21. "Paysage" (nineteen-article anthology), *L'Architecture d'aujourd'hui* (April 1989) 262: 32–89.
22. Rose, James C. "Articulate Form in Landscape Design," *Pencil Points* 20 (February 1939): 98–100.
23. Schermerhorn, Richard. "Landscape Architecture: Its Future," *Landscape Architecture* 22 (July 1932): 281–87.
24. Sears, William R. "The Past and Future," *Landscape Architecture* 22 (July 1932): 288–89.
25. "Shades of Green" (three-article anthology), *Abitare* (March 1989) 272: 218–37.
26. Steele, Fletcher. "Landscape Design of the Future," *Landscape Architecture* 22 (July 1932): 299–302.
27. Steele, Fletcher. "New Pioneering in Garden Design," *Landscape Architecture* 20 (April 1930): 159–77.
28. Tomlinson, David. "Design in the Twentieth Century: Start with Art," *Landscape Architecture* 72 (May 1982): 56–59.
29. Tunnard, Christopher. "Art and Landscape Design," *Landscape Architecture* 39 (April 1949): 105–110.
30. Tunnard, Christopher. "Modern Gardens for Modern Houses," *Landscape Architecture* 32 (January 1942): 57–64.
31. Turner, Frederick. "Cultivating the American Garden: Toward a Secular View of Nature," *Harper's* (August 1985): 45–52.
32. Voigt, L. B. "Modern Gardens," *Landscape Architecture* 42 (April 1952): 116–19.
33. Wrede, Stuart. "Landscape and Architecture: The Work of Erik Gunnar Asplund," *Perspecta* 20 (1983): 195–214.
34. Zach, Leon Henry. "Modernistic Work and Its Natural Limitations," *Landscape Architecture* 22 (July 1932): 292–95.

INDEX OF NAMES